# Praise for The McNally Me[thod]

"It is a very complete, unders[tandable explanation of] the most complex mazes of ru[les, regulations one] is likely to encounter."

> Patrick M. Carter, M.D., M.B.A.
> Family Practice Physician
> Chairman, Department of Family Practice
> Kelsey-Seybold Clinic

"This book proved to be very enlightening for me and three colleagues in other specialties who also reviewed it. Health care consumers and all members of the health care professions need to be aware of the options available to patients in an ever-changing health care environment. Consumers also need to become effective patients by communicating with their health care providers, as the author proposes. Both the patients and the health care providers will be better off by their having done so."

> Dr. Robert L. King, M.D., F.A.C.O.G.

"*The McNally Method*$^{SM}$ *for Managing Your Health Care* has helped me personally and in my teaching. It has helped bring my extended family up-to-date on our health care system, its terminology, and the insurance options available to them. It has also helped my family to effectively communicate with their health care providers. Professionally, it has served as an easy to read tutorial textbook and reference guide for my nursing students. Its practical insights and methods have been invaluable to my students and the clients they serve. This is the "how to" consumer friendly book for clients and medical professionals to use together to plan their care."

> Mary Lou DiNatale, Ed.D., R.N.

"William McNally is willing to tackle issues that are common to consumers faced with the broadest range of public sector, mixed, and private health care providers and insurers. He does it with a clarity of style and organization that makes the reader feel empowered to systematically seek and receive the best care possible from an often chaotic health care system."

> Stan Weisner, Ph.D., M.S.W.
> Program Director, Behavioral and Health Sciences
> University of California, Berkeley Extension

"As someone dealing with complications from spinal cord surgery, I found *Managing Your Health Care* gave me the hands-on advice I needed to again take charge of my life. It's an invaluable tool."

> Suzanne Tamasie, M.Ed.
> Manager of Support Services
> Facilities Department
> Stanford University

### THE MCNALLY METHOD FOR

# MANAGING YOUR HEALTH CARE

## William F. McNally

Warde Publishers, Inc.

Portola Valley, California

The McNally Method^SM for Managing Your Health Care

Copyright © 1997 by William F. McNally. Warde Publishers, Inc. publishes *The McNally Method for Managing Your Health Care* under an exclusive worldwide license of the copyright from the copyright holder. All rights reserved. No part of this publication may be reproduced, stored in a retrieval system, or transmitted in any form or by any means, electronic, photocopying, recording, or otherwise without the prior written consent of the Publisher, except in the case of brief excerpts in critical reviews and articles. For permission requests, write to the Publisher, addressed "Attention: Permissions," at the address below.

Warde Publishers, Inc.
3000 Alpine Road
Portola Valley, CA 94028

The reader of this book has the publisher's permission to reproduce the forms in Appendix D. If you are borrowing this book from a library, please be considerate of the next reader by not marking on the forms.

*Publisher's Cataloging-in-Publication Data*
William F. McNally,
    The McNally method for managing your health care : a consumer guide for navigating today's health care systems / William F. McNally. — 1st ed.
    p. cm.
    Includes bibliographical references and index.
    ISBN 1-886346-20-8

    1. Insurance, Health—United States.  2. Health maintenance organizations—United States.  3. Medical care—United States
I. Title.  II. Title: Managing your health care

RA411.M36 1997                                368.38'2'0029773
                                                                                   QB197-40689

Printed in the United States of America
10  9  8  7  6  5  4  3  2  1   99  98  97

While this publication is intended to provide accurate and useful information with regard to the subject matter in question, it is not intended as a substitute for legal, accounting, medical, psychological, or other professional services or advice, and this book is sold with the understanding that neither author nor publisher are engaged in rendering professional services. The reader is encouraged to seek such professional advice as is appropriate to the reader's circumstances. Author and publisher, and their respective affiliates and assigns, disclaim any responsibility of any kind or in any amount for any errors or omissions herein and any liability for any harm, loss, or damages of any kind caused or alleged to be caused, directly or indirectly, by the contents of this publication or by any party's reliance thereon.

The tables in this book that provide information on Medicare and Medigap coverage are compiled from a variety of U.S. government sources. The information available is, to the best of the author's information, the latest available at the time of publication.

This book contains tables that provide sample coverage from various health care plans. While the samples are representative of typical health plans, they are not actual data from any specific plan. The author has also made interpretations in preparing these tables. Before selecting any health care plan, it is imperative to read in full the plan summaries and disclosure documents describing the plans you are considering.

Produced by Professional Book Center, Denver, Colorado
Cover design by Penna Design and Production

# Contents

**Foreword**     ix

**About the Author and the People Who Helped Him**     x

**Chapter 1**    Introduction: The Importance of Managing Your Health Care     1

**PART I: The Health Care System in the United States: What It Is and What It Is Not**

**Chapter 2**    The U.S. Health Care System     9
     Status   *9*
     Legislative Activity   *10*
     Health Care Delivery Systems   *11*
     An Historical Perspective   *13*

**PART II: Insurance Plans: Options and Informed Decisions**

**Chapter 3**    Insurance Plan Options     19
     My Experience   *19*
     The Range of Available Options   *20*
     Health Insurance–Risk Sharing   *21*
     Health Care Terminology   *24*
     Insurance Plans   *26*
     Health Care Terminology Update   *34*
     Fee-For-Service Summary   *36*
     Health Maintenance Organization (HMO) Introduction   *37*
     Types of Health Maintenance Organizations   *39*
     HMO Quality Measurements   *46*
     Health Care Terminology Update   *46*
     The Good News of the Range of Options   *48*
     Where Have We Been?   *51*
     Where Are We Going?   *52*

**Chapter 4**  The Decision-Making Process                53

The Importance of Asking Questions  *53*
The Health Insurance Decision Process  *54*
The "Sample" Example  *58*
Back to the Decision Process  *67*
A System for Evaluating Insurance and HMO Plans Through Questioning  *71*
Private and Employer-Provided Insurance  *81*
Decision Process Glossary Update  *83*

**PART III: Medicare, Medicaid, and Other Insurance: Options and Informed Decisions**

**Chapter 5**  Medicare and Medicaid                     87

Introduction  *87*
Medicare Part A—Hospitalization  *88*
Medicare Part B as Medical, Physician, or Provider Insurance  *91*
Additional Medicare Reading Material  *92*
The Medicare Decision Process  *94*
Filling the Medicare Gaps  *97*
Medicaid  *99*
Sources of Medicare, Medicaid, and Other Information  *101*

**Chapter 6**  Medigap                                   105

Introduction to Medigap Plans  *105*
Evaluating Medigap Options  *108*
Detailed Medicare–Medigap Tables  *110*

**Chapter 7**  Medicare HMOs                             117

Medicare HMOs Introduction  *117*
Medicare HMO Contracts  *119*

**Chapter 8**  A System for Evaluating Local Medigap Insurers and Medicare HMOs                         123

Narrow Down Your Options  *123*
Get Ready to Ask the Right Questions  *124*
Use Questions to Grade and Compare  *124*

**Chapter 9**  Making Your Medicare Decisions            137

Completing the Medicare Decision Process  *137*
Glossary Update  *148*

## Chapter 10 Other Insurance — 151
Supplemental Insurance Considerations  *151*
Glossary Update  *155*

# PART IV: Getting the Most Out of the Medical Systems

## Chapter 11 U.S. Health Care Status and Directions, What You Can Do About It — 159
The Information Age Changes All Our Lives  *159*
Nothing Is Like It Was in "The Good Old Days"  *163*
Vesting Others with Decision-Making Power  *164*
Getting the Most Out of the Medical System  *165*

## Chapter 12 Enhancing Your Health Care — 167
Introduction  *167*
Getting Answers from Your Doctor  *169*
Chronic Illness  *170*
Prolonged Serious Illness  *173*
Glossary Update  *182*

## Chapter 13 Managing Medical Bills and Insurance Reimbursement — 185
The Business Relationship with Health Care Providers and Insurers  *185*
Explanation of Benefits (EOB)  *191*
Working with the Billing/Reimbursement System(s)  *194*

## Chapter 14 Summary — 207

# PART V: Appendices

**Appendix A** Glossary — 211

**Appendix B** Information Directory — 221

**Appendix C** Reading List — 227

**Appendix D** Forms — 231

**Index** — 275

The McNally Method℠ Educational Services

# Foreword

With the rapidity of changes taking place in the organization and delivery of health care in the United States, *Managing Your Health Care* is a timely publication. Bill McNally has researched and written a comprehensive guide to all aspects of taking responsibility for your personal health care. This manual is both well-researched as well as practical, and is written in a very readable and personal style. As a physician and friend of Bill, I have experienced firsthand the application of the techniques found in the book. I have also received favorable comments from other consulting physicians regarding the usefulness of the organized approach used by Bill McNally. A well-planned and informed approach to patient–physician interactions greatly facilitates the timely and precise delivery of health care.

Another extremely valuable contribution of this manual is the lucid description of the menu of insurance plan options that are available and the explanation of Medicare, Medigap, and Medicaid. Bill McNally also provides a very practical approach to working with the various billing and reiumbursement systems. As a physician often divorced from the specific financial details of health care, I was brought up to date by this comprehensive and clear description of available health insurance plans.

As is emphasized throughout, it is better to understand and plan your personal health care before the development of a major medical illness. All that you need to know on this important topic can be found in *Managing Your Health Care*.

Emmet B. Keeffe, M.D.<br>
Professor of Medicine<br>
Stanford University Medical Center

# About the Author and the People Who Helped Him

 **The Medical Background for the Book**

I was raised in Chicago and graduated from Loyola University of Chicago in 1956. I have worked in computer industry sales, support, and management since 1957. In 1991 I became jaundiced. A rare autoimmune system disease was destroying my liver. My transplant on January 31, 1994 was a success, but six days later I fell, shattering many bones. That's when I learned that I had osteoporosis. I have had over 120 medical procedures not including lab work. In 1994 my medical bills exceeded $637,000.

Before acknowledging those who made direct contributions to this book, I need to recognize the contributions of my medical professionals. They made this book possible by saving my life. Their goal always was and still is, not just to keep me alive but also to return me to a very acceptable quality of life. There were dozens of them: physicians from many disciplines, registered nurses, practical nurses, and nurses' aides. I empathized with the nurses' aides as they had to move me, clean up after me, and bathe me. They also had to do it gently. They treated me like a 200-pound baby with many sources of pain, and they did so beautifully.

A big share of credit goes to Gayle, my wife of 38 years. She was my caretaker during my inpatient hospitalizations and never left my side. She stayed in a nearby hospital-owned facility so she could be with me day and night helping me and making sure that I received the proper care. Even now she hovers over me like a young mother with her first child. It's no wonder I'm in love with her.

There are a few doctors who deserve special thanks. It starts with my gastrointerologist, Michael C. Kushlan, M.D., who called in a colleague, David Stein, M.D. Their combined diagnostic efforts indicated that my autoimmune system was destroying my liver. Dr. Kushlan told me I had one to two years to live and referred me to a liver transplant team.

Emmet B. Keeffe, M.D., the medical director of the liver transplant team, agreed with Dr. Kushlan's prognosis and put me on the waiting list for a blood type "B" liver. Six months later, Carlos Esquivel, M.D., Ph.D., the team's chief surgeon, performed a successful transplant. I had a number of rejection problems, which Drs. Keeffe, Waldo Conception, Samuel So, and other staff members worked on tirelessly.

Whether from the pain medication, toxicity, or both, I hallucinated and was paranoid. The day after the operation I pulled out my drainage tubes. Dr. So operated to correct the problem. While still in the hospital, I fell in the bathroom shattering my right shoulder, pelvis, and both hips. I also crushed three vertebrae and broke my tailbone. My old liver had left me with "profound osteoporosis." In the time since then, Felix O. Kolb, M.D., an endocrinology and metabolic disease specialist, has improved my bone density to "near normal for a man my age." Dominic Tse, M.D. put my right shoulder together 45 days after the fall. He inserted a prosthesis, even though my bones were like "tofu." He did a great job. My right shoulder's range of motion is near normal.

In late 1994, I started retaining fluid next to my right lung. S. J. Salfen, M.D. and Dr. Kushlan provided symptomatic relief. After a few months, I asked for a new diagnosis and treatment plan in one of my Status Reports. Dr. Keeffe pulled together a diagnosis team of physicians from select medical disciplines. Drs. Razavi and Semba, cardiovascular and interventional radiology specialists, inserted stents in two collapsed veins in my liver in a seven-hour operation. I lost 34 pounds of fluid in five days.

Family and friends frequently dropped in or even stayed up to three weeks at a time, making sure that Gayle was not alone during her anxiety-ridden role as my caretaker. It started with Ann Funabashi, who sat up all night with Gayle in the hospital lobby during my transplant operation. Another friend, Marie Loncasty, visited with Gayle for days at a time. Our three daughters from Birmingham, Alabama, Cindy Mahoney, Patty Scollard, and Ann Henson, Gayle's sister, Gwen Canepa from New Orleans, and my aunt and uncle from Alaska, Marion and Leo Oberts, visited multiple times.

Other friends, including parishioners of Holy Spirit Church of San Jose, dropped in from time to time. Friends who couldn't be with us remembered us with cards and their prayers. Some people still come up to me, ask me how I'm doing, offer an encouraging word, and say "I'm praying for you."

Thank you all for your continuing support and help and for the continuation of my happy life here on Earth.

 ## Acknowledgments

The idea for this book came to Jim Woolever during my stent insertion and inpatient stay in Stanford University Medical Center in May 1995. While he was sitting with Gayle during my operation, she explained how I managed my health care by going through the forms I created and took to medical encounters. The next day he observed me asking a floor nurse about the compatibility of a pill she was going to give me with my daily medications.

Shortly after those experiences he started encouraging me to write a book about how I manage my health care. I started the research and writing project in September 1995. Jim has been a big help in taking me through the research and publication process.

I quickly learned that writing a nonfiction book required considerable research and editing by health care professionals and by consumers. I had to set up an editing process by signing up medical professionals and consumers to edit and critique my manuscripts. Before sending manuscripts to them, I explained that I expected them to be exacting and toughminded in their critique. I wanted them to tell me how I could improve the content and style of the book. They would make their comments on the manuscript and return them to me. I would review their recommendation, do more research, produce the next version, and go through the process again. We did this several times.

Let me thank all of you who spent so much of your time and expertise in contributing to making *The McNally Method*$^{SM}$ *for Managing Your Health Care* a reality that can help both consumers and providers.

| | |
|---|---|
| Peggy Adams | Roy Adams |
| Karen Bryant | Gwen Canepa |
| S. Joseph Canepa | Patrick M. Carter, M.D., M.B.A. |
| Mary Lou Di Natale, Ed.D., R.N. | Charles Fahey, M.S.W. |
| Toni Lynn Gallagher, M.A. | Ann Henson, R.N., B.S. |
| Frank Jirik | Emmet B. Keeffe, M.D. |
| Robert L. King, M.D., F.A.C.O.G. | Joseph Kinsella, M.B.A. |
| Felix O. Kolb, M.D., F.A.C.B. | Diana Laurent, M.P.H. |
| Cynthia A. Mahoney | Tom McMahon |
| Gayle L. McNally | Richard Middaugh |
| Frederick Parrella, Ph.D. | John Renner, M.D. |
| Michael Riordan, M.D. | Beth Robinson, R.N., B.S. |
| Joan Sarringhaus, R.N., B.S. | Patricia A. Scollard |
| Dudley Scott, M.D. | Suzanne Tamasie, M.Ed. |
| Jeanne Taylor | Jake J. Warde |
| Stan Weisner, Ph.D. | Joan White, R.N., M.A. |
| Karen Wolf, R.N., M.A. | James J. Woolever, Ph.D. |

In addition to all these contributors, a number of families struggling with serious medical problems asked for a copy of my book. When I sent them the manuscript, I made sure that they knew that it was preliminary and under copyright. I also encouraged them to call if they had any questions. To me they were simply people who were involved in a difficult medical situation like mine and needed help. As these families reported that the book was very helpful, I realized that this amounted to a good field test of the manuscript. I hope you too find the book helpful in *Managing Your Health Care*.

Bill McNally
Health Care Consumer

# Introduction: The Importance of Managing Your Health Care

---

Sooner or later you or a member of your family will have to
deal with a serious medical problem
emotionally, medically, and financially.
Don't worry about it, but be prepared to deal with it.

---

Living is dangerous. As a matter of fact, it's 100% fatal. It's not a question of whether you and your family are going to have one or more life-threatening illnesses or serious injuries during your lifetime. The only real questions are "When?" and "How are you going to deal with them?"

There are books, videotapes, cassette tapes, television shows, classes, exercise facilities, and spas concerned with helping us to achieve and maintain a healthy lifestyle. The food industry has provided us with fat-free, cholesterol-free, sugar-free, salt-free, and sometimes flavor-free foods. By now most of us know what we need to do in the way of nutrition and exercise, and we know what we should not do. We also should realize that our lifestyle decisions have a cumulative effect on our lives. What we do about our lifestyle comes down to personal choices.

This is not another "Eat healthy and exercise frequently to stay healthy" book. This book is about what happens when you or a family member has health problems in the United States. I have written this book based on my own experience with sudden, catastrophic illness. I want to share with you the lessons I learned and the techniques I developed for managing my health care from a medical and a financial standpoint. It will help you now, and someday you could really need it.

The steps you take now in preparing for medical problems in your family will largely determine whether you will have access to quality and affordable medical care. My preparation for potential medical problems consisted of selecting the most flexible and expensive insurance option my employer offered, in the belief that it had to be the best option. I was lucky. When I became ill, I had excellent insurance coverage. But I did not know what to expect, was not an effective patient, and was totally unprepared for the medical billing and insurance reimbursement task that awaited me.

You are taking an important first step in managing your health care by preparing for health problems now. To help you prepare, I'm going to cover the following topics:

- The importance of managing your health care
- The current health care systems in the United States
- Options among health insurance plans
- The health insurance decision-making process
- Medicare and Medicaid
- Medigap Plans
- Medicare HMOs (aka Senior Plans)
- The questions to ask about your Medicare options
- Making your Medicare decision
- Supplemental insurance
- The status and direction of health care in the United States
- Enhancing the health care you receive
- Managing your medical bills and insurance reimbursement

***DANGEROUS ATTITUDES!** "I can't spend time on health care issues. I have more urgent issues to deal with right now." and "Why should I worry about managing my health care? I have insurance; the doctors in the U.S. are the best; the health care system in the U.S. is the best; and I'm in great shape."*

These two attitudes were very common among Americans up until a short time ago. In the last few years, we have become aware of problems with availability and affordability of health care insurance. And we realize that without insurance most Americans cannot afford health care. Nevertheless, we tend to not personalize the problems that we see others having. At least, I never did.

I saw others who had family members struck down with life-threatening diseases or with a family member in a nursing home for years, but I just did not identify with their problems. I never believed it could happen to me.

When my wife wanted me to go to a doctor with flu problems, or whatever, I'd refuse to see a doctor or even to take over-the-counter medications in the dosage and frequency recommended. I placed great faith in the fact that I "come from good stock" and had a great immune system and a strong will.

"Why should I worry about managing my health care? I have insurance." This is exactly what I said five years ago. The only time I had been in a hospital was to have a tonsillectomy in 1942, at age 7. My parents checked me in at 6:00 AM and checked me out at 3:00 PM the same day. Once I was rid of my troublesome tonsils, I enjoyed good health until 1991. I started 1991 as a 56 year old and in great shape. I was working long hours, traveling internationally, golfing, and enjoying an active social life. I looked good and felt great at the time.

Then out of nowhere I became jaundiced. I ignored the problem for months, but my wife finally persuaded me to see a doctor. After eight months of tests and consultations with specialists, my problem was diagnosed. My immune system was attacking and destroying my liver as though it were a foreign body. I was told that this condition occurred very rarely in women and ten times more rarely in men. The doctors called it PBC (primary biliary cirrhosis). At the time it was diagnosed, I was advised that as my symptoms worsened I would have to have a liver transplant or die. A year later I nearly bled to death with an internal hemorrhage. My doctors said I had one to two years to live.

---

*Isn't it ironic that my immune system, of which I have always been so proud, caused my downfall. On the other hand, someone once said, "Pride goes before a fall."*

---

Six months later, I had a liver transplant. The operation was a success. Because PBC had left me with osteoporosis, however, my problems were far from over. While in the hospital recuperating from the transplant, I fell, shattering many of my bones. My shoulder, pelvis, hips, three of my vertebrae, and my tailbone were all broken. Five years after the original appearance of jaundice, I still have skeletal and liver problems and osteoporosis.

During the last five years, I have had to deal with many medical and financial issues. You will, too, when you or a member of your family has a major illness or a serious, life-threatening injury. Except for the good fortune of having selected a very comprehensive health insurance plan provided by my employer, I was totally unprepared for having a liver transplant, even though I knew it had to happen.

Between the second and third draft of this book I made a decision to "write the book I should have read six years ago." Unfortunately, no such book existed. I believe that even the healthiest of us can benefit from the lessons I have learned. As part of the process of writing this book and publishing it, 40 people have read multiple drafts and have given me detailed suggestions for improvements and corrections. They include doctors, nurses, insurance utilization review personnel, educators, and consumers. A number of the reviewers have reported deriving personal benefits from some part of the book, such as

- Being able to get more information from a doctor by knowing how to ask the right question the right way
- Understanding how the health care billing system works
- Knowing how to read "Explanations of Benefits" (EOBs)
- Being better able to make health care insurance or HMO decisions
- Making better "Open Enrollment" selections by knowing the questions to ask
- Understanding Medicare, its gaps and how to fill those gaps (Medigap and Medicare HMOs)

I hope that you, too, will begin deriving benefits today and be better prepared to help family, friends, and yourself when a medical crisis occurs.

---

*From my own passage through the health care system, I developed some tools and techniques to maximize the effectiveness of my visits with my physicians and to protect my financial position. I want to share this information with you.*

---

Television, newspapers, and magazines provide us with facts and opinions about health care and insurance on a daily basis. For many of us, it's more than we can absorb and relate. It can be a bewildering array of disjointed facts. In my opinion, this is one of the reasons that people don't pay enough attention to health care and insurance issues. It is also one of the reasons that I have written this tutorial and reference book and I plan to publish a bi-monthly newsletter. In the newsletter I will sort out the latest facts and relate them to this text. (You will find information about the newsletter in the mailer included at the end of this book.)

Throughout this book I have pulled facts together and presented them in tables and forms (in Appendix D) to help you understand and relate the health care and insurance information I am presenting. On complex subject matters I will start with simple tables, giving you an overview. Then I will build to more detailed tables. The Medicare subject matter is an example of this technique. Hopefully, the tables will enhance your understanding of the topic, and the forms will help you apply the information to your situation.

One prefatory note: This book is about consumer management of one's own health care. It is not about the clinical side of medical care, such as disease research and reports. You can, however, find a listing of firms you might want to contact for clinical information in the "Information Directory" (Appendix B). You will find names and voice, fax, internet, and mailing information listed under the heading "Medical Database Access and Report Services."

 **KEY POINTS** — **Introduction**

1. Take charge of your health care with *The McNally Method*.
2. It will help you now with doctors' office visits, insurance open enrollment periods, understanding your medical bills and explanations of benefits (EOBs), and making sure that your insurance company properly reimburses your expenses.
3. Someday you will have a medical crisis in your family.
4. Be ready to deal with it.

# PART I

# The Health Care System in the United States: What It Is and What It Is Not

# 2

# The U.S. Health Care System

> I often hear and read:
> "The United States has the finest
> health care system in the world."
> If this is true, then why did the President and Congress
> spend so much time on our health care system in 1994,
> accomplishing little if anything?

 **Status**

If you look in a dictionary you'll find that the word "system," as used in "the health care system," is defined as "an orderly way of getting things done." According to this definition, there are hundreds of health care systems in the United States, but not one overall Health Care System.

Why is this distinction between a national system and hundreds of local systems important to you? It's important because the phrase "The Health Care System," as used throughout the world, implies that there is a national process by which every citizen or taxpayer has access to a consistent standard of health care, regardless of medical history, delivered whenever and wherever it is needed, with affordability assured through the guaranteed availability of insurance at a reasonable cost, with or without governmental subsidies. Medicaid and Medicare, with their commercial companion insurance plans, Medigap and Medicare HMO Plans, are such systems for subsets of the population. The rest of us do not have this kind of reassuring health care insurance security.

We have over forty million Americans who are uninsured. They cannot afford individual health insurance, are not poor enough to join the ranks of the thirty-eight million who are covered by Medicaid, are not disabled or old enough to qualify as one of the thirty-eight million who have Medicare insurance, and do not have health insurance from their employer.

Some nations, which we might call welfare states, guarantee lifetime health care. Their citizens may also have employer-provided private health and retirement benefits. They can move from job to job without having any concern about insurance coverage or affordable medical care. Their benefits are said to be "portable." If their corporations downsize, the employees who are fired at least have continuation of their health care coverage, public or private, and in some countries vested retirement rights as well. With the exception of our 401K or equivalent plans and a short-term insurance option called COBRA, we do not have either of these safety nets. On the other hand, the countries who have these benefits also have tax structures that we would call "un-American."

COBRA (Consolidated Omnibus Budget Reconciliation Act), is designed to provide short-term health insurance coverage while we are between jobs, whether we resigned or were terminated. Through COBRA, we have the ability to convert group health insurance to individual insurance upon leaving the group (our employer). It provides coverage at a rate equal to the cost of coverage plus 2% administrative cost for 18 months (36 months in certain medical situations). COBRA is expensive. Nevertheless, it at least protects those of us who have employer provided health insurance until we find employment with an organization offering similar benefits or until the coverage period ends (18–36 months), whichever comes first.

 ## Legislative Activity

*"Tis better to light a single candle than to curse the darkness."*

Senators Kassebaum and Kennedy cosponsored a bill that passed both Houses of Congress on August 2, 1996, and was signed into law by President Clinton on August 20, 1996. The bill is known as *The Health Insurance Portability and Accountability Act*. Although it is not the health care reform envisioned by President and Mrs. Clinton in 1992, it is an important first step toward guaranteeing coverage to those with preexisting medical conditions in their family. An employee who is a member of an employer's group health care plan can change jobs with the assurance that he or she cannot be denied coverage by a new employer's group health care plan. The law's effective date is July 1, 1997, and it has five provisions as follow:

1. Requires group insurance plans to provide coverage within a year of starting a new job for employees with preexisting medical conditions.

2. Prohibits group insurance plans from dropping coverage for a sick employee or for an employer who has a sick employee.

3. Requires insurance companies to make individual coverage available to people who have group plans.

4. Sets up, on an experimental basis, some tax-deductible medical savings accounts for small businesses, the self-employed, and the uninsured.

5. Expands the tax-deductibility percentage allowable for health insurance premiums paid by the self-employed, from the current 30% to 80% by 2006.

Covered employees can continue coverage for 18 months through COBRA. If COBRA coverage is not available to them, they can continue coverage through the provisions of the Health Insurance Portability and Accountability Act as this act is written. I caution that the Health Insurance Portability and Accountability Act goes into effect on July 1, 1997. We won't really know how this act will be implemented until that time.

The law doesn't address the needs of every person who becomes permanently unemployed before age 65 with a personal or family history that includes a medical condition. Nevertheless, it provides our President and Congress with a framework for solving this serious health care insurance problem. I believe they will address this issue.

## *So if there isn't a National Health Care System, what is there?*

 **Health Care Delivery Systems**

We are fortunate to have excellent health care available to us in the United States, undoubtedly the best in the world. We have well-trained and informed specialists who have amazing diagnostic and treatment equipment at their disposal. Our teams of medical care providers can solve almost any problem, if they become involved early enough.

With the new age of technology, the benefits of research in teaching hospitals, where much of the nation's research takes place, can be made available electronically. For example, if Sloan Kettering Hospital for Cancer in New York acquires new research information about the timing or effectiveness for a chemotherapy protocol, this information will be available on electronic libraries (databases), making the findings available to other medical centers immediately. The key is that doctors have to be aware of the findings from their reading or have the curiosity to search the databases for the latest developments. You, too, can search the medical libraries and databases or have it done for you. Recently, there have been newspaper articles pointing out ways in which you can gain access to these medical databases. More about this later.

In addition to these major research and care centers, there are community-based health care systems. These community systems consist of several components, including a hospital or group of commonly owned or otherwise associated hospitals, designed to provide for your health care needs. They also include specialists and laboratory, ambulance, therapeutic, and other services. All of these professionals, services, and facilities are answerable to your doctor for providing what is required to meet your medical needs.

Before going any further, I need to briefly tell you about the range of health care and health insurance options available in the marketplace. You may obtain medical care through traditional fee-for-service. In this arrangement, you go to the doctor of your choice and pay for the services provided. You pay for the services yourself, unless you have a health insurance policy. Fee-for-service offers you the most freedom of choice and flexibility at the highest cost.

Or, at the other end of the health care spectrum, you may become a member of a Health Maintenance Organization (HMO). An HMO charges you a monthly or quarterly membership fee and then manages your health care. Access to specialists and other medical providers (e.g., hospitals, laboratories, clinics) is controlled by your HMO Primary Care Physician (PCP). When you join a managed care plan or an HMO, a Primary Care Physician, usually a general practitioner, internist, or family doctor, will either be assigned by your HMO or chosen by you. By managing your health care, the HMO is able to contain costs. There are a number of other health care and insurance choices, which I will discuss in later chapters. They are variations of the freedom of choice the patient has with fee-for-service and the cost-savings of managed care plans, including HMOs. At this point, I just want to familiarize you with the terms "fee-for-service" and "health maintenance organization."

If you're a fee-for-service patient and a specialist is required, your doctor may refer you to other providers he or she knows from being on the same hospital staff, from going to medical school together, from attending the same seminars or conferences, or from a variety of sources. Perhaps your doctor may refer you to someone known by reputation. In the HMO environment, your primary care physician will refer you to one of the HMO's specialists. Depending on the coverage your HMO offers, you could be referred to a non-HMO specialist for highly specialized health care procedures, such as a transplant. Whether in a fee-for-service based community system or as a member of an HMO, you will be referred to someone in whom your doctor has confidence. These networking systems can work well.

*Let's put health care in the United States in an historical perspective. Let's also look at the current trends and what they bode for the future.*

## An Historical Perspective

My parents did not have health care insurance until they were old enough for Medicare. They were able to pay for health care out of pocket. They may have had to pay the doctor a dollar or two a week for awhile if it was something relatively big. Nevertheless, they were self-insured and it worked for them. Today we call this the "Fee-For-Service" (FFS) model.

My wife and I had three children in the early to mid 1960s. Our family doctor charged $100 for prenatal care and delivery of our first daughter. It cost $125 to have an obstetrician provide prenatal care and delivery of each of our other two daughters. My employer-provided insurance paid for these expenses, the equivalent of one week's wages at the time. The five-day hospital stays were also covered and cost about $250 to $300 or just over two weeks' pay. Like our parents, my wife and I have always paid on a fee-for-service basis, meaning that we have gone to the doctors of our choice and paid for services rendered. Unlike our parents, we have always had health care insurance.

For those who earn $40,000 a year today, the same care would cost the equivalent of a month's salary for the doctor and two months' salary for the hospital stay, and the hospital stay would be 24 hours, not five days, as it was for my wife and daughters. Even though health care technique is better and hospital stays have shortened dramatically, the cost per unit of health care measured in earning power puts health care out of reach for the middle class unless they have insurance, which they may not be able to afford on their own. Fortunately, many of us work for an organization that provides some form of affordable health insurance.

When Medicare was enacted, medical costs started going up immediately and they've never stopped. In 1965 our doctor apologetically explained his 75% increase in the charge for an office visit (from $4 to $7) as resulting from Medicare, which was willing to pay $7. Medicare costs us in taxes and in the rising cost of health care. Recently the rate of inflation in health care has slowed somewhat, but it is still going up. There have been a number of other factors which have also contributed to the rising cost of health care. Among them are:

- High technology medical equipment for diagnosis and treatment
- Drug and genetic research
- Highly specialized treatment and surgical procedures (e.g., transplants, cancer treatment)
- Malpractice insurance cost
- The cost of having over 50% more hospital beds than are required
- The fact that we live longer and experience more medical problems than our forebears did

In response to the rising cost of health care, we have seen an increase in the managed care approach for the delivery of health care services. This movement has its roots in the clinics of the coal mining communities of West Virginia in the 1920s, where unions demanded that employers provide for the health care needs of their members. In turn, employers demanded that insurance companies lower cost of employee health care and find ways to improve employee wellness. Clinics were set up for the coal miners, and, over time, HMO benefits became part of their union contracts.

In the 1970s this innovative way for delivering lower cost health care started to show up in communities around the country, especially in California. Doctors and hospitals joined with HMOs to provide medical care for a fixed monthly fee. Their approach to providing health care was based on preventive medicine to maintain their members good health and catch problems early. This approach, combined with better utilization of resources, enabled them to provide health care for less. With rising costs and the pressure of helpful legislation, employers started offering this form of insurance to their employees. HMOs saved employers money and provided health care benefits to employees at lower out-of-pocket expense than the coverage being provided to them under a fee-for-service plan.

With the rapidly increasing cost of health care, more and more employers wanted plans by which they could continue to provide the same level of health care insurance to their employees, without increased cost to themselves or their employees. Health care insurance companies and HMOs responded with new options. As a result, my employer, for example, has found ways to increase our health care insurance coverage during this period of rising costs. They offer employees a choice of plans on a cost sharing basis. If I want fee-for-service insurance and am willing to pay more to get it, I can have it. On the other hand, I can have more benefits with very little cost to me if I sign up for a more structured HMO plan. There are also other options available to me with varying degrees of flexibility and cost.

The insurance plan options available to me from my employer are representative of the choices available in the health care marketplace to other employers and individuals alike. Many employees have found, however, that the insurance plan options offered have become more limited. Cost increases have put the more expensive options out of reach of many employers' benefits budgets. In the next chapter, "Insurance Plan Options," I will go into detail on the options available for consideration and some of the things you need to consider before making your health care insurance decision.

## ▼ KEY POINTS    The Health Care System

1. United States health care is technically great.
2. Expressed in middle-class earning power, medical care today costs four times what it did in the 1960s.
3. Except for the elderly, disabled, and very poor:
   No money + No insurance = No health care.
4. Not everyone can buy health insurance, even if they can afford it.

▲

# PART II

# Insurance Plans: Options and Informed Decisions

# Insurance Plan Options

---

Soothing words from the modern day Lorelei:
"Don't worry: you're covered."

---

 **My Experience**

At the time I became ill I didn't even know what my insurance covered. In 1993, when I was told I would die in one to two years at the outside unless I had a liver transplant with a 90% chance of survival, I blurted out that I didn't know if my insurance would cover it. There was a possibility that liver transplants could be considered "experimental" under the terms of my policy, meaning that they were not covered. It was something that I should have checked out a year earlier when I was told I would eventually need a transplant, but I didn't. Dumb, but true.

My medical bills totaled $637,921.12 for 1994. In 1995, I had a three-day hospital stay. The doctors' charges were $4,707.00; room and board, $5,583.00; hospital incidentals, $35,679.05. That's right—incidentals! The insurance provided by my employer has taken care of these bills and others, except for a modest expense which I paid, gladly.

Without insurance or with a policy that did not cover transplants, I would have had a tough decision in 1994. A liver transplant with a 90% chance of living would have financially decimated my family. My alternative was to continue losing liver function and die. But I was lucky, I had the coverage I needed. Today I am very aware of what insurance coverage I have and how it works.

Hopefully, your family has not had to deal with serious medical problems and never will. When a personal medical crisis does occur in your family, it's not just your life and your ability to return to good health that could be at risk. You also face the potential loss of all your assets, as the price you pay to get the medical help you or a family member needs.

In this chapter, I will provide you with information on the range of options available, how insurance plans work, key differences in the various plans, insurance terminology, and questions to use in evaluating options. Then I will guide you through a decision process to get you started on your insurance decision, and I will close with a summary. The topical outline follows:

- The Range of Available Options
- Health Insurance—Risk Sharing
- Insurance Plans and Terminology
- Fee-For-Service
- Health Maintenance Organization (HMO)

 ## The Range of Available Options

Let's start our insurance options evaluation with a comparison of the types of health care insurance currently available to employers and individuals. If you have employer-provided insurance, the options available will undoubtedly be limited. My employer offers employees a choice of plans, including Fee-For-Service with a Preferred Provider Option, a Managed Care Plan, and several Health Maintenance Organization plans. With rising health care costs, however, it's not uncommon for an employer to select a single HMO to maximize the health care available to employees at a cost that is affordable to the employer and the employees. Even in this situation, you may have some latitude if you are willing to pay for it. Nevertheless, a recent report states that 75% of those having employer group insurance receive their health care from HMOs.

Fee-for-service is at one end of the health care insurance spectrum. With this type of insurance offering, you are able to go to the doctor of your choice and self-refer to other health care providers (e.g., specialists), if you are willing and able to pay for the privilege of having this much flexibility and control. Many of us grew up with this approach to health care and are very comfortable with it.

Receiving your health care through an HMO is at the other end of the spectrum. This is especially true in the case of an HMO that has its own doctors, medical staff, hospitals, laboratories (labs) and other facilities. This type HMO organization is the model that was used for the initial HMOs. It's what many still visualize when they hear the term HMO. It's the least flexible and least patient-controlled option. On the other hand, it offers us low cost health care and provides preventive care.

Each of these two approaches, fee-for-service and HMO, has inherent advantages and disadvantages. Although the fee-for-service approach is expensive and provides financial incentive for overuse of tests and procedures, it has the advantage of being the traditional approach. We seem to be conditioned to think that when we get sick the more tests, procedures, and medications we have, the better. In the 1980s, having had a triple bypass was a badge of honor for some. Some men proudly showed off their scar. That mentality seems to have lost favor. Nevertheless, we still tend to measure health care by our recovery from illness. It's "the old way."

For years dentists, ophthalmologists, optometrists, and gynecologists have sent their patients reminders of the need for a checkup, something we all seem to appreciate. They make it easy for us to dutifully show up for our appointment. It's a system that works. HMOs in their very name spell out the fact that they take the same approach raised to a higher level—Health Maintenance Organizations. Yet they have not gained the public acceptance that they might have. Many of the reasons given seem to boil down to a lack of flexibility, having to go through a primary care physician for all medical services, and a mistrust of the insurer's also being the provider.

The two objections to joining an HMO that I *hear* most frequently have to do with being forced to change doctors and not being able to self-refer. As you will see when we discuss the various types of HMOs available today, you may not have to change doctors. In addition, the chronically ill who must regularly see a specialist, as in my case, may not have to be referred to the specialist each time. Women who want or need to see their gynecologist also may not need a referral from a primary care physician (PCP). In fact, a woman might be able to keep her gynecologist as her PCP. There are HMOs who are able to offer these options, given the nature of their organization. Whether or not you have access to one is another question.

Over the years, HMOs have developed a number of variations in their health care delivery systems. If you grew up in a fee-for-service world, as I did, you need to look at what's available today. There are a number of employer and individual options. HMOs have not changed their preventive medicine principle, but there are some options that provide more latitude in provider selection. There are also many more private practice specialists who provide medical care to HMO members. I will show you these variations later in this chapter.

## Health Insurance–Risk Sharing

Health insurance protects you against the possibility of having unaffordable medical expenses. In return for your premium payment, an insurer agrees to pay your health care expenses. The insurer is said to indemnify its policyholders, thus the term "indemnity insurance company." Your premium amount is based on the odds (actuarial risk) that the insurer will have to pay health care bills and on the potential amount of those bills.

To the extent that you are willing to share in the risk, the insurer's risk and, therefore, your premium go down. There are several ways in which traditional/indemnity health insurance companies write their policies to have you share the financial risk. The most commonly used risk-sharing policy provisions follow:

- *Annual deductible* You pay all expenses up to a preset annual limit (e.g., $200).
- *Copayments* You pay a set amount for each office visit, or other designated procedure, throughout the year (e.g., $15).
- *Out-of-Pocket (OOP) Expense* After your annual deductible is paid, you pay a percent of the expenses for all procedures, except those for which you make a copayment, up to an annual limit (e.g., 20% of the cost until you have paid $1,000).
- *Cap* The insurer pays according to the terms of your policy up to a pre-set amount, as specified in your policy. The amount will be the maximum the insurer will pay per disease, per incident, or in your lifetime (e.g., $250,000 for a liver transplant). Once the insurer has paid the limit, you are on your own for that disease or that incident or your lifetime. If you have a maximum amount for which the insurer will pay "per lifetime" stipulated in your policy or agreement and you reach it, you no longer have health insurance.

HMOs insure against medical expense in return for membership dues or fees. They use a variety of techniques for risk-sharing. Of the risk-sharing techniques listed above, HMOs tend to only use copayments. They also control costs by making sure that each member has a primary care physician (PCP) who manages the member's health care and makes all referrals, as specified in the HMO's membership agreements. HMOs place heavy emphasis on maintaining the health of their members with fitness programs, patient education, and preventive medicine procedures (e.g., physical examinations). Through their commitment to these "wellness" programs, HMOs try to keep their members healthy. If they are successful in maintaining the good health of their members, HMOs will not have to restore good health with expensive tests and procedures. In this way, the successful HMO accomplishes its mission for the membership and enjoys financial benefits as a result.

HMOs have ways to share risks with insurance companies. They may elect to protect themselves against the high cost of catastrophic illness by buying "stop-loss" insurance from indemnity insurance companies. This means that the HMO will bear the expense of a major illness up to a limit. When the limit has been reached, the stop-loss insurance takes over, meaning the indemnity insurance company pays the costs incurred from that point forward.

They also share risk with doctors, hospitals, and laboratories through a variety of financial arrangements. One of these arrangements is called "capitation" (a dollar amount per member). For example, an HMO will contract with a laboratory to provide services to any and all its members, as frequently as needed, in return for a flat amount per member per month or quarter. The payment is calculated by multiplying the capitation rate per patient (e.g., $1/member/month) by the number of members within an HMO (e.g., 50,000). In this example, the HMO would pay the laboratory $50,000 per month.

If none of the HMO's members need laboratory work in a given month, the laboratory does well financially. On the other hand, if all members needed tests run several times a month, the laboratory could have a problem. In this example, the HMO has limited its cost, or risk, to a flat amount paid to the laboratory each month, and the laboratory has a guaranteed monthly cash flow. When HMOs have this type contractual arrangement with hospitals, laboratories, and other providers, their patients do not have to be involved in the billing and insurance reimbursement process. This is a significant benefit to the members.

Some HMOs pay hospitals on a "per diem" basis. This is a monthly payment to the hospital for the number of member days spent in the hospital over the course of the month. This payment is part of a contract between the HMO and the hospital. The rates per day per member are specified in the contract, with different rates based on the type care provided (e.g., surgery, critical care, maternity).

You might hear the term "carve-out" in relation to HMOs. This is another risk-sharing technique some HMOs use. It refers to an HMO's practice of "carving-out" the treatment of certain diseases (e.g., cancer) or certain highly specialized surgical procedures (e.g., transplants). If the HMO makes the decision to "carve-out" the treating of cancer from their area of specialization, they would contract with a cancer practice and refer members with cancer to that practice. They might use a form of capitation as the basis for the contract. In other words, they would pay the cancer practice an amount per member per month, multiplied by the number of members in the HMO. The specific amount per patient would be based on the demographics (e.g., age, gender) of the HMO's membership.

An important point to remember about the range of health care insurance choices available to you is that insurance policies, whether from indemnity insurance companies or from HMOs, have rules you must follow. If you do not follow the rules spelled out in your policy, be prepared to pay a financial penalty. It's not a question of whether you can self-refer (e.g., go to see a specialist without your doctor's referral); go to a doctor who is not under contract to the insurance company or the HMO; get emergency room treatment without pre-authorization; or whatever. It's a question of whether you can do so within the terms of your insurance policy or your HMO membership agreement.

Your premium payment or monthly membership fee is based on your policy or HMO plan. If you do not follow the rules, you unilaterally expose your insurance carrier or HMO to risk (cost). You will not have paid them to take that risk by paying a higher premium or membership fee. If you're lucky, you may only have to pay a higher copayment percentage, but it's more likely that you will have to pay all costs, unless you can prove that extenuating circumstances justified incurring the unauthorized costs.

You might apply for an exception to the rules for a case in which you were taken to an emergency room by paramedics without pre-authorization because you had serious injuries and were unconscious. Even though you should have to pay based strictly on the wording of your contract, your insurer or HMO might override the terms of your policy because of the circumstances and seriousness of your injury. Contractually, they do not have to grant an exception, and might not.

*When you first become involved with the world of medicine, health insurance, and HMOs, you'll find it's like being in a somewhat familiar foreign country. You understand some of the words being used, but not enough of them to make sense out of what is being said. You can ask for an English translation, but there are some words and phrases you are going to have to learn to survive. There's no better time to learn the language than now.*

 ## Health Care Terminology

Our next section is about the variations in health care insurance plans that are available. I will be explaining and using some new terminology in that section. Therefore, I thought I should provide a summary of the terminology used so far for your review. You might want to scan it, just to make sure you're familiar with these terms. This will be the first of a series of definitions that I will include throughout the book. These definitions are combined to form a Glossary, which can be found in the appendices, for your reference.

### Laws

**COBRA**—The law (Consolidated Omnibus Budget Reconciliation Act) that allows employees having employer health insurance to convert it, at the time of their resignation or involuntary termination from employment, into personal and family health insurance for 18 months (36 months with certain health problems).

**The Health Insurance Portability and Accountability Act**—The law that assures employees having employer group health care insurance, that they and their covered dependents will be insurable under a new employer's health insurance plan within one year of employment and that they can buy the insurance coverage they had until their new employer insurance becomes effective.

## Insurance Plans

**Fee-For-Service**—The practice of going to a medical provider (e.g., doctor, laboratory) of our choice and paying for the service performed, personally or through insurance. It offers maximum flexibility and choice for the patient, at maximum cost.

**Health Maintenance Organization (HMO)**—A form of health insurance based on preventive medicine and maintaining of the wellness of its enrollees. Individuals join as members and receive their care through the personnel and facilities that are part of the organization or are under contract to provide health care to the organization's members. Though this health maintenance plan is the least flexible and patient-controlled option, it is a relatively low-cost health care option.

## Health Care and Insurance Terminology

**CAP**—The limit on the amount of coverage that the insurance company will provide (e.g., $250,000 lifetime limit per patient).

**Capitation**—One of the techniques used by HMOs to pay for specific services performed for members of the HMO. The HMO pays a set amount per member per month or quarter multiplied by the number of members in the HMO (e.g., $1/month × 50,000 members = $50,000).

**Copayments**—A stipulated amount that the patient must pay each time he or she receives a specified service (e.g., $15/office visit).

**Carve-Outs**—An HMO practice of contracting with a highly specialized practice (e.g., cancer treatment center, liver transplant team) to treat members needing their services. The HMO is said to "carve-out" in this example, cancer treatment and liver transplants.

**Deductible**—The amount a patient must pay for health care within a year (e.g., $200) before receiving insurance benefits (e.g., reimbursement).

**Indemnity Insurance Company**—An organization that will indemnify (pay for) pre-identified types of losses, which you may incur, in return for your payment of premiums, based on the indemnity insurance company's actuarial risk of incurring losses.

**Out-of-Pocket Expense (OOP)**—The amount of money a patient must pay annually as a percentage of the cost of his or her health care, after having paid an annual deductible amount, if that provision is also part of the patient's insurance policy. OOP is sometimes referred to as coinsurance.

**Per Diem**—The arrangement HMOs sometimes make with hospitals to pay a fixed rate per day of hospital occupancy, per member, per type of care provided by the hospital (e.g., surgery, critical care, maternity).

**Provider**—A professional or facility that provides health care.

**Self-refer**—The right of a patient to determine when and to whom to go for health care.

**Stop-Loss**—An insurance policy that indemnifies the policy buyer (e.g., HMO) from losses above a pre-set limit (e.g., $250,000), at which level the indemnifying organization starts to pay.

## KEY POINTS         The Range of Available Options

1. Traditional Approach = Fee-For-Service
   Go to any doctor when sick
   Recover from illness
   Pay for services rendered (Insurance and Patient)
2. Preventive Approach = Managed Care & HMO
   Pay membership fee
   Prevent illness with diet, exercise, and physical examinations
   Medical services provided by Primary Care Physician
   Services prepaid by membership fee
3. Know how your insurance works
4. Make an informed insurance decision now, when you don't need it and can get it.

### Insurance Plans

I am going to use diagrams in this section to explain the most common types of fee-for-service insurance policies and health maintenance organizations. Instead of giving you a long list of health care and insurance terminology, I will define and explain the new terminology as we go. Terms and phrases that have not previously been explained or defined will be shown in quotes (e.g., "Provider") throughout the insurance option we are discussing at the time (e.g., Fee-For-Service), but not in subsequent text.

As you go through this section, there is no need to memorize definitions. You will probably become quite familiar with the basic terminology as we go along. If from time to time you're not sure of the meaning of a word or a phrase, look it up in the glossary.

Health care insurers are innovative. Expect to find hybrids or combinations of the plans I'm going to show you. The examples I use are only intended to explain the types of insurance plans available and the terminology used in the industry. You may never find the exact plans I have shown you, however, armed with the following diagrams, terminology definitions and explanations, I think you should be able to understand other offerings.

For each insurance plan or option in this section, I will provide the following:

- Introductory comments
- Diagram of professional and financial relationships
- Description of the diagram
- Summary of key points

We will start by explaining three forms of fee-for-service health insurance.

- Fee-For-Service in its purest form
- Fee-For-Service with a Preferred Provider Option (PPO)
- Managed Care based on a fee-for-service plan with a primary care physician

*"Years ago, my first employer group health insurance did not restrict my choice of doctors and hospitals. Is that type of insurance available today?" Yes, it is. Read on.*

### Fee-For-Service

Fee-for-service health insurance lets you to go to any health care provider for your medical needs, including specialists. The ability to go to a specialist, without a referral from your primary care physician (e.g., general practitioner, family doctor, internist) is known as the ability to "self-refer." It is unlikely that you will find many insurers offering fee-for-service in this form as a stand-alone policy. I am going to explain fee-for-service insurance, because it is the cornerstone on which other insurance plans are built, but you will more likely find this as a defined form of service covered within another type of policy. Fee-for-service coverage, in that case, would be available at extra expense (payment of a higher copayment or out of pocket expense). The insurer offering this option would most often be a health care insurance company, but this option could also be stipulated within the terms of an HMO agreement, as I will discuss later.

Refer to the diagram, as you read the following explanations. The diagram has four significant parties or class of parties on it. They are:

1. the "Patient"
2. the "Insurance Company"
3. the "Claims Office"
4. the "Providers"

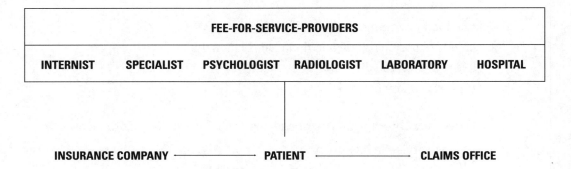

1. You as the "Patient" are the focal point of a fee-for-service insurance policy. You are the decision maker, the communications hub, and the payment hub. You decide which "Providers" to use and when to use them. When you receive services from a "Provider," you pay the bill and send a copy of it with the "Insurance Company" claim form to the "Claims Office."

The "Claims Office" adjusts the "Provider's" charges to the "Usual and Customary" amounts for your community. You are reimbursed based on those amounts and the terms of your insurance policy. You will receive an "Explanation of Benefits" ("EOB") listing the services, the amounts billed for each of them, the "Usual and Customary" amount for each charge, the amount of reimbursement for each line item on the bill, and codes explaining any exceptions that the "Claims Office" has taken to the billed amount. If you don't agree with the amount reimbursed, you will need to call the "Claims Office." Whether you are reimbursed in full or not, you are responsible for the total amount shown on your "Provider's" bill.

2. The "Insurance Company" is the organization from which you bought your policy, even though you may have signed up for it through your employer. If you bought it directly from the "Insurance Company,"

you would contact them directly to get questions answered. If you bought the insurance through your employer, your initial contacts will probably be with your employer's Human Resource or Personnel organization. You'll find that on a day-to-day basis, most of your questions will have to do with claim reimbursement, and you typically will call the "Claims Office" to discuss an "Explanation of Benefits."

3. The "Claims Office," in a fee-for-service environment, primarily works with the "Patient." There may be "Providers," however, who will file claims with the "Claims Office" on your behalf. When that happens, the "Claims Office" will send its reimbursement directly to the "Provider" with an "Explanation of Benefits." They will also send a copy to you. You should then wait to be billed by the provider for the balance due from you, before you pay it.

4. The "Provider" is the professional or organization from whom you receive health care. Many use the term "Provider" interchangeably with the word "Doctor." The definition of a "Provider" which prevails is the one used by your insurance policy. It will undoubtedly include hospitals, laboratories, skilled nursing facilities, and others. It may or may not include people you rely on for health care, such as chiropractors or alternative medicine practitioners. The definition of "Providers" in your insurance policy is the definition that prevails. It is not a question of who *should* be included as a "Provider," it is a question of who *was* included in writing and pricing your policy.

---

### ▼ KEY POINTS                           Fee-For-Service

1. You can use any "Provider."
2. The "Provider" bills you.
3. You file for reimbursement with the insurance "Claims Office."
4. "Claims Office" adjusts provider's charges to "Usual and Customary" amounts.
5. "Claims Office" reimburses you for "Usual and Customary" charge amounts.
6. You pay the "Provider's" bill.

---

*"My spouse and I both have chronic conditions. We have been going to the same family physician for years. Each of us has also been going to our own specialist for a long time. We don't want to change doctors, but want to cut our medical expenses. What is there for us?" You may want to look into a Preferred Provider Option.*

### Fee-For-Service With Preferred Provider Option

Fee-For-Service with "Preferred Provider Option" (PPO) is just what its name implies. This plan is usually called the "Preferred Provider Option" or "PPO Plan." With this plan, the patient has all the options open to him or her as under a fee-for-service plan. In addition, the patient can elect to use preferred providers, who have agreed to discount their services under terms of their "Preferred Provider Organization Contract" with the patient's insurance company. (Note: You might find a "Preferred Provider Option" insurance plan that does not include fee-for-service provisions.)

I have said that I have had a fee-for-service plan, and I do, but to be more specific my plan is a Fee-For-Service plan with a preferred provider option. In my community, most of the providers are included in my insurance company's preferred provider plan. You will probably find the same to be true in your community, if you look into this option.

The entrepreneur physicians do not have a lot of choice. A doctor friend of mine in another community told me of a friend of his who lost 510 out of 512 patients that he had from one employer in town. The employer signed up for an insurance plan with another insurer, and the doctor was not part of that insurer's plan. The patients who worked for that employer, or their spouses, simply could not afford to come to him anymore.

If you refer to the diagram on the next page, you will notice that its top half is the same as in the Fee-For-Service diagram. The patient interactions with the Fee-For-Service providers, the insurance company, and the claims office are unchanged from what they were in the Fee-For-Service (only) plan.

The "Preferred Providers" half of the diagram looks similar to the "Fee-For-Service" half, but there are different relationships of the parties shown in the diagram, based on the "Preferred Provider Organization Contract" that the "Preferred Providers" entered into with the insurance company. The difference is depicted on the diagram by the "Preferred Provider Organization Contract" line between the "Preferred Providers" and the patient, insurance company, and claims office.

The "Preferred Provider Option" differences from Fee-For-Service are in the following:

1. The insurance company's interaction with the "Preferred Providers"

2. The "Preferred Provider Organization Contract"

3. The claims office interaction with the "Preferred Providers"
4. Your interaction with the "Preferred Providers"
5. Your interaction with the claims office relative to the "Preferred Providers"

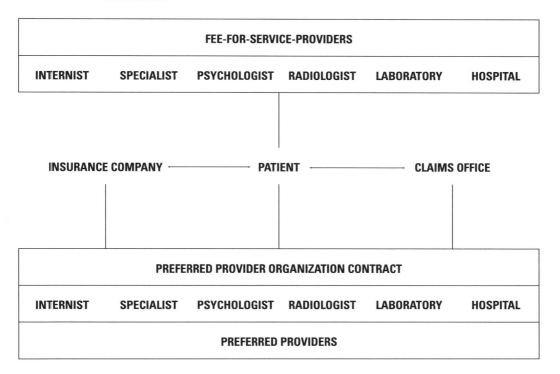

1. With this plan, the insurance company's relationship with those providers who are not "Preferred Providers" does not change. The insurance company has a direct relationship, however, with the "Preferred Providers." It recruited them and had them sign a "Preferred Provider Option Contract," which defines their relationships.

2. Under the terms of the "Preferred Provider Organization Contract," the "Preferred Providers" accept discounted fees for services performed for "Preferred Provider Option" policyholders.

3. "Preferred Providers" send their claims directly to the claims office. The claims office adjusts the "Preferred Provider's" charges to the usual and customary amounts for your community. The claims office discounts the charges as agreed in the "Preferred Provider Organization Contract." They send an EOB and reimbursement to the "Preferred Provider."

4. You do not pay "Preferred Providers" at the time the services are performed (known as the "Date of Service"). You will receive a copy of the

EOB sent to the "Preferred Provider." At that time you know the amount of the usual and customary balance due. Wait for a bill from the "Preferred Provider." If it does not match the amount you owe as shown on the EOB, pay the EOB amount.

5. You are responsible for payment of your bill in the "Preferred Provider" environment. As the responsible party, you may have to call the claims office or the "Preferred Provider's" billing service. On a number of occasions, I have had to call the claims office either because I spotted an error on the EOB or because the "Preferred Provider" billed me after being unsuccessful in their efforts to get payment from the claims office.

### ▼ KEY POINTS    Preferred Provider Option

1. Insurance company signs providers to a "Preferred Provider Organization Contract."
2. Contract discounts services to "Preferred Provider Option" patients.
3. "Preferred Provider" sends bills to claims office.
4. Claims office adjusts charges to usual and customary amounts and applies discounts.
5. Claims office sends EOB and payment to "Preferred Provider," with a copy to the patient.
6. Patient pays balance of discounted usual and customary charges when billed by "Preferred Provider."

▲

*"Friends of ours have an 'Exclusive Provider Option.' It sounds expensive. Is it?" As a matter of fact, it's a health insurance plan designed to save money. I'll explain.*

 **Exclusive Provider Plan**

The "Exclusive Provider Plan" is a "Managed Care Plan" that a major employer in a community negotiates with a local physician network. You may find that you have this plan available to you if you are in your employer's headquarters location or in a community having a substantial population of employees (e.g., plant site). Your employer must have a substantial number of employees to be able to negotiate a favorable contract with a local physician network, including their associated hospitals, laboratories, clinics, surgical centers, and so forth. The employer would probably offer other standard plans, available from health insurance companies or HMOs, to employees in remote sites.

When looking at the diagram for the "Exclusive Provider Plan," you will find that, except for the absence of a Fee-For-Service option, it is similar to the Preferred Provider Option. It's unlikely that you will find a Fee-For-Service option combined with an "Exclusive Provider Plan."

The key differences between the "Exclusive Provider Plan" and a Fee-For-Service Plan with a Preferred Provider Option follow:

1. The Employer's involvement
2. The "Exclusive Provider Organization Contract"
3. The role of the "Insurance Company" and its "Claims Office"
4. The role of the "Primary Care Physician" ("PCP")
5. The patient's access to specialists and other providers

| EMPLOYER | | | | | |
|---|---|---|---|---|---|
| EXCLUSIVE PROVIDERS | | | | | |
| PCP | SPECIALIST | PSYCHOLOGIST | RADIOLOGIST | LABORATORY | HOSPITAL |
| EXCLUSIVE PROVIDER ORGANIZATION CONTRACT | | | | | |

INSURANCE COMPANY ——— PATIENT ——— CLAIMS OFFICE

1. The "Employer" negotiates directly with a local physician network and their associated provider facilities to provide managed health care to its employees, at low cost to the employer and its employees.

2. The "Exclusive Provider Organization Contract" is between the employer and the local physician network.

3. An Insurance Company and its Claims Office administer the provisions of the "Exclusive Provider Option Contract" for the "Employer."

4. A "Primary Care Physician" (e.g., general practitioner, internist, family physician) is your doctor, who manages your health care and makes all referrals for you. The "Exclusive Provider Organization Contract" provisions determine whether or not you can select your "Primary Care Physician."

5. Your access to specialists and other providers is through your "Primary Care Physician," sometimes referred to as a "Gatekeeper" because of the role he or she fills as your access to the local physician network with whom your "Employer" negotiated the "Exclusive Provider Organization Contract."

---

### ▼ KEY POINTS     Exclusive Provider Option

1. Your "Employer" signs up a local physician network as "Exclusive Providers."
2. "Exclusive Provider Organization Contract" discounts health care services.
3. "Insurance Company" and its "Claims Office" administer the contract.
4. "Primary Care Physician" manages your health care.
5. "Primary Care Physician" ("Gatekeeper") makes all referrals for you.

▲

---

 ## Health Care Terminology Update

Here's a summary of the terminology we used in the section just completed on Fee-For-Service, Preferred Provider Plan, and Exclusive Provider Plan. You may want to scan these definitions just to make sure you are familiar with them, before moving on to the section on Health Maintenance Organization variations.

### Insurance Plans

**Exclusive Provider Option**—A health care insurance plan in which the providers are members of a local physician network which has been recruited by an employer to provide discounted managed care to the employer's employees.

**Managed Care Plan**—A Fee-For-Service type plan in which the policyholder sees an assigned doctor who manages his or her care and who, as needed, refers the patient to providers who participate in the plan.

**Preferred Provider Option (PPO Plan)**—An option provided as an adjunct to a Fee-For-Service Plan. The insured can use any of the Preferred Providers who have signed a contract with the insurance company to accept discounted fees for their services and file for reimbursement directly with the insurance company's claims office.

## Health Care and Insurance Terminology

**Claims Office**—The insurance claims processing and reimbursement function of an insurance company.

**Explanation of Benefits (EOB)**—The form that the claims office sends to the provider claimant and/or the patient as a transmittal and explanation of its claim reimbursements. It shows the charges, reimbursements, and any explanations required.

**Gatekeeper**—A colloquial name given to the "Primary Care Physician" who, in a managed care or an HMO environment, controls access to other providers.

**Preferred Provider**—A professional or facility that provides health care and has signed a contract with an insurance company to do so at a discount for its policyholders.

**Preferred Provider Organization (PPO)**—The insurance company's view of the "Preferred Providers." The insurance company signs providers to a contract as "Preferred Providers" and is then able to sell a "Preferred Provider Plan."

**Preferred Provider Organization Contract**—A document signed by health providers agreeing to file claims directly with a claims office and to accept discounted reimbursement for their services.

**Primary Care Physician (PCP)**—The physician assigned as a health care manager to each patient having Managed Care Insurance and to each member of an HMO. He or she also functions as a "Gatekeeper," controlling all access to other providers.

**Usual and Customary**—The phrase that describes allowable insurance claim charge amounts for the procedures performed in the provider's community.

## Fee-For-Service Summary

As I mentioned, most Fee-For-Service plans also include a Preferred Provider option. With this type of plan, you are free to go to the doctor of your choice, but it's to your financial advantage to use only Preferred Providers. From my experience, most providers in the community will accept Preferred Provider rates, even though they have not signed my insurance company's Preferred Provider organization contract. Whenever I am referred to another doctor or facility and I call for an appointment, I always ask if the doctor or organization is one of my insurance company's Preferred Providers.

There are a couple who have said that they were not, but that they would accept the Preferred Provider fee rate. I make a note of the date, time, and name of the person with whom I spoke. Later, I use this information when I call them to write-off the balance due (charges billed less discounted reimbursement).

With all the procedures and tests I have had, and all the providers I've seen, I have only found one provider who does not accept the Preferred Provider reimbursement rate. He requires cash on delivery of services. This particular physician is a renowned specialist who started treating me while I was hospitalized after my liver transplant and fall. When I see this provider, I pay him and have to file for insurance reimbursement. It's a bit of a nuisance and more expensive for me, but in this case, well worth it. Using Preferred Providers has not been a problem for me. It has been a benefit.

Your employer may provide a managed care plan, which uses Exclusive Providers or Preferred Providers. In this case, you would have a primary care physician who, in the role as your case manager, controls access to other providers. The provisions of your policy will determine whether you may select your Primary Care Physician or will have one assigned to you. A Managed Care plan should be less expensive than a Fee-For-Service plan with a preferred provider option because the insurer has a more controllable risk.

A number of different types of policies have evolved from the original fee-for-service policies. Demands for lower cost health care insurance brought this about. We have policies with a variety of options, from freedom of choice in the selection of providers, to selection from a network of preferred providers, to a plan which has a primary care physician.

Less flexible, lower cost policies evolved from the fee-for-service base. At the same time, HMOs started offering more flexible, somewhat higher cost, managed care plans. I will talk about the HMO offerings next.

---

*The more freedom of choice, the more it costs.*
*The more managed your care, the less it costs.*

## Health Maintenance Organization Introduction

Although I have discussed the functioning of a Health Maintenance Organization in the "Health Insurance—Risk Sharing" section, that was from the perspective of the HMO as an insurer. Now I want to discuss HMOs from your perspective, as a patient and a member. I will use the same format that I used in explaining Fee-For-Service, Preferred Provider Option, and Exclusive Provider Option, with one exception. The newer HMOs contract with physicians and facility organizations to provide care. I am going to explain some of the terminology, functions, and services of these physicians and facility organizations before explaining the range of HMO plans available.

From your perspective, there are two types of Health Maintenance Organizations. The first one is called the "Staff Model HMO." The term refers to the way in which the original HMOs were organized. They had their own staff of physicians and medical personnel, as well as their own hospitals, clinics, laboratories, and other facilities. The "Staff Model HMO" is no longer the prevalent Health Maintenance Organization.

Today most of the HMOs that you are likely to encounter either do not have their own medical staffs and facilities, or, if they do, they augment their resources with those of other organizations. With hospital occupancy rates hovering at the 50% level, even "Staff Model HMOs" are starting to send their members to underutilized hospitals and do so at very favorable rates. In this way, "Staff HMOs" are able to avoid building new hospitals for their growing member populations. In some cases, they are even able to shut down their own hospitals. With the profit squeeze on small non-profit hospitals and their low occupancy rates, this is a trend that you can expect to continue.

Most HMOs enter into contracts with other organizations to have them provide primary care, specialist care, hospital services, and other services to their members. The HMO specifies the "protocols" (rules for any procedure) that the physician organization must follow in treating the HMO's members. These HMOs are given a name corresponding to the type of medical organization that provides physician care to the HMOs' patients. For example, a Health Maintenance Organization that enters into a contract with a "Medical Group" of doctors, is called a "Group Model HMO." A Medical Group, sometimes referred to as a "Group Practice," consists of physicians organized as a partnership, professional corporation, or other association.

Similarly, an HMO that contracts with an "Independent Physician Association" or "IPA," is referred to as an "IPA Model HMO." An Independent Physician Association is just what its name implies, an association of entrepreneurial doctors. The "Association" part of the organization provides administrative and other services to the "Independent Physicians." One of these "other" services is "Credentialing." This is the determination of whether or not a physician has proper credentials to practice medicine and, if a specialist, to practice as a specialist. You and I want to know if the doctors and specialists to whom we are referred are doctors in good standing, and the reputation of "Independent Physician Association" requires that all their physicians are "qualified physicians" and all specialists are "qualified specialists."

When "IPAs," HMOs, and other organizations monitor their "Credentialing," they use objective measurements to determine the qualifications of their physicians to provide patient care, in general and in their specialty. Each physician is required to pass a multi-day series of written and oral tests, the "Boards," within 5 years of completing his or her residency. Residency is served on the staff of a hospital as the last phase of a physician's training. Passing or failing of the "Boards" is a very important part of "Credentialing."

The physician who elects to become a specialist must have additional training and must pass another battery of tests in his or her chosen specialty. Physicians and specialists who have completed their required training but have not yet passed their "Boards" are said to be "Board Eligible," as opposed to "Board Certified."

"Credentialing" is very important to you as a prospective HMO member, because you may not have any voice in the selection of your "Primary Care Physician" and your specialists. This is particularly true in a "Staff Model HMO." Whether you are considering membership in a "Staff Model HMO" or an HMO that contracts with other organizations for their physicians, you need to know that your "Primary Care Physician" and the specialists to whom you will be referred are fully qualified. More about this later.

"Utilization Management" is another important management service provided by the "Independent Physician Association." It refers to the evaluation of a procedure proposed by a physician for a specific patient before it is performed. The physician must be able to justify that, given the patient's problem, it is a needed, appropriate, and effective procedure. This is a management technique used by the health insurers, "IPAs," and HMOs to make sure that the patient is not being subjected to unnecessary and costly procedures.

The diagnostic, treatment, and billing practices that a physician has used over a period of time are also evaluated, using "Utilization Management" techniques. For example, on a national basis, 22% of full-term pregnancies are terminated by caesarian section delivery. This has trended up from 11% in 1972, which raises a concern about the increasing number of mothers who are incurring additional risk in delivery, not to mention their increased and lengthened postpartum discomfort. An obstetrician on an "IPA" or HMO staff who was found to have a 70% caesarian delivery rate would, at a minimum, be asked some questions as to why.

Before moving on to descriptions of HMOs as you would see them, I need to familiarize you with two more HMO terms, "Case Management" and "Formulary." "Case Management" is a technique used by HMOs to monitor and coordinate the treatment of patients who are seriously or chronically ill, have long term hospital stays, or have other problems calling for multi-specialty long-term care. This function is over and above the health care management role of your "Primary Care Physician" ("PCP").

Some HMOs offer prescription drug coverage to their members. The amount of coverage and the cost will vary from one HMO's plan to another. The prescription drug benefit, however, will undoubtedly have a cost limit. The HMO will provide your doctors with a list of low-cost drugs from which they can prescribe. That list of drugs is referred to as the "Formulary."

##  Types of Health Maintenance Organizations

*"We have three generations in our family and need to save money on health care. I would also like to be able to take everyone to the same place to see the doctor. If we have to change doctors to meet our needs, that's OK with me. Is there any combination of insurance and medical association for us?" Yes, there is. Read on.*

### Staff Model Health Maintenance Organization (HMO)

From your perspective as a potential HMO member and patient, there are two types of Health Maintenance Organizations. One has its own medical staff and facilities. The other uses the staffs and facilities of other organizations to provide health care to the HMO's patients, according to the HMO's protocols (rules for dealing with any situation that can occur). First, I will discuss the workings of the "Staff HMO," the key elements of which follow:

1. Your "Membership Agreement"
2. The charges for which you are responsible
3. The role of the "Primary Care Physician" ("PCP")
4. Your access to specialists and medical facilities
5. Your access to emergency care

| STAFF MODEL HMO | | | | |
|---|---|---|---|---|
| SPECIALISTS | LABORATORIES | EMERGENCY CARE | HOSPITAL | OTHER FACILITIES |
| PRIMARY CARE PHYSICIAN | | | | |

MEMBERSHIP AGREEMENT

MEMBER/PATIENT

1. Your "Membership Agreement" will specify your monthly or quarterly membership fees and any other charges you might have to pay (e.g., copayments for office visits) as a "Member/Patient." You should not receive any other bills unless you incur costs without the pre-authorization or referral of your "Primary Care Physician."

2. A "Primary Care Physician" (e.g., general practitioner, internist, family physician) is your doctor, who manages your health care and makes all your referrals to specialists and facilities.

3. The "Staff Model HMO" "Membership Agreement" will specify your rights as they apply to your "Primary Care Physician." Specifically, it will determine whether you can select your "Primary Care Physician," the terms under which you may change your "Primary Care Physician," and whether the "Primary Care Physician" for you and your family members may be selected from certain specialists (e.g., gynecologist, pediatrician).

4. Your access to specialists and other providers is through your "Primary Care Physician," who is sometimes referred to as a "Gatekeeper" because of the control he or she has over your access to other physicians and facilities.

5. "Emergency Care" pre-authorization access procedures, allowable exceptions, and penalties for not getting pre-authorization will also be specified by your "Membership Agreement." Generally speaking, you need pre-authorization for emergency room care.

## KEY POINTS  Staff Model HMO

1. Your "Membership Agreement" specifies your dues and other charges.
2. Your "Primary Care Physician" manages your health care and makes all referrals.
3. You may be able to select your "Primary Care Physician."
4. Some HMOs permit gynecologists and pediatricians to be "PCPs."
5. Pre-authorization is required for "Emergency Care," but exceptions may be allowed.
6. Penalties for self-referral are spelled out in the "Membership Agreement."

*There are HMOs and then again there are HMOs.*

*"We would like to join an HMO, but both my spouse and I have specialists who do not see HMO patients. We cannot afford to give them up, regardless of the benefits offered by an HMO. I suppose we're out of luck, aren't we?" No, not necessarily.*

### Other Model HMOs

When you look at HMOs that are not "Staff Model HMOs," you will find a seemingly endless number of variations in their organization and "Membership Agreement" provisions. There are too many types of HMOs and combinations of types to show them individually (e.g., "Group Model" HMO, "Independent Physician Association" or "IPA" HMO). If I could show them all and did, it would just be confusing. It would be like any history class I ever took, in which we memorized names, places, and dates instead of learning the lessons history had to teach. I am trying to show and explain the organizational elements that can comprise an HMO and the impact they can have on the HMO's services. I want to help you understand how the make-up of an HMO might relate to you, so you will be better able to understand and evaluate HMO offerings.

I will show and discuss an HMO that is comprised of different provider types (e.g., Staff, Group Practice, Independent Physician Association) and combinations of these and other types of providers. I will use the terminology I explained, before starting this section on Health Maintenance Organizations, and terminology we used earlier in this chapter (e.g., Fee-For-Service, Preferred Providers). I will also introduce you to some new terminology.

I am going to use a different approach in explaining the "Other Model HMOs." I will go through the diagram from top to bottom to explain the variations you might find as you investigate Health Maintenance Organizations. It's unlikely that you would have access to an HMO having all the options shown on the diagram. Nevertheless, you need to understand the different resources an HMO might use, because the make-up of an HMO determines the services that the HMO is able to offer to you as I explained.

Before explaining the diagram, let me assure you that it's not as complicated as it might look to you. We'll go through it a step at a time. If you found an HMO with all the variations shown on the diagram, it would have flexibility and easy access to all health care providers. It would also be expensive, when compared to a "Staff Model HMO."

**The "Other Model HMOs" Diagram**

1. "Other Model HMOs" refers to HMO variations that use non-HMO medical personnel and facilities. The HMO may have some employee staff members and own some facilities, but if it also contracts with others for physicians, medical staff, and facilities, it is not a "Staff Model HMO."

2. "Facility Sources" refers to ways in which HMOs provide their members with access to health care facilities such as hospitals, laboratories, and other facilities.
   - "HMO Owned" refers to facilities that the HMO may have.
   - "HMO Contracted" refers to facilities under contract to an HMO.
   - "Group Contracted" refers to facilities under contract to "Medical Groups." If an HMO contracts with a "Medical Group" for physicians, their hospital(s) are available to the HMO's members.

3. "Facilities" refers to facility health care providers including
   - Laboratories (e.g., chemical, radiology)
   - Emergency care centers
   - Hospitals
   - Clinics
   - Other facilities

4. "Physician Sources" refers to the doctors who are available to an HMO's members.
   - "Staff" physicians are those on the payroll of the HMO.
   - "Group Practice" refers to physicians who contract to treat the HMO's patients based on a reduced set of fees, negotiated with the HMO, and to arrange for an HMO member's hospitalization when needed. You might currently go to doctors who are members of a "Group Practice." If you join an HMO who contracts with the same "Group Practice," you may not have to change doctors. It would depend on the rules of the HMO. If all of an HMO's physicians belong to a "Group Practice," the HMO is a "Group Model HMO."
   - "IPA" or "Independent Physician Association" refers to an organization formed by independent physicians to serve their common good, which to that end might contract with HMOs to have their physicians treat HMO patients, at a reduced rate or based on capitation. The physicians might still be treating their own "IPA" patients. If all the HMO's physicians are members of "Independent Physician Associations," the HMO is an "IPA Model HMO." There are more "IPA Model HMOs" than all other types combined, including the combinations which follow.
   - There are other HMOs who contract with multiple "Group Practices" and some who contract with both "Group Practices" and "Independent Physician Associations." You may find some advantage in signing up with one of these HMOs because of the selection of physicians they can offer.
   - "Preferred Providers" may also sign up with an HMO. If you sign up for a plan that offers "Preferred Providers" as well as "Primary Care Physicians" and HMO physicians, you will find that you have the ability to go to "Preferred Providers" instead of seeing your "Primary Care Physician" and the HMO physicians and facilities to whom you are referred. Your costs would be higher, as spelled out in your HMO agreement.
   - Health Maintenance Organizations may even have provision for their members to go to "Fee-For-Service" providers as well as "Preferred Providers." If you join such a plan, you will have the ultimate flexibility. This option will be expensive to use. If you have a specialist who has treated you for a chronic ailment over the years and you want to join an HMO but not change all your doctors, this type of plan might be a good solution for you.
5. "Physician Types" include the following:
   - "Primary Care Physicians" are key to the HMO preventive approach to medicine and are always part of HMOs.

- "Specialists" are critical to modern health care and to all health care plans.
- "Carve-Out" teams are sometimes used by HMOs to provide care when needed to treat critical medical problems, such as cancer and transplants. These "Carve-Out" teams help provide the highest quality care available and protect the HMO from very high costs, as I discussed in the "Health Insurance—Risk Sharing."
6. "Membership Agreement" spells out the details of your coverage and restrictions. It is very important that you study the agreement or a detailed spreadsheet of your agreement.

| OTHER MODEL HMOs | | | | |
|---|---|---|---|---|
| **FACILITY SOURCES** | | | | |
| HMO OWNED | | HMO CONTRACTED | | GROUP CONTRACTED |
| **FACILITIES** | | | | |
| LABORATORIES | EMERGENCY CARE | HOSPITAL | CLINICS | OTHER FACILITIES |
| **PHYSICIAN SOURCES** | | | | |
| STAFF | GROUP PRACTICE | IPA | PREFERRED PROVIDERS | FEE-FOR-SERVICE PROVIDERS |
| **PHYSICIAN TYPES** | | | | |
| PRIMARY CARE PHYSICIANS | | SPECIALISTS | | "CARVE-OUT" TEAMS |
| **MEMBERSHIP AGREEMENT** | | | | |

**MEMBER/PATIENT**

## ▼ KEY POINTS           Other Model HMOs

1. For the most part, HMOs and health insurance plans use the same medical facilities.
2. Most HMOs use "Group Practice" or "Independent Physician Association" doctors.
3. Some HMOs offer "Preferred Provider" and "Fee-For-Service" options.
4. Some HMOs set aside funds to have specialists provide catastrophic disease care (e.g., cancer, transplant).
5. The "Membership Agreement" can contain many desirable options in HMO care.

### Health Maintenance Organization Summary

HMOs that provide health care using their own medical staff and facilities require their members to use only the HMO's resources. This staff model HMO might be appealing to the three-generation family. The whole family can be taken to the same clinic for doctors' appointments and referrals are within the organization. This plan might not be for everyone, however, and it doesn't have to be. As other HMO models have become popular, some organizations that began as staff model only HMOs now offer other type plans.

It's quite possible that you will find an HMO that contracts with your current doctor(s) as a member of a medical group or IPA. You might not have to change doctors in that case. Your current family doctor, internist, or family practitioner might take on the role of PCP. Female members of your family may be able to go to their gynecologist for an annual examination and mammogram without a PCP referral, or even have their gynecologist as their primary care physician. You may even be able to have your child's pediatrician serve in the role of PCP. From my own experience I can tell you that even the most highly specialized providers (e.g., liver transplant teams) are available on referral from certain HMOs, should you need them.

Not every HMO provides all the options that I have mentioned, but some do. And with the competition among HMOs, more and more options are going to be made available to the buying public. I think this will be especially true when it comes to the provisions that people covered by fee-for-service insurance find troublesome, including not being able to choose one's own PCP, not being able to have specialists such as gynecologists or pediatricians as a PCP, and having to change doctors.

Some HMOs offer a "Point of Service Plan," whereby their members are free to go to doctors who are part of a preferred providers network whenever they wish, at an additional cost in the form of a copayment. For an even larger copayment, the members can go to any licensed physician or provider. In other words, the HMO provides the two levels of access of a fee-for-service plan with a preferred provider option. They offer freedom of access at additional costs.

## HMO Quality Measurements

The National Committee for Quality Assurance (NCQA) evaluates HMOs based on common criteria and stores their findings in a database. It measures hundreds of HMOs on quality of care provided to their 56 million members. The measurement data are stored in the "Health Plan Employer Data and Information Set" ("HEDIS"), which is made available to employers and HMOs. "HEDIS" is a computer-resident library of facts, which can be repetitively updated and referenced. "Database" is the computerese word for this kind of computer-resident library. Some employers who use "HEDIS" to evaluate HMOs publish a report card on them to their employees. If you're considering an HMO, ask your employer or the HMO for their "HEDIS" report card. Information is also available from the National Committee for Quality Assurance, 2000 L Street NW, Washington, D.C. 20036; or call them at 202-955-3515 or 202-955-3500; or check the Internet World Wide Web at http://www.ncqa.org.

Recently, the NCQA Vice President for Quality Measurement, Dr. Carry Seined, announced the availability of the "Quality Compass." It's a computer database of dozens of quality measurements on 200 of the 600+ Health Maintenance Organizations around the country. It shows national averages and the best marks for each measurement. It's intended to provide employers with on-going measurements of HMO quality when they select and negotiate with Health Maintenance Organizations to provide the best possible HMO value to their employees. It will be available on paper and on CD-ROM with an expected price of $3,200.00.

## Health Care Terminology Update

Here's a summary of the terminology we used in the section just completed on "Staff Model HMO" and "Other Models HMO." You may want to scan these definitions just to make sure you are familiar with them, before moving on to the next section.

## Insurance Plans

**Direct Contract Model HMO**—An HMO that contracts with individual physicians to provide health care services to its patients under protocols defined by the HMO.

**Group Model HMO**—A Health Maintenance Organization whose members receive medical care, under protocols defined by the HMO, from doctors belonging to a "Medical Group," also known as a "Group Practice."

**IPA Model HMO**—A Health Maintenance Organization whose members receive medical care, under protocols defined by the HMO, from doctors who are part of an "Independent Physician Association."

**Network Model HMO**—A Health Maintenance Organization that contracts with two or more group practices to provide health care services to the HMO's patients under protocols defined by the HMO.

**Point of Service HMO Plan**—A plan that offers its members the benefits of an HMO with the freedom to go to preferred providers at an additional cost and to go to any licensed provider at still greater cost. This plan offers greater access in return for greater cost.

**Staff Model HMO**—A Health Maintenance Organization that has physicians and medical personnel on its payroll and operates its own hospitals, laboratories, clinics, and other facilities to minister to the preventive and other health care needs of its members.

## Health Care and Insurance Terminology

**Case Management**—An HMO function that monitors and coordinates the treatment of patients who are seriously or chronically ill, have long term hospital stays, or have other problems requiring multi-specialty long-term care. This function is over and above the health care management role of the "Primary Care Physician" ("PCP").

**Credentialing**—An on-going assessment of a physician's qualifications to practice medicine and in the doctor's chosen specialty, if he or she is considered a specialist.

**Formulary**—The list of low-cost drugs your HMO physician may prescribe for you, if you have prescription coverage with the HMO.

**Group Practice**—A number of physicians who are organized as a partnership, professional corporation, or in some other type association. The group's administrative function compensates its physicians and enters into contractual relationships with other organizations (e.g., hospitals, HMOs) on their behalf.

**Health Plan Employer Data and Information Set (HEDIS)**—A computer-resident database containing individual HMO's data on 60 "quality of care measurements" (e.g., credentialing, average duration of appointments, specialist appointments average wait times).

**Independent Physician Association (IPA)**—An organization formed by entrepreneurial doctors to perform services for its member physicians, with the bargaining power of an association and at a reduced cost to the individual physicians.

**National Committee for Quality Assurance (NCQA)**—An organization made up of representatives from HMOs and large corporations. It has its roots in the 1980s, when a number of employers wanted a way to evaluate the HMO plans that they had begun offering as part of their employees' benefits plans. This group developed HEDIS for this purpose and have continued to refine it and expand its usage.

**Pre-Authorization**—The requirement for an HMO member to obtain permission from his or her "Primary Care Physician" before visiting an emergency room or other facility for medical care.

**Protocols**—The set of written procedures that are to be followed under given medical situations.

**"Quality Compass"**—A report on the quality of care provided in 200 HMOs, as measured using HEDIS.

**Utilization Management**—A process used by insurance companies and HMOs to evaluate the diagnostic, treatment, and billing practices that a doctor has used over a period of time.

**Utilization Review**—An insurance company's or HMO's evaluation of a procedure proposed by a physician. The evaluation is based on the patient's problem, the need to perform the procedure, and a judgment of the effectiveness of the proposed procedure in the given situation. The physician may be required to personally justify the procedure proposed for the patient. If he or she cannot justify it, it will not be allowed.

## The Good News of the Range of Options

### Fee-For-Service

It was not too many years ago that the options available to employer group plans or to individuals were limited. The choice was either Fee-For-Service or Staff Model HMO—unlimited choice and ability to self-refer at high cost, or no choice or ability to self-refer at low cost. Employers and individuals wanted more choices, and insurance companies and HMOs both responded with plans that gave choices between the two extremes.

Fee-For-Service insurers offered lower-cost plans, based on discounted fees for the services of a subset of physicians, other medical personnel, and facilities in the community. Over time, these insurers also developed Managed Care plans, which borrowed from the wellness, preventive care, and Primary Physician techniques established by Staff HMOs.

With these lower-cost plans, the providers file claims for the fees associated with the services they rendered. This benefits the policyholders or patients in two ways. First, they do not have to pay their providers up-front. Second, they do not have to file claims, interact with the Claims Office, and wait to be reimbursed. Nevertheless, in all variations of fee-for-service health insurance plans, the patients or policyholders are the responsible parties for payment, regardless of the claims processes and reimbursement procedures used.

### Health Maintenance Organizations (HMO)

The Fee-For-Service insurers had to devise ways to lower their prices, if they were going to be competitive, so they developed some creative discount variations. The Health Maintenance Organizations needed to win over more of the fee-for-service and preferred provider population.

The Staff Model HMO attracted a membership who believed in the concept of maintaining wellness with preventive care. They were willing to put up with limited choice and flexibility, in return for the benefits that could accrue to those who followed the HMO "wellness" regimen. Others were attracted to the low and fixed cost. Members paid their monthly fee and, except for copayments, there were no financial surprises.

Mainstream America, however, has a fee-for-service mentality: "I'll buy what I want, from whom I want to buy, and pay for what I get!" albeit through insurance. HMOs recognized that many more people would sign up for the benefits of the HMO model of "wellness" health care if they had more freedom to go to non-HMO Staff providers at an additional cost. And we now have other models of the HMO organization and the "Point of Service Plan." Health insurance policyholders can sign up for an HMO and still have the freedom of access to other providers, albeit at an increased price.

### Maybe a Picture Is Better Than 10,000 Words—You Be the Judge

Perhaps the following diagram will be far more eloquent in saying what I have tried to say in the past "10,000 Words" . . . or so.

|  THE RANGE OF AVAILABLE PLANS  |
| --- |
| **INSURANCE**                                                                                              **HMO** |
| High Access & Cost                                                                                  Low Access & Cost |
| FFS        PPO        EPO        M/C        IPA        GROUP        DIRECT        STAFF |
| Insurance – – – – – – – – – – – – – – – –> |
| <– – – – – – – – – – – – – – – – – – – – – – – – – – – – HMO |
| POS                                                                        NET |

Legend
- FFS — Fee-For-Service
- PPO — Preferred Provider Option
- EPO — Exclusive Provider Option
- M/C — Managed Care
- IPA — Independent Physician Association
- GROUP — Medical Group (aka Group Practice)
- DIRECT — Individual doctor HMO contracts
- STAFF — Staff (as in "Staff Model HMO")
- POS — Point of Service Plan
- NET — Network of Groups

## *BEFORE WE GO ANY FARTHER:*
*Where have we been? Where are we going?*
*Good Questions Bill—Let Me Try to Answer Them*

**Where Have We Been?**

In Chapter 1, I discussed how important it is to be prepared for a potential medical crisis in your family:—not worried about it, but prepared.

In Chapter 2, I tried to give you a realistic assessment of the status of health care and health insurance in the United States. We have some shortcomings, particularly as far as insurance availability is concerned. Our medical systems have great potential to help us if we know how to get the most out of them by being an effective patient.

Here in Chapter 3, I told you how big my medical bills have been. The point was that anyone could be hit with huge medical expenses. I encouraged you to make an "informed decision." I did not. Make sure you know what insurance you are buying and why. I was lucky in my choice of an employer and an insurance option. You may not be as lucky.

Next I discussed "Health Insurance—Risk Sharing." Armed with an understanding of how "risk sharing" principles impact on coverage and cost, you should be less likely to make assumptions about what's unsaid in the description of coverage. In short, you should be able to make a better decision.

In the section just completed, "Insurance Plans and Terminology," I took you through a range of health insurance and HMO plan types. My intent was to prepare you for your review of specific health care plans. Hopefully, you picked up the language of the health care insurance industry as you went through the plans. There's a glossary in the appendices, if you need to refresh your memory.

### ▼ KEY POINTS          Insurance Options

1. Anyone can be hit with huge medical bills.
2. Make an "informed decision" when selecting your insurance.
3. Understand the risks that you and your insurer are each taking.
4. Know the details of your coverage: DON'T ASSUME!
5. Fee-For-Service, PPO, and HMO provider options are beginning to overlap.

## Where Are We Going?

The next chapter is titled: "The Decision-Making Process." It will start you through a process of deciding on the health care plan that is the best of the affordable and available options for your family. It places emphasis on the importance of asking questions. Then it provides you with some questions you should ask in your process of evaluating options. I will take you through the following topics and processes:

- The Importance of Asking Questions
- The Health Care Decision Process
- HMO and Insurance Company Questions
- Health Care Plan Enrollee Questions
- Questions to Ask Your Doctor
- Private and Employer-Provided Insurance Decision Summary

# The Decision-Making Process

> "I keep six honest serving men (They taught me all I knew); Their names are What and Why and When and How and Where and Who."
> (from Rudyard Kipling's story, "The Elephant's Child," in his book The Just-So Stories, 1902)

 **The Importance of Asking Questions**

I don't remember when I first heard this quote, but it has stuck with me. Sometimes I scramble the words, but I always remember the questions and the point of the quote. Rudyard Kipling's writing was reinforced for me by a professor who taught an entire course on a question and answer basis. It was a required course, and I was not looking forward to taking it. The course had always been taught and tested based on the memorization of names, places, quotes, and time frames. I enrolled in the section being taught by a professor who was just joining the faculty that term, hoping he would take a different approach. He took a very different approach.

The professor introduced the topic on the first day by saying that this was the first class for the course: "The Study of *The Old Testament*," in case anyone was in the wrong room. Two people left to find their classrooms. The professor then said: "We will start with the *Book of Genesis*. What do you want to know about it?"

That was in the fall of 1953. I still remember that classroom situation in my mind's eye. I enjoyed the class and remember lessons learned, including the learning power of asking the right question, in the right way.

Six years later, when I started teaching computer programming, I remembered that professor's teaching approach, and I used the same question asking technique. If they did not ask questions, I asked questions for them. It worked well for my students and for me. As far as I'm concerned, Rudyard Kipling and my college professor were right: We do learn and retain much of what we learn by asking questions. This chapter is largely based on this principle.

I will pose a series of questions for you to answer as you decide on the health care coverage you want, need, and can afford. As you are making these decisions, you will need to review brochures about health insurance coverages and HMO plans. You will find the brochures are good, but they will not anticipate every question you might have. You will need to ask the right questions. I will provide you with questions to ask about the available health insurance and HMO plans. You will need to select the questions that are important to you and ask any other questions you may have.

## The Health Insurance Decision Process

With the number of choices available, selecting the insurance plan that is right for you and your family can be difficult. Here are some questions you should ask yourself and answer to narrow in on the insurance or HMO plan you should have. If you think of others, ask them too.

- How much does my current health care insurance or HMO cost?
- How much can I afford?
- What coverage do I have now?
- What coverage do I need that I don't have now?
- What's available?
- Which plan meets my needs?
- Is it better than what I have now?
- Can I live with its rules?
- Is it worth the price?
- Can I afford it?

And then, decide.

No one can tell you what you need. You and your family know your situation and will be able to make that decision after you've studied your options. Whether you're deciding what to buy, reevaluating what you have, or are signed up for the only option provided by your employer, start the decision process now. Why start the decision process if you have no options from your employer? Because you may have a critical need that can be met with a supplemental policy of some sort. If you have an employer's open enrollment period coming up later, prepare now. Be ready to make an informed decision when you get the opportunity.

It should be easy to determine the amount of money that you are spending for medical care today. I have included a form to guide you in your calculations. A sample of it follows. You will find a full-sized version in Appendix D.

## MEDICAL EXPENSES

| Expense Item | Monthly or Quarterly Expense | X 12 or X 4 Expenses | Annual Expense |
|---|---|---|---|
| Premium Expense | | | |
| Chiropractor | | | |
| Dentist | | | |
| Doctor | | | |
| Durable Equipment | | | |
| Hospital | | | |
| Laboratory | | | |
| Medicine | | | |
| Total Insurable Expenses | | | |
| Food | | | |
| Housing | | | |
| Mileage | | | |
| Total Other Expense | | | |
| Total Medical Expenses | | | |

Notice that the form has three sections. The first lists expense items that could be covered in whole or in part by health insurance or by an HMO. The second section lists travel expenses you and your family could incur, including mileage to and from the doctor's or other provider's office. Make sure that you can substantiate all expenses with receipts and written explanations of the reason for your incurring the expense. When the nature of an illness or injury takes your family away from home overnight, these expenses can mount up. In my case, my wife stayed near my out-of-town hospital for three months, so she could help take care of me. The third section of the form is the grand total of the other two sections.

If you qualify for tax deductions in a calendar year, the expenses in both sections of the form might be qualifying deductions. Hopefully, you will never have enough medical expenses to deduct, but if your medical expenses start to mount up, consult with the IRS or a qualified tax advisor to find out what the current tax deductibility requirements are.

Back to the question. All you are trying to do is determine how much your medical costs are each year. You are doing it for your own benefit. You may want to look at your last full year of medical expenses, or the average of several years, or the current year extrapolated to a full year, or any other way that makes sense to you.

Start by listing the insurance premiums you pay. If you pay by payroll deduction, get the amount of your premiums from your pay stubs. If you pay your premium or membership fee personally, look at your check stubs for the monthly or quarterly premium paid and multiply it, to arrive at the annual cost. Keep your detailed data handy for later use.

The rest of the form lists likely medical expense items to look for in reviewing your check book and your receipts. Show the amount spent on each expense item (e.g., dentist, prescriptions). If you have others that are not listed (e.g., alternative medicine practitioners), add them to the list and show the annual expenses for their services.

Your completed "Medical Expenses" form answers the first question: "How much does my current health insurance or HMO cost?" Make sure you list expenses not covered by insurance (e.g., dental, prescription). You may find a health care plan that offers one or both of these benefits. By itemizing your expenses, you will have an estimate of how much you can afford to spend for dental and prescription coverage premiums, copayments, and out-of-pocket expenses.

### What Can I afford?

To answer this question you will need your completed "Medical Expenses" form. Assuming you have insurance, you will also need to refer to the document your insurer, HMO or employer gave you when you signed up for coverage. It could look something like the following "Insurance Options Summary," to which I will refer in this section.

## INSURANCE OPTIONS SUMMARY

| | Fee-For-Service with Preferred Providers $110/month | | Managed Care Plan $60/month | | HMO $70/month |
|---|---|---|---|---|---|
| | **PPO Provider** | **Non-PPO Provider** | **M/C Provider** | **Non-M/C Provider** | **HMO Provider** |
| **Annual Deductible** | | | | | |
| Individual | $200 | $300 | $0 | $150 | $0 |
| Family | $600 | $900 | $0 | $450 | $0 |
| **Annual Out-of-Pocket (OOP)** | | | | | |
| Individual | $1,000 | $1,500 | 0 | $1,200 | $0 |
| Family | $3,000 | $4,500 | 0 | $2,400 | $0 |
| **Amount or Percent You Pay** | | | | | |
| After Out-of-Pocket | 0% | 0% | 0% | 0% | N/A |
| After Deductible | See Below | See Below | See Below | See Below | N/A |
| **Hospitalization** | | | $100 CoPay | | |
| Room & Board | 15% | 30% | 0% | 30% | 0% |
| Surgery | 15% | 30% | 0% | 30% | 0% |
| Anesthesia | 15% | 30% | 0% | 30% | 0% |
| **Outpatient** | | | | | |
| Surgery | 15% | 30% | 0% | 30% | 0% |
| Office Visits | $15 CoPay | 30% | $10 CoPay | 30% | $5 CoPay |
| X rays | 15% | 30% | 0% | 30% | 0% |
| Laboratory Tests | 15% | 30% | 0% | 30% | 0% |
| **Preventive Care** | | | | | |
| Bi-annual Physicals | $15 CoPay | 30% | $10 CoPay | 30% | $5 CoPay |
| Well-Baby Care | $15 CoPay | 30% | $10 CoPay | 30% | $5 CoPay |
| Baby Immunizations | 0% | 0% | 0% | 0% | 0% |
| **Psychiatric Care** | | | | | |
| Annual Limit | 12 Visits | 12 Visits | 12 Visits | 12 Visits | 12 Visits |
| Treatment | 0% | 0% | 0% | 0% | 0% |
| **Physical Therapy** | | | | | |
| Annual Limit | $1,500 | $1,500 | $1,500 | $1,500 | 60 Visits |
| Therapy | 20% | 20% | 0% | 30% | $5 CoPay |
| **Chiropractic Care** | | | | | |
| Annual Limit | 26 Visits | 26 Visits | 26 Visits | 26 Visits | No Cvge. |
| Treatment | 20% | 40% | 20% | 40% | No Cvge. |
| **Emergency Room** | | | | | |
| Emergency | 0% | 0% | 0% | 0% | $25 CoPay |
| Non-emergency | 30% | 30% | 30% | 30% | $50 CoPay |
| **Ambulance** | 0% | 0% | 0% | 0% | 0% |

You should have a document which explains your coverage and costs. It has the same type of coverage and cost information as this small sample form, "Insurance Options Summary." Your form undoubtedly is more detailed, and may show just the option you selected or all the options that were available to you at the time you chose your health insurance. Or it could be a brochure with narrative information about your plan. Its format is not important, as long as you know what your coverage and costs are.

If you are a member of an employer group health insurance policy or HMO, you should have received your coverage information from your employer. If you have misplaced it or never received one, contact your employer's Personnel or Human Resources representative to get a copy. If you signed up for coverage directly with an HMO or an insurance company, look at the material you received when you signed up. Your explanation of coverages may be part of the sales literature you received at that time. If not, call the HMO or insurance company to get your coverage information.

In any case, make sure that you get a copy of your coverage information. You need it for your reference. If you have your coverage information, keep it handy as we go through the rest of this chapter. Follow along with me as I use the sample "Insurance Options Summary" to

- show you how to read a summary of available insurance options
- show you how to estimate your annual medical expense exposure
- demonstrate that coverage documents tend to show you only what they *do* cover
- point out that you need to know what the plans you are evaluating *do not* cover

## The "Sample" Example

To get started, let's set up a sample family situation. They will need a name, so let's call them Mr. & Mrs. I. M. Sample and sons. They will be in good health, except for a couple of problems. After giving you their brief medical history for last year, I am going to use three example situations with charts to demonstrate different points.

Before getting into the examples of the Samples, I need to explain a term used by the medical profession to refer to meetings which medical professionals have with patients for consultation or the dispensing of medical care. The word is "encounter." It is a good generic word for physicians, medical staff, and claims office personnel. They can use it to refer to office visits, examinations, or whatever without going into detail. The detail will be specified in the doctor's notes and in the code used to bill for services. As I've said before, "more about this later." In this case it will be in Chapter 13, where I explain how medical billing and insurance reimbursement work.

Here's a summary of the Samples's health problems and last year's encounters:

- The Sample family consists of a father, mother, and two teenaged sons.
- Mrs. Sample has chronic back problems and sees a chiropractor once a month.
- Mr. Sample hurt himself last year and required minor surgery as an outpatient.
- Mr. & Mrs. Sample believe in preventive medicine and had physicals.
- The two sons had four office visits for flu bugs between them.

**The Sample Family Expenses**

The Sample family medical expenses for last year would have varied based upon their health care experience and the plan they chose. If no one needed medical care, they would just have the expense of insurance premiums, as shown on the coverage form's column headings:

Fee-For-Service with Preferred Provider Option = $1,320/year
Managed Care = $ 720/year
HMO = $ 840/year

Based on these annual premiums, it looks like Managed Care would have been the best choice for the Sample family. But that's not necessarily true. If the Sample family does not need any medical care, Managed Care is the least expensive. Otherwise, it all depends on the doctors the Sample family uses and how much medical care they need. If any of the Samples require a doctor's care, the HMO plan quickly becomes the least expensive, because it has no "Annual Deductible" and no "Annual Out-of-Pocket" expense. This is true if the care they need is offered by their HMO. I need to discuss these two expense items before going back to the Samples.

Notice that if there is an annual deductible for a plan on the "Insurance Options Summary" there is an "Individual" amount and a "Family" amount. An individual must pay his or her deductible amount for the year or be a member of a family that in aggregate has met its "Family Deductible," which in this example is three times the "Individual" amount. A couple would not have to meet the "Family Deductible," because they would each meet their deductible obligation by paying their "Individual" amount.

The deductible amounts vary according to the plan and the type of providers the Samples use. If their insurance plan has an "Annual Deductible," it is the amount they must pay in a calendar year, before their insurance plan makes any contribution. When the Samples have paid their deductible for the year, their insurance starts to help out. It then pays their bills except for a percentage as shown on the coverage summary, or in this case "Insurance Options Summary."

The "Insurance Options Summary," has a number of expense categories with percentages in them. For example, the "Fee-For-Service with Preferred Provider Option" has 15% for PPO Provider hospitalization items and 30% for Non-Preferred Provider. This means that once the Samples have met their individual or family deductible expense requirements for the year, their insurance will reimburse all but that percent of the charges incurred (15% or 30%), until they have also met their "Out-of-Pocket" annual expense requirement. The "Out-of-Pocket" expense requirement, in this example, has annual "Individual" and "Family" provisions. The individual pays out-of-pocket expenses until his or her "Individual" or "Family" "Out-of-Pocket" expenses have been paid for the year.

If the Samples have serious medical problems, it will not take very long before they will have met their "Out-of-Pocket" requirements for the year. In the case of the "PPO Provider" the amount is $1,000. If they use "Non-PPO Providers," the "Out-of-Pocket" requirement is $1,500. Once the out-of-pocket limit for a provider type is met for a Sample family member, the insurance reimburses 100% of the "usual and customary" bills.

Let me add an exception to what I just said. In this example, items showing a copayment amount do not participate in the deductible or out-of-pocket provisions. For example, in the "PPO Provider" column, under "Outpatient," the "Office Visits" box shows "$15/CoPay." In these cases, the Samples pay the copay amount every time they have an "Office Visit," regardless of the status of their deductible and out-of-pocket expense. They do not pay deductible or out-of-pocket expense based on their ProPlan.

## *There's one answer on which you can always rely: "It depends."*

I know these provisions can get confusing, but bear with me. They should become clearer as I go through the following examples:

- Mrs. Sample's non-discounted chiropractic back adjustments
- Mr. Sample's preferred provider outpatient surgery
- Mrs. Sample's preferred provider physical examination
- The Sample sons' office visits

### Mrs. Sample's Back Problems

Last year, Mrs. Sample went to her chiropractor every month for a back "adjustment." She uses a chiropractor who is not part of any insurance plan or HMO. Therefore, her costs would fall under the "Non-PPO" or "Non-M/C" or "HMO" provisions as shown on the "Insurance Options Summary." He charges $70 per adjustment. Her costs under the three options of the "Insurance Options Summary" would be as shown on the following table, depending on the plan her family chose.

## "MRS. SAMPLE CHIROPRACTIC COSTS"

| | Charge | Non-PPO | Non-M/C | HMO |
|---|---|---|---|---|
| Deductible & OOP→ | | $300 & $900 | $150 & $450 | $0<br>No Cvrge |
| January | 70 | 70 D | 70 D | 70 |
| February | 70 | 70 D | 70 D | 70 |
| March | 70 | 70 D | 34 * | 70 |
| April | 70 | 70 D | 28 O | 70 |
| May | 70 | 40 * | 28 O | 70 |
| June | 70 | 28 O | 28 O | 70 |
| July | 70 | 28 O | 28 O | 70 |
| August | 70 | 28 O | 28 O | 70 |
| September | 70 | 28 O | 28 O | 70 |
| October | 70 | 28 O | 28 O | 70 |
| November | 70 | 28 O | 28 O | 70 |
| December | 70 | 28 O | 28 O | 70 |
| | 840 | 516 * | 426 * | 840 |

Legend:  D—deductible expense
 O—out-of-pocket expense
 *—combined deductible and out-of-pocket expenses

**Notes about the table:**

1. Mrs. Sample's chiropractor is not part of any insurance or HMO plan.

2. Mrs. Sample was charged the same $70 fee for each chiropractic back adjustment.

3. If the Sample Family had selected the "Fee-For-Service with Preferred Provider Option," her costs would have been as follows:

   - She paid $280 of her $300 deductible by paying $70 for each of the first four fees.
   - Mrs. Sample paid the last $20 of deductible for the May fee, leaving a $50 balance of the fee due.
   - She paid an additional $20 as an out-of-pocket payment for a total of $40, computed as follows: deductible balance ($150 − $130 paid ytd = $20), then fee ($70 − $20 = $50), then out-of-pocket ($50 × 40% = $20), for a total of ($20 + $20 = $40) payment in May.
   - From June on, Mrs. Sample paid "Out-of-Pocket" at 40% of $70 = $28. (See "Insurance Options Summary"—"Chiropractic Care" "Non-PPO" @ 40%.)

4. If the Sample family had chosen the "Managed Care" option, her costs would have been as follows:

   - Mrs. Sample paid $140 of $150 deductible by paying for first two $70 fees.
   - Mrs. Sample paid the last $10 of her $150 deductible for the March fee, leaving a $60 balance due.

- She paid an additional $24 as an out-of-pocket payment for a total of $34, computed as follows: deductible balance ($150 − $140 ytd = $10), then fee ($70 − $10 = $60), then out-of-pocket ($60 × 40% = $24), for a total of ($10 + $24 = $34) payment in March. The Claims Office paid the balance of $36 ($70 − $10 − $24 = $36).
- From April on, Mrs. Sample paid "Out-of-Pocket" at 40% of $70 = $28. (See "Insurance Options Summary"—"Chiropractic Care" "Non-PPO" @ 60%.)

5. If the Sample family had chosen the "HMO" option, her costs would have been as follows:
    - Mrs. Sample as an HMO member paid the $70 fees in full, because the "Insurance Options Summary" HMO plan does not cover chiropractic fees. This would not necessarily be the case in the real world.

6. Managed Care would have been less expensive, because its "Non-M/C" deductible is less than that of "Non-PPO" ($150 vs. $300).

7. Sample family health care expenses, based on this first example and depending on their plan, would have been as follows:

|  | PPO Plan | Managed Care | HMO |
|---|---|---|---|
| Annual Premium | $1,320 | $ 720 | $ 840 |
| Chiropractic Care | 516 | 426 | 840 |
|  | $1,836 | $1,146 | $1,680 |

8. So far, on a cost basis, it looks like the Samples should have selected "Managed Care" coverage, but we cannot judge a health care plan by one set of encounters.

You may have to go through this example and explanation a couple times, slowly. By understanding the example, however, you should have a better feel for the impact and interaction of health insurance and HMO provisions.

Premiums, deductibles and out-of-pocket expenses are big cost factors which dramatically affect the cost per unit of care. In the table that follows, I compare the costs of the three plans depicted on the "Insurance Options Summary." For simplicity sake, I assume that the policyholders, or members in this example, only use "Preferred Providers," "Managed Care Providers," or "HMO Providers" based on "Primary Care Physician" referral.

|  | PPO Plan | Managed Care | HMO |
|---|---|---|---|
| Annual Premium | $1,320 | $ 720 | $ 840 |
| Deductible | 200 | 0 | 0 |
| Cost of first $200 of care | $1,520 | $ 720 | $ 840 |
| Out-of-Pocket | 1,000 | 0 | 0 |
| Cost of $6,667 care at 15% OOP | $2,520 | $ 720 | $ 840 |

In this example, assuming that no copay services were used, the PPO Plan patient would pay $1,520 for the first $200 of care. That's roughly twice the cost of the other two plans. The first $6,667 of care would cost $2,520 for the Preferred Provider patient. I used the cut off points of $200 and $6,667 of care, because that's where, under the PPO Plan, deductible and out-of-pocket payments, respectively, were paid in full for the year. PPO Plan costs at the $6,667 level of health care in any given year are 300% of what the HMO's costs and 350% of the Managed Care's costs would have been in this example.

*As I said, premiums, deductibles, and out-of-pocket expenses can be big cost factors.*

Of course, cost saving is not the only reason you should buy any particular insurance or join an HMO. The primary reason to buy any kind of insurance is to indemnify yourself against major financial losses. But if several of the available options provide you with what you want and need in the way of protection against loss, cost is a consideration when weighing the various insurance plans and HMOs against each other. It's something you should keep in mind.

Let's look again at Mrs. Sample's use of a non-preferred, non-managed care, and non-HMO chiropractor. Sticking to her old chiropractor cost Mrs. Sample money. She had to pay the non-PPO or non-M/C (Managed Care) deductible before her insurance paid anything. In addition, as you will see in the third Samples family example, she went to a preferred provider for her other care. This meant that she had to pay another deductible and start paying another out-of-pocket expense. It's a point to consider before going to a provider who is not a Preferred Provider, a Managed Care Provider, or an HMO Provider, depending on the plan to which you belong.

### Mr. Sample Goes to the Doctor

If you remember, Mr. Sample injured himself and needed surgery. He also had a physical last year. I am going to set the scene for this example and the next one by saying that last year was the first year that the Samples had this insurance plan. The plan is "Fee-For-Service with Preferred Provider Option." The Samples were allowed to have physicals last year, but not this year, because it's a biannual benefit. In these two examples, the whole family used preferred providers.

## "MR. SAMPLE PREFERRED PROVIDER COSTS"

| Procedure | Billing | Paid By Mr. Sample | Paid By Insurance | Comments |
|---|---|---|---|---|
| **Injury** | | | | |
| Office Visit | 90 | 15 cp | 70 | Discounted fee |
| X rays | 260 | 200 d | | Annual Ded. paid |
| | | 3 op | 17 | Discounted fee |
| Hospital Outpatient | 3,400 | 510 op | 2,890 | Annual OOP paid |
| Surgeon | 1,050 | 0 | 1,050 | Ins. paid in full |
| Anesthesiologist | 250 | 0 | 250 | Ins. paid in full |
| **Physical** | | | | |
| X rays | 150 | 0 | 105 | Discounted fee |
| Blood Tests | 275 | 0 | 142 | Discounted fee |
| Sigmoidoscopy | 210 | ? | ? | Covered? |
| Doctor's Exam. | 150 | 0 | 110 | Discounted fee |
| | 5,835 | 728 | 4,634 | |

Legend:  cp—Copayment @ $15
 d—Annual Deductible @ $200
 op—Out-of-Pocket expense @ $1,000

**Notes about the table:**

1. The Claims Office discounted Mr. Sample's Office Visit from $90 to $85.
   - Mr. Sample made a $15 copayment for his Office Visit and no deductible payment.
   - The Claims Office paid off the balance of the discounted amount, $70.

2. The Claims Office discounted the X rays from $260 to $220.
   - Mr. Sample paid $200 deductible for X rays leaving $20 due.
   - He paid $3 out-of-pocket ($20 × 15%), leaving $17 due.
   - The Claims Office paid the $17 balance due.

3. The Claims Office did not discount the $3,400 hospital bill.
   - Mr. Sample paid the rest of his out-of-pocket expense ($510) for his hospital bill.
   - The Claims Office paid the balance of the hospital bill ($2,890).

4. The Claims Office paid all other bills after discounting, except the sigmoidoscopy.
   - Is Mr. Sample covered for a sigmoidoscopy?
   - Is it part of the biannual physical exam benefit?
   - Is there an age requirement?
   - If so, is Mr. Sample old enough?

It would seem that we don't know enough about Mr. Sample's coverage from the summary sheet. Is he covered for a sigmoidoscopy or not? He should have asked some questions before he signed up for this insurance plan. All Mr. Sample can do now is hope he's lucky. Thank goodness his exposure is not more than $210.

## Mrs. Sample and Sons Go to the Preferred Provider

Throughout the year Mrs. Sample has gone to her chiropractor for back adjustments. He is not a preferred provider. She paid her non-preferred provider deductible for the year and some of her out-of-pocket expense. Now she is going to go to a preferred provider for her physical. Mrs. Sample will have to start paying her $200 preferred provider deductible and her $1,000 out-of-pocket expense. She will take her sons to the same physician for office visits during the year.

### "MRS. SAMPLE AND SONS PREFERRED PROVIDER COSTS"

| Procedure | Billing | Paid By Mrs. Sample | Paid By Insurance | Comments |
|---|---|---|---|---|
| Office V sit (Son #1) | 90 | 15 cp | 70 | Discounted fee |
| **Physical Exam** | | | | |
| Office V sit | 140 | 15 cp | 92 | Discounted fee |
| X rays | 195 | 195 d | 0 | Annual Deduct. |
| Blood Tests | 161 | 5 d | 85 | Disc. fee to $105 |
| | | 15 op | | |
| Mammogram | 160 | ? | ? | Covered? |
| Pap Smear | 35 | ? | ? | Covered? |
| Office V sit (Son #1) | 90 | 15 cp | 70 | Discounted fee |
| Office V sit (Son #1) | 90 | 15 cp | 70 | Discounted fee |
| Office V sit (Son #2) | 90 | 15 cp | 70 | Discounted fee |
| | 1,151 | 290 (?) | 457 (?) | |

Legend:  cp—Copayment @ $15
  d—Annual Deductible @ $200
  op—Out-of-Pocket expense @ $1,000

### Notes about this table:

1. The Claims Office discounted Son #1's Office Visit from $90 to $85.
   - Mrs. Sample paid a $15 copayment for Son #1's Office Visit.
   - The Claims Office paid the balance of $70.

2. The Office Visit part of Mrs. Sample's physical was $140, which the Claims Office discounted to $107.
   - Mrs. Sample paid a $15 copayment for her Office Visit.
   - The Claims Office paid the remaining $92.
3. Mrs. Sample's X rays were $195.
   - The Claims Office did not discount her X rays.
   - Of her $200 PPO Provider deductible, Mrs. Sample paid $195 for her X rays.
4. Mrs. Sample's blood tests were $161.
   - Charges of $46.25 are being held, pending receipt of more information.
   - A charge of $50.00 was rejected as not allowable under PPO contract terms.
   - The Claims Office discounted the balance of the blood tests down to $105.
   - Mrs. Sample paid the last $5 of her preferred provider deductible for the year.
   - She paid 15% of the $100 balance ($15) out-of-pocket expense.
   - The Claims Office paid the blood tests balance due after discount ($85).
5. Once again the Samples don't have enough information on coverage.
   - It looks like Mrs. Samples could owe $195 for her mammogram and Pap smear.
   - Mammograms and Pap Smears are not always covered.
   - There may be a multi-year interval requirement, or a need to be "at risk," or an age requirement, or "all of the above."
6. The Sample sons had four Office Visits between them at $90 each.
   - The Claims Office discounted them to $85 each.
   - Mrs. Sample paid $15 copayments for each of the four Office Visits.
   - The Claims Office paid the balance due of $70 for each of them.

### What Should We Learn from the Sample Family?

Let's see what wisdom "The Great Bright Light of Retrospect" can shine on the Samples' experiences.

- Both Mr. and Mrs. Sample believe in preventive care. HMOs are based on wellness and preventive care. I wonder if they considered an HMO?
- Do you suppose they know that physicals are every other year?
- Apparently, the Samples did not ask many specific questions about their coverage. Sigmoidoscopy? Mammogram? Pap smear? If I were in their shoes, I think I would wonder what else I don't know.
- Mrs. Sample spent at least $300 extra by going to her fee-for-service chiropractor.
- Would she consider another chiropractor if she knew how much extra she spent.

*It's time to focus on your family's needs once again. Learn from the "Sample Example" that you and your family must ask the right questions before signing up for any health care plan.*

 ## Back to the Decision Process

We need to go back to "The Decision Process." When we left it to go through the "Sample Example," you were asking the question, "What can I afford?" We went through the example to show you how to estimate your medical expenses, as expressed on the "Medical Expenses" form and your insurance coverage summary. You should have received the details of your coverage and costs from your employer's group or from your insurance company or HMO if you contracted directly with them. If you don't have it, you must get a copy.

Having gone through the "Sample Example," you should now be able to work through your own insurance coverage summary. Go through your situation with your expenses and coverage summary, in much the same way that we worked with the Sample family situation and the "Insurance Option Summary." As you do, you will be answering the "What can I afford?" question by putting down your actual medical and health insurance costs on paper.

You should also learn how to test other health care insurance or HMO plans, using your situation. How would your family have made out with the specific coverages and costs of other health care options. I'm getting ahead of myself, but after you evaluate your own insurance, you should use the same techniques to get the answers to "What happens if" questions. "What would happen if we had 'Brand A' health insurance or the 'Brand B' HMO plan, with the 'Medical Expenses' we had last year?" You can test the plan you are considering with your "Medical Expenses" before you buy it, but let's get back to evaluating your current situation first.

### Evaluate Your Own Situation Now

While the lessons learned up to here are fresh in your mind, determine where you stand now. Use your completed "Medical Expenses" form to help you reconstruct your family's health care experiences. You will find a lined blank form similar to form we used for "Mr. Sample Goes To The Doctor." It's called "Health Care Plan Evaluation." Make copies of it. Fill in the "Date of Service," "Family Member," "Encounter," and "Billed" columns, then make a set of these partially completed forms for each plan you might want to evaluate for your family. Chronologically within family member (i.e., by date within an alphabetical listing of family members) fill in the "Family Paid," "Insurance Paid," and "Comments" columns to complete an analysis of your current coverage. When the form is completed, you will have a tool for measuring other plans. (A "Health Care Plan Evaluation" form follows.)

## HEALTH CARE PLAN EVALUATION

| Date of Service | Family Member | Encounter | Billed Amount | Family Paid | Insurance Paid | Comments |
|---|---|---|---|---|---|---|
| | | | | | | |
| | | | | | | |
| | | | | | | |
| | | | | | | |
| | | | | | | |
| | | | | | | |
| | | | | | | |
| | | | | | | |
| | | | | | | |
| | | | | | | |
| | | | | | | |
| | | | | | | |
| | | | | | | |
| | | | | | | |
| | | | | | | |
| | | | | | | |
| | | | | | | |
| | | | | | | |

After you have completed this written evaluation of the coverages and costs of your current health care plan in your family situation, ask yourself the first four questions of "The Decision Process." Your answers might not be complete, but write down what you know. You will find that these questions will bring up other questions. Although, I have provided some prompts for you in parenthesis after each question, you will have to revisit your answers after you ask and get the answers to the final six Decision Process questions.

*Before we go any further, the questions I'm providing are not "The Questions." If you have better, fewer, additional, or other questions, use them.*

### Answer the First Four Questions of the Decision Process

Write down the answers to the following questions:

- How much does my current health care insurance or HMO cost?
    (See completed "Medical Expenses Form.")
    (See completed "Health Care Plan Evaluation.")
- How much can I afford?
    (Is what I'm spending on health insurance a burden on my family finances?)
    (Could we spend more for more coverage?)
    (Have I found some medical expenses which other plans might cover?)
    (Can I get those other coverages through some other type of plan for less?)
    (If yes, do I need to do so to get other coverages?)
- What coverage do I have now?
    (See my insurance option summary.)
    (Am I prepared for a family medical crisis?)
    (If not, what coverages am I lacking?)
- What coverage do I need that I don't have now?
    (What coverages do I see specified on other plans that I don't see on mine?)
    (Can I get those other coverages through some other type of plan for less?)
    (Do I want to?)
    (Do I really know what my options are?)
    (Do I know what questions to ask to get the information I need?)

### The Final Six Decision Process Questions

Before you can answer the final six "Decision Process" questions, you will still need information which you probably do not have today. I will try to show you how to get that information. You will need to know whom to contact, what to ask about, what questions to ask, of whom to ask them, and how to ask them. When you finish asking questions and doing your homework, you should be able to answer the unanswered portion of the first four questions and the next six questions:

- What's available?
- Which plan meets my needs?
- Is it better than what I have now?
- Can I live with its rules?
- Is it worth the price?
- Can I afford it?

### Collect Written Information from Insurers and HMOs

Get copies of all the literature on the options available from your employer or from your local health care insurers and HMOs. This is easy to do. You may already have the information you need to evaluate your employer's group options. If not, get them from your employer's Human Resources or Personnel staff. They should have the information on hand.

If you are going to deal directly with the insurance carriers or HMOs in your community, you can get information by writing or calling them. They're easy to find. Look in the yellow pages under "Health Plans Insurance" and under "Insurance." Even if you have an employer provided health care plan, you may want to call a few plans listed in the yellow pages to get information. We did and received some very detailed coverage information.

Make sure that the HMOs and insurers who offer prescription coverage send you a copy of their "Formulary" (the list of the prescription drugs included in their coverage) to check your family's needs against it.

The "Sample Example" pointed out what can happen if you don't know what your coverage is before you sign up for a health care plan. But there's more than coverage to ask about. The questions I would ask of the health care insurers, HMOs, and the people who are their policyholders or members follow. These questions, and others which you add, should give you the answers you need before making a decision. You will find a blank question form in the appendices for your other questions.

## ▼ KEY POINTS      The Decision-Making Process

1. Evaluate your situation now, as described in this chapter.
2. List your medical expenses for a year.
3. Know what your insurance covers.
4. Know what your insurance does not cover.
5. Use and follow "The Decision-Making Process."

### A System for Evaluating Insurance and HMO Plans Through Questioning

#### Get Ready to Ask the Right Questions

At this point you should have evaluated the health care insurance or HMO plan you have today, using your "Medical Expenses." You should have asked yourself some questions about what you can afford and what you need. You should have gathered coverage and cost information on other employer options or insurance and HMO plans available to the general public. Now, I'm going to give you some questions to help determine the value the plans might hold for you. Add to the list and reword it to meet your needs. Go through the list of questions before asking them. Make prompting notes on the question lines as needed. You will need to do some homework on three of the questions.

1. Preexisting conditions: Write your family's preexisting conditions on the line for that question to make sure you don't forget to mention them.
2. List the special needs of your family members. There is a question about special needs. Either write the needs on its question line or keep the list handy when you ask that question.
3. List your family's prescription medications. Have the list handy when you ask about prescription coverage. Check it against the "Formularies" you received from the HMOs and insurance plans. Determine whether each of the plans you are investigating has exactly the same drug. If not, you will need to ask if they have a generic of each drug, a substitute (different medication to treat the same symptom or malady), or nothing to meet your family's needs. Ask your doctor about any generic or substitute offered by the HMO or insurance plan before you make your decision about the coverage you are considering.

### Use Questions to Grade and Compare

You are going to use the answers you get to your questions to arrive at a numerical grade for each question and for the interview as a whole. By using the same system with all the insurers and HMOs, you will have a basis for comparing their plans. There are sets of questions to ask various types of health care coverage plans. I have tried to put the questions in a priority sequence, at least for the first few questions. If you get the wrong answers early in the questioning, you can save some time by dropping the plan from consideration quickly.

As you get answers to your questions, you will grade the plan. Let me explain how it works. There is a line above each question. Before you start your interview process, you will assign an "Importance" level to each question you intend to ask. As the respondent answers a question, you give the answer a "Score." Sometime after the interview, multiply the "Score" for each answer by its "Importance" to develop a "Weighted Score." Add up the weighted scores and divide by the number of questions you asked. You will have reduced the answers to a numeric value, which can easily be used for comparison to the values from others that you interviewed. Use the system as follows.

**Plans** will show for whom the question is intended. In the first set of questions, the word "Plans" will be followed by "HMO" or "PPO" or "M/C" or "All." The "M/C" refers to a fee-for-service "Managed Care" plan.

**Importance** has a line for your entry of the question's importance in your decision process. I suggest that you use a scale of 1 to 5, with 5 being very important. If it has no importance to you, don't ask the question. After assigning an importance level to each question, make copies of the forms for your use.

**Score** has a line for your entry. I suggest that you use a scale of 0 to 10, with 10 being the best score. If you heard exactly the right answer and you really liked the way the respondent answered it (e.g., with enthusiastic understanding of its importance), write in a 10 as soon as you have your answer. If the plan does not have the coverage, put down a 0 for their score. (If they don't have the coverage, it doesn't matter how the question was answered.) Don't at any time tell the person who answers the questions that you have assigned importance levels to the questions or the relative level assigned to any of them.

It's important that you write in the score before you go to your next question. The score will show how you felt about the answer at that moment and will have the least chance of being contaminated by your impressions of answers to other questions.

**Weighted Score** has a line for your entry. When you finish with all your questions, multiply the "Score" for each question by its "Importance," then write in its "Weighted Score." When you have all the "Weighted Scores," add them up and divide by the number of questions you asked. You will now have a numeric evaluation based on the questions you asked. It should be interesting to compare the weighted score of your current plan to these other plans.

*All the following questions are provided as forms with more room for your use in Appendix D.*

### HMO AND INSURANCE COMPANY QUESTIONS

| Plans: All | Importance: _____ | Score: _____ | Weighted Score: _____ |
|---|---|---|---|
| Is there a maximum lifetime benefit? | | | |
| If yes, how much is it? | | | |
| Is it for each patient or for my whole family? | | | |

| Plans: All | Importance: _____ | Score: _____ | Weighted Score: _____ |
|---|---|---|---|
| Do you have disease or procedural limits? | | | |
| If yes, what are they? | | | |
| How much are they by disease or procedure? | | | |

| Plans: All | Importance: _____ | Score: _____ | Weighted Score: _____ |
|---|---|---|---|
| What procedures are considered "experimental"? | | | |

| Plans: All | Importance: _____ | Score: _____ | Weighted Score: _____ |
|---|---|---|---|
| Do you have carve-outs for certain diseases? | | | |
| If yes, what are they? | | | |
| Where do you send the patients for each disease? | | | |

| Plans: All | Importance: _____ | Score: _____ | Weighted Score: _____ |
|---|---|---|---|
| Is this a national policy or HMO? | | | |
| If not, am I insured outside of your region? | | | |
| How does that coverage work? | | | |

| Plans: All | Importance: _____ | Score: _____ | Weighted Score: _____ |
|---|---|---|---|
| Will I have worldwide health care coverage? | | | |
| If yes, how does it work? | | | |
| If no, what happens to my family or me if we need care while abroad? | | | |

## HMO AND INSURANCE COMPANY QUESTIONS

| Plans: All | Importance: _____ | Score: _____ | Weighted Score: _____ |
|---|---|---|---|

May I have a list of your providers?

If not, why not?

| Plans: All | Importance: _____ | Score: _____ | Weighted Score: _____ |
|---|---|---|---|

What percentage of your providers out of residency for 5 years are board certified?

What percentage passed their Boards on the first try?

What percentage failed and are not Board Certified?

| Plans: HMO & M/C | Importance: _____ | Score: _____ | Weighted Score: _____ |
|---|---|---|---|

May I select my own Primary Care Physician?

If yes, will the PCP I want be available? (Ask before you sign up.)

| Plans: HMO & M/C | Importance: _____ | Score: _____ | Weighted Score: _____ |
|---|---|---|---|

From what fields do you draw your Primary Care Providers?

Can women have a gynecologist as their PCP?

Do you have pediatricians as PCPs?

| Plans: HMO & M/C | Importance: _____ | Score: _____ | Weighted Score: _____ |
|---|---|---|---|

Are patients with chronic problems allowed to have a specialist as their PCP?

| Plans: HMO & M/C | Importance: _____ | Score: _____ | Weighted Score: _____ |
|---|---|---|---|

If being treated by a specialist for a problem that requires follow-up or continuing care, can my specialist become my PCP either temporarily or permanently?

| Plans: HMO & M/C | Importance: _____ | Score: _____ | Weighted Score: _____ |
|---|---|---|---|

If being treated by a specialist for a problem that requires follow-up or continuing care, do I have to have a PCP referral for each follow-up visit?

| Plans: HMO & M/C | Importance: _____ | Score: _____ | Weighted Score: _____ |
|---|---|---|---|

Are annual gynecological examinations and mammograms allowed without referral?

If not, why not?

| Plans: HMO & M/C | Importance: _____ | Score: _____ | Weighted Score: _____ |
|---|---|---|---|

Can infants and children be taken to pediatrician without a referral?

If not, why not?

## HMO AND INSURANCE COMPANY QUESTIONS

| Plans: HMO & M/C | Importance: _____ | Score: _____ | Weighted Score: _____ |
|---|---|---|---|
| What is the average wait (days) for a PCP appointment? | | | |
| Plans: HMO & M/C | Importance: _____ | Score: _____ | Weighted Score: _____ |
| What is the average length (minutes) of PCP office visits? | | | |
| Plans: HMO & M/C | Importance: _____ | Score: _____ | Weighted Score: _____ |
| When a referral to a specialist occurs, what is the average length of wait (days) between being seen by the PCP and a specialist? | | | |
| Plans: HMO & M/C | Importance: _____ | Score: _____ | Weighted Score: _____ |
| What is the average length (minutes) of specialist office visits? | | | |
| Plans: All | Importance: _____ | Score: _____ | Weighted Score: _____ |
| What specialties participate in your plan? <br> What specialties do not participate in your plan? | | | |
| Plans: All | Importance: _____ | Score: _____ | Weighted Score: _____ |
| What percentage of your specialists are Board Certified in their specialty? <br> What percentage passed on their first try? <br> What percentage failed and never have been Board Certified? | | | |
| Plans: HMO & M/C | Importance: _____ | Score: _____ | Weighted Score: _____ |
| Where will I be referred if I need highly specialized medical care (e.g., rare disease treatment, transplant)? | | | |
| Plans: All | Importance: _____ | Score: _____ | Weighted Score: _____ |
| May I request and receive a second opinion? <br> If yes, how would I go about getting the second opinion? | | | |
| Plans: All | Importance: _____ | Score: _____ | Weighted Score: _____ |
| What hospitals do you use? | | | |
| Plans: All | Importance: _____ | Score: _____ | Weighted Score: _____ |
| What are the rules regarding Emergency Room care? | | | |

## HMO AND INSURANCE COMPANY QUESTIONS

| Plans: All | Importance: _____ | Score: _____ | Weighted Score: _____ |
|---|---|---|---|

What is the procedure for pre-authorizations?

Emergency Room?

Outpatient?

Inpatient?

| Plans: All | Importance: _____ | Score: _____ | Weighted Score: _____ |
|---|---|---|---|

What are the coverage provisions if I have a life-threatening emergency (e.g., heart attack, hemorrhage, serious accident) and do not get a pre-authorization? If I'm unconscious? If my family is too distraught?

| Plans: All | Importance: _____ | Score: _____ | Weighted Score: _____ |
|---|---|---|---|

What is the procedure for pre-authorization exceptions?

| Plans: All | Importance: _____ | Score: _____ | Weighted Score: _____ |
|---|---|---|---|

What is the prescription drug benefit?

| Plans: All | Importance: _____ | Score: _____ | Weighted Score: _____ |
|---|---|---|---|

I have a list of my current prescriptions and need to know which of my medications are not in your formulary?

| Plans: All | Importance: _____ | Score: _____ | Weighted Score: _____ |
|---|---|---|---|

Do you have other brands of the same drug?

If so what are they?

| Plans: All | Importance: _____ | Score: _____ | Weighted Score: _____ |
|---|---|---|---|

Do you have substitute drugs?

If so, what are they?

| Plans: All | Importance: _____ | Score: _____ | Weighted Score: _____ |
|---|---|---|---|

What are the caps on your prescription benefits?

| Plans: All | Importance: _____ | Score: _____ | Weighted Score: _____ |
|---|---|---|---|

Does your prescription benefit have copayment or coinsurance provisions?

If yes, what are they?

Is that all I have to pay?

| Plans: All | Importance: _____ | Score: _____ | Weighted Score: _____ |
|---|---|---|---|

Do you have a formal complaint program?

If yes, please describe it.

THE DECISION-MAKING PROCESS ■ 77

## HMO AND INSURANCE COMPANY QUESTIONS

| Plans: A I | Importance: _____ | Score: _____ | Weighted Score: _____ |

Do your patients have an Advocate to whom they can appeal?

If yes, please describe how that function works.

| Plans: A I | Importance: _____ | Score: _____ | Weighted Score: _____ |

If after going through your advocacy or grievance program I am not satisfied with the answer, to whom do I go in your management?

To whom do I go for outside advocacy or arbitration?

| Plans: All | Importance: _____ | Score: _____ | Weighted Score: _____ |

What measurement criteria are used in the evaluation of your doctors?

What is the weighting for each of the measurement criteria?

| Plans: HMO | Importance: _____ | Score: _____ | Weighted Score: _____ |

What was the NCQA rating by your HMO membership for each of the last 3 years?

| Plans: HMO | Importance: _____ | Score: _____ | Weighted Score: _____ |

What was your overall NCQA rating for each of the last 3 years?

| Plans: | Importance: _____ | Score: _____ | Weighted Score: _____ |

| Plans: | Importance: _____ | Score: _____ | Weighted Score: _____ |

| Plans: | Importance: _____ | Score: _____ | Weighted Score: _____ |

| Plans: | Importance: _____ | Score: _____ | Weighted Score: _____ |

| Plans: | Importance: _____ | Score: _____ | Weighted Score: _____ |

### Health Care Plan Enrollee Questions

The questions we have to ask of the health care insurers and the HMOs should help us find out the "What" and "Why" and "When" and "Where" and "Who." If we want to get the answer to the question "How," we have to ask someone else. For that answer we have to ask the policyholder, the patient, or the member. And that's what we are going to do next.

## HEALTH CARE PLAN ENROLLEE QUESTIONS

| | | | |
|---|---|---|---|
| Plans: All | Importance: _____ | Score: _____ | Weighted Score: _____ |
| How do you like the plan? | | | |
| Plans: All | Importance: _____ | Score: _____ | Weighted Score: _____ |
| How long have you been receiving care under this plan? | | | |
| Plans: All | Importance: _____ | Score: _____ | Weighted Score: _____ |
| What plan did you have before this one? | | | |
| Plans: All | Importance: _____ | Score: _____ | Weighted Score: _____ |
| Why did you change over to this plan? | | | |
| Plans: HMO & M/C | Importance: _____ | Score: _____ | Weighted Score: _____ |
| How do you like your Primary Care Physician? | | | |
| Plans: HMO & M/C | Importance: _____ | Score: _____ | Weighted Score: _____ |
| How long do you have to wait to get an appointment with your Primary Care Physician? | | | |
| Plans: HMO & M/C | Importance: _____ | Score: _____ | Weighted Score: _____ |
| How are you treated on the phone when you call for an appointment? | | | |
| Plans: HMO & M/C | Importance: _____ | Score: _____ | Weighted Score: _____ |
| Have you ever had any problems that required help from a specialist? If yes, how long did it take to get to see the specialist? | | | |
| Plans: HMO & M/C | Importance: _____ | Score: _____ | Weighted Score: _____ |
| Does your Primary Care Physician listen to you? | | | |
| Plans: HMO | Importance: _____ | Score: _____ | Weighted Score: _____ |
| Have you ever been sent a bill that you should not have received? If yes, how did your HMO deal with it? Was it a problem? Or did one phone call take care of it? | | | |

## HEALTH CARE PLAN ENROLLEE QUESTIONS

| Plans: PPO & M/C | Importance: _____ | Score: _____ | Weighted Score: _____ |
|---|---|---|---|
| When the Claims Office sends out an erroneous Explanation of Benefits (EOB); ||||
| Do they admit the error and take charge of correcting it? ||||
| Does it take more than one call from you? ||||
| Do you have to manage communications between the Claims Office and the Provider? ||||
| **Plans: All** | **Importance: _____** | **Score: _____** | **Weighted Score: _____** |
| Have you ever received an incorrect statement from your insurer? ||||
| If yes, how did your insurer deal with it? ||||
| What caused the problem? ||||
| Did one phone call take care of it? ||||
| Who corrected it? ||||
| How long did it take to straighten it out? ||||
| **Plans: All** | **Importance: _____** | **Score: _____** | **Weighted Score: _____** |
| What do you like most about the plan? ||||
| **Plans: All** | **Importance: _____** | **Score: _____** | **Weighted Score: _____** |
| What do you like least about the plan? ||||
| **Plans: All** | **Importance: _____** | **Score: _____** | **Weighted Score: _____** |
| I'm thinking of signing up for this plan; do you recommend it? ||||
| If yes (for HMO and M/C), who is your PCP? ||||

### Questions To Ask Your Doctor

Your doctor is an excellent source of information about HMOs if he or she treats HMO patients. If your physician has worked under contract with several HMOs, that's even better. Tell your doctor that you are considering switching to an HMO and ask the following questions. Some of the questions for your doctor can be answered by his or her staff. Get as many answers as you can from them to save your doctor's time.

## QUESTIONS OF YOUR DOCTOR ABOUT COMMERCIAL HMOS

| Plans: HMO | Importance: _____ | Score: _____ | Weighted Score: _____ |
|---|---|---|---|

Do you have HMO patients?

If yes, from which HMOs?

| Plans: HMO | Importance: _____ | Score: _____ | Weighted Score: _____ |
|---|---|---|---|

Are you a Primary Care Provider for any HMOs?

If yes, which ones?

| Plans: HMO | Importance: _____ | Score: _____ | Weighted Score: _____ |
|---|---|---|---|

In your opinion, which HMOs do the best job on utilization reviews?

| Plans: HMO | Importance: _____ | Score: _____ | Weighted Score: _____ |
|---|---|---|---|

Do you feel that any of the HMOs intrude on your professional judgment?

| Plans: HMO | Importance: _____ | Score: _____ | Weighted Score: _____ |
|---|---|---|---|

With which HMOs are you able to refer patients to specialists by name?

Do you or your staff arrange for the appointment?

If not, does the HMO let you know when they have set it up?

| Plans: HMO | Importance: _____ | Score: _____ | Weighted Score: _____ |
|---|---|---|---|

If you were running an HMO and had a choice of how to pay physicians (e.g., capitation, hold backs, fees, salary), how would you do it?

Why?

| Plans: HMO | Importance: _____ | Score: _____ | Weighted Score: _____ |
|---|---|---|---|

How are you compensated by the HMOs with whom you work?

| Plans: HMO | Importance: _____ | Score: _____ | Weighted Score: _____ |
|---|---|---|---|

With which of the HMOs do you have the best working relationship?

| Plans: HMO | Importance: _____ | Score: _____ | Weighted Score: _____ |
|---|---|---|---|

With which of the HMOs do you not have a good working relationship, if any?

| Plans: HMO | Importance: _____ | Score: _____ | Weighted Score: _____ |
|---|---|---|---|

If you were going to recommend an HMO to a family member who had a choice of several HMOs offered through an employer benefits program, which one would you recommend?

**Private and Employer-Provided Insurance**

### The "Decision Process" Questions, One More Time

Once again, here are the "Decision Process" questions.

- How much does my current health care insurance or HMO plan cost?
- How much can I afford?
- What coverages do I have now?
- What coverages do I need that I don't have now?
- What's available?
- Which plan meets my needs?
- Is it better than what I have now?
- Can I live with its rules?
- Is it worth the price?
- Can I afford it?

### Decision Process Summary

Let me sum up the steps involved in making your informed health care decision, as you go through the balance of the "Decision Process" and make your decision. You may not have finished some of the steps. If not, now is a good time to do so.

1. List one year of your family's medical expenses on a "Medical Expenses" form, found in the Appendices. (See "How Much Does my Current Insurance Cost?")

2. Make sure that you have the detailed coverage information for your health care insurance plan or your HMO plan. (See "What Can I Afford?")

3. If you don't have your coverage information, get it from your employer's Human Resources or Personnel representative, or from your insurance company or HMO if you deal directly with them. (See "What Can I Afford?")

4. Using your completed "Medical Expenses" form and the document showing your detailed coverage and cost information, document your family's situation on a "Health Care Plan Evaluation" form, found in the appendices. (See the "Sample Example.")

5. Obtain coverage and cost information on other health insurance plans and HMO plans, either from your employer or directly from insurers or HMOs. (See "Getting the Answers to Make Your Decision.")

6. Prepare to evaluate other plans against your current plan by filling in the "Family Member," "Encounter," and "Billed" columns of a "Health Care Plan Evaluation" form, found in the appendices. (See "Evaluate Your Own Situation Now.")
7. Make copies of the partially completed "Health Care Plan Evaluation" forms for your use in evaluating other plans. (See "Evaluate Your Own Situation Now.")
8. Go through the information you obtained on other plans, eliminating the ones that obviously do not meet your needs based on your answers to the "Decision Process" questions.
9. Select some plans for further investigation. Call or visit in person to get answers to the "HMO and Insurance Company Questions." You may eliminate some plans based on the early questions.
10. Evaluate the insurance and HMOs that remain attractive after questioning.
11. If any of the plans look better than what you have on a coverage or cost basis, ask some of their policyholders, patients, and members the "How" questions. (See "Health Care Plan Enrollee Questions.")
12. Finish answering the "Decision Process" questions.
13. Decide.

### ▼ KEY POINTS  Asking the Right Questions

1. Prepare to ask the right questions for your situation.
2. Draw from the questions provided for:
   Health care insurers & HMOs
   Policyholders and members
   Your doctor and his or her staff
3. Prioritize the questions you will ask.
4. Score the answers you receive by phone or in person.
5. Divide the sum of weighted scores by the number of questions you asked to arrive at a grade for each insurer and HMO.

**Decision Process Glossary Update**

**Encounter**—A term used by physicians, medical staffs, and claims office personnel to refer to interactions with patients without disclosing the nature of the patient's visit (e.g., office visit, consultation, examination).

**Out-of-Pocket (OOP)**—An annual patient cost built into the health care insurance contract. The patient pays a percentage of provider charges until the OOP amount is paid. Out-of-pocket expense is also referred to as "coinsurance."

# PART III

# Medicare, Medicaid, and Other Insurance: Options and Informed Decisions

# Medicare and Medicaid

> "Thank goodness when we reach 65 we will
> have the insurance we need.
> That is how it works, isn't it?"
> Well, in all candor, not quite.

 **Introduction**

Medicare is a federally sponsored insurance program which provides health care insurance coverage for approximately 39 million Americans. It provides benefits to those who are 65 and older who have paid into Social Security and to their spouses once they reach age 65. It also provides benefits to younger people who qualify for coverage on the basis of being disabled and having been eligible for Social Security Administration (SSA) disability payments for two years. Those who receive continuing dialysis for permanent kidney failure or who have had a kidney transplant may also qualify for Medicare.

Medicare provides both hospitalization and medical insurance coverage. Medicare hospitalization is referred to as Medicare Part A; the medical coverage is Medicare Part B. Part A is automatic and free to those who qualify on their 65th birthday or their second anniversary of being eligible for Social Security Administration Disability payments. Part B coverage starts on the same date, provided that the qualifying individual accepts coverage and agrees to pay for it. There is a monthly premium for Part B. In 1997, the premium is $43.80, up from $42.50 in 1996. The Medicare beneficiary may still have insurance coverage from his or her employer and elect to not accept

Part B. The beneficiary may sign up for Part B at a later date under provisions spelled out by Medicare.

About 90 days before the date of enrollment in Medicare, the eligible person is mailed a Medicare identification card showing the date upon which benefits begin. Instructions for rejecting Part B are contained in the mailer sent to the enrollee. If the beneficiary wants both parts of Medicare, he or she only needs to sign the card and carry it. The monthly premium for Part B coverage is automatically deducted from the Medicare beneficiary's Social Security check. Under certain circumstances a disabled person may be a Medicare enrollee while employed and not receiving monthly Social Security disability checks. In this case a disabled person would pay the Part B monthly premium by check.

---

*"That sounds good. All I have to do is wait until my Medicare card arrives in the mail. I'll have free hospitalization insurance and medical, too, if I want to pay $43.80 per month. And I don't have to tell anyone my life story or take a physical. It sounds like a good deal to me. . . . Are there any other costs?"*

*Yes, there are deductibles and copayments. I will explain.*

---

 ## Medicare Part A—Hospitalization

There is no premium for Part A. It provides partial coverage for inpatient hospital bills. In addition, it helps with the cost of care received in a skilled nursing facility or a hospice. It will also pay 100% of the approved amount for home health care and 80% of the approved amount for durable medical equipment if the patient meets restrictive eligibility and review requirements. Medicare approved facilities and firms must be used.

For hospital stays, the beneficiary is responsible for paying an annual deductible expense and, on long stays, will not receive full coverage. There is 100% coverage for the first 60 days except for any portion of the inpatient hospital deductible which may not have been paid. In 1997, this annual deductible amount is $760. There are some flat rate daily payments for extended hospital stays as there are for other types of facilities. In all cases, I used the 1997 rates. Current rates are available from the Social Security Administration.

After day 60, the hospitalized patient is responsible for a daily copayment amount. For days 61–90, it's $190 per day. There is no coverage beyond day 90 unless the beneficiary draws from the one-time 60-day reserve. The 60-day reserve can be used as required to extend hospital stays beyond 90 days. They can be used a day at a time or in a 60-day block. The copayment is $380 per day. After day 90, the beneficiary could draw from the one-time 60-day reserve to pay for days 91–150. You will see an example of how this would work in the Part A chart which follows. Otherwise, there is no coverage after day 90.

The duration of hospice coverage for the terminally ill is unlimited with a doctor's certification of need, on a patient-by-patient basis. In most cases, the attending physician is required to certify that, in his or her best medical judgment, no more effective medical treatment exists in the patient's case and the patient has less than 6 months to live. There are some limits on payment for outpatient drugs and inpatient respite care. "Respite" means a time of relief and rest. It describes the care a terminal patient receives in a hospice.

Skilled nursing is covered at the 100% rate for 20 days. After that, the patient must pay a fixed amount of $95 per day for the next 80 days. After day 100, there is no coverage.

There is no Medicare coverage for custodial nursing home care. "Long-term care insurance" is available commercially. It helps protect you from the financial impact of long-term nursing home care. It is one of the supplemental insurance topics covered in Chapter 10.

## Medicare Coverage and Costs Tables

Medicare Part A coverage and costs are shown in a table on the next page. The Part A and Part B column headings and their meanings are as follows:

"Services" column defines the limits of what's included in the benefit.

"Benefit" column shows the number of days for each level of Medicare-paid expenses.

"Medicare Pays" is the amount Medicare pays for the "Benefit" column periods.

"You Pay" shows the amount you must pay for the periods shown under "Benefit."

## MEDICARE PART A COVERAGE

| Services | Benefit | Medicare Pays | You Pay |
|---|---|---|---|
| **Hospitalization** | | | |
| Semiprivate room & board, general nursing, other services & supplies | Day 1–60<br>Day 61–90*<br>Day 91–150**<br>Day 151 on | All but $760<br>All but $190/day<br>All but $380/day<br>$0.00 | $760<br>$190/day<br>$380/day<br>All costs |
| **Skilled Nursing Facility** | | | |
| Semiprivate room & board, skilled nursing, therapy, & other services & supplies | Day 1–20<br>Day 21–100<br>Day 101 on | 100%<br>All but $95/day<br>$0.00 | $0.00<br>Up to $95/day<br>All costs |
| **Home Health Care** | | | |
| Part-time skilled care, home care, aide services, durable medical equipment, supplies, & services | Unlimited as long as you meet Medicare conditions | 100%<br>80% durable medical equipment | $0.00 for Services<br>20% of approved cost of durable medical equipment |
| **Hospice Care** | | | |
| Pain relief, symptom management, & support services for the terminally ill | As long as doctor certifies need | All but ~ $5.00/Rx outpatient drugs<br>All but ~ $5.00/day for inpatient respite care | ~ $5.00/Rx outpatient drugs<br>~ $5.00/day for inpatient respite care |
| **Blood** | | | |
| When furnished by a Hospital or skilled nursing facility during a covered stay | Unlimited | All after First 3 Pints during year | First 3 Pints |

\* There is no coverage beyond day 90 unless the beneficiary uses some of his or her one-time pool of 60 "reserve days."

\*\* Each beneficiary has a one-time pool of 60 "reserve days," which can be used to supplement coverage beyond the 90-day Medicare coverage for each hospital stay. The reserve days can be used for a single extended hospitalization or can be spent as needed, over the years, for a number of hospitalizations exceeding 90 days each.

## Medicare Part A—Table Summary

**Hospitalization** costs are based on an annual deductible and the number of days you stay in the hospital. The first 60 days are free after you pay your deductible ($760 in 1997). After the first 60 days, you pay $190 per day for the next 30 days. Then there is no coverage after day 90, unless you use your 60 reserve days. You can spend your reserve days all at once or over the years, but you can only spend them once. As you use them, you pay $380 of the hospitalization daily costs.

**Skilled Nursing Facility** costs are paid in full by Medicare for the first 20 days. For days 21–100, Medicare pays all but $95 per day. After day 100, you have no coverage.

**Home Health Care** benefits are provided to patients who are confined to their homes; are under physician's care; and need periodic skilled nursing, physical therapy, or speech therapy. These services are provided without charge by a Medicare-approved home health agency's skilled nurses or home health aides. If your doctor prescribes durable equipment (e.g., wheelchair, oxygen), you pay 20% of the cost.

**Hospice Care** is paid for by Medicare with two exceptions. There can be a copayment of up to $5.00 for each prescription drug and about $5.00 for each day as an inpatient.

**Blood** is free after you pay for the first 3 pints during the calendar year.

**Custodial Care** is not covered.

## Medicare Part B as Medical, Physician, or Provider Insurance

Part B will pay some of the expenses for a number of medical services. Included are such things as physicians services, outpatient hospital care, physical therapy, mental health services, laboratory tests, and biannual mammography screenings. It will also assist with the cost of medical equipment and ambulance service. It provides limited coverage for medically required chiropractic, podiatric, optometric, and dental surgery procedures.

In addition to the monthly premium for Part B, there is an annual deductible of $100 and a patient responsibility for 20% of the amount that Medicare approves for each of the patient's medical bills. Medicare determines the amount it is willing to pay for each medical procedure. The patient is responsible for at least 20% of this amount and could be responsible for most outpatient mental health services.

The medical provider may or may not agree to accept the amount that Medicare has set for reimbursement. If the provider has agreed to accept the Medicare rates, he or she is said to have "accepted assignment" for a particular service. In this case the patient is responsible for a copayment equal to 20% of the rate set for each procedure after his or her Part B annual deductible has been paid.

Your local Social Security Administration office has a list of the doctors in your area who accept assignment. It's called the *Medpard Directory*. Call your local office and ask for it. Your library may also have a copy. The *Medpard Directory* may not be up-to-date. If you have a provider whom you would like to see as a Medicare patient, call his or her office. Ask whether the provider accepts assignment. Your local hospital is another source of names of doctors who accept assignment. Hospitals are required to furnish Medicare beneficiaries with a list of their specialists who accept assignment. Ask for it.

If the medical provider does not accept assignment, the provider is allowed by Medicare to charge the patient up to 115% of the Medicare set rate. The patient is responsible for the extra 15% as well as the 20% copayment.

*Outpatient billing differs from the other 20% copayment rules. It is 20% of what the hospital billed, not 20% of what Medicare considers to be reasonable.*

There are three major areas of coverage exclusion for the Medicare patient. First, custodial nursing home and long-term nursing home care are not covered. Second, the Medicare beneficiary is not covered when outside the United States. Third, Medicare does not cover all services and procedures that are preventive in nature. Examples of preventive services not covered are routine physicals, routine dental services, dentures, eye examinations and glasses, hearing tests and hearing aids, and routine foot care. Call your local Medicare carrier for current coverage information.

*Your Medicare Handbook* has a listing of the toll free telephone numbers and addresses of local Medicare carriers. The local Medicare carrier processes Medicare claims in your area. You also call your local Medicare carrier if you have any claim questions or problems.

There are a number of special circumstances that can affect your Medicare costs. You need to talk to your local Medicare carrier before incurring out of the ordinary medical expenses. There are too many special circumstances to list and they are subject to change, so I'll give you a couple examples to show you the type of circumstances I have in mind.

For example, certain states have "Charge Limit" laws. If you are a resident of one of these states, you may have additional protection on what you can be charged by doctors who do not accept assignment. Also, there's a special rule for doctors who perform elective surgery and do not accept assignment. If the charge is going to be $500 or more, your doctor is required to give you a written estimate. If the physician did not give you the estimate, he or she is limited on the amount he or she can collect from you.

"Medicare Part B Coverage" table is on the next page.

---

*So there you are. If you don't mind paying for the gaps and the deductibles and the copayments, make your decision on Part B and you're done. On the other hand if you want to hear about plugging those gaps and not paying some or all of the cost-sharing, read on.*

---

 **Additional Medicare Reading Material**

These two Medicare coverage charts are intended to show you that Medicare provides basic health care insurance coverage, but requires beneficiaries to pay for a portion of their care. There is much more you need to know

## MEDICARE PART B COVERAGE

| Services | Benefit | Medicare Pays | You Pay |
|---|---|---|---|
| **Medical Expenses** Doctor services, inpatient & outpatient medical & surgical services & supplies, therapy, tests, durable medical equipment & other services | Unlimited if medically necessary | 80% of approved amount after $100 deductible reduced to 50% for most outpatient mental health services | $100 deductible 20% of approved amount & limited charges above approved amount (Notes 1 & 2) |
| **Clinical Laboratory Tests** Blood tests, urinalysis, and more | Unlimited if medically necessary | Generally 100% of approved amount | Nothing for services |
| **Home Health Care** Part-time skilled care, home care, aide services, durable medical equipment, supplies, & services | Unlimited as long as you meet Medicare conditions | 100% of approved amount & 80% of approved amount for durable medical equipment | $0.00 for services 20% of approved amount for durable medical equipment |
| **Outpatient Hospital Treatment** Services for diagnosis or treatment of illness or injury | Unlimited if medically necessary | Medicare payment to hospital based on hospital cost | **20% of billed amount (after $100 deductible) (Note 1 & 4)** |
| **Blood** | Unlimited if medically necessary | 80% of approved amount (after $100 deductible and starting with fourth pint) | First 3 pints plus 20% of approved amount for extra pints (after $100 deductible) (Note 3) |

1. Part B requires the beneficiary to pay up to $100 deductible each calendar year for services delivered under Part B coverage.
2. The amount "You Pay" is dependent on whether or not your doctor "accepts assignment."
3. Blood paid for or replaced under Medicare Part A during the calendar year does not have to be paid for or replaced under Medicare Part B.
4. **Beneficiary is responsible for 20% of billed amount, not 20% of what Medicare considers reasonable.**

before making decisions about your Medicare coverage. I will go into greater detail in the following pages and will include some very detailed tables. Before you make any decisions about Medicare, however, you need to get detailed and current information from Medicare. And you need to consult with your Medicare representatives.

You'll find *Your Medicare Handbook* to be helpful, though it will probably leave you with questions about your specific situation. It tells you how to get help and provides pertinent phone directories. I suggest that you read it through quickly to get a general feel for the coverage provisions of Medicare. Reread it, this time writing down your questions. Call the Medicare insurance carrier for your region, state, or territory to get your questions answered. There's a list of the carriers in *Your Medicare Handbook*. The carrier's number is also available from the Social Security Administration's hotline: 1-800-638-6833.

The 1995 edition of *Your Medicare Handbook* provided a list of free publications available by writing to the Consumer Information Center, Department 33, Pueblo, CO 81009. Since they are not listed in this year's *Handbook*, I have included a list of these publications for you here. They are also listed in the Information Directory. You will undoubtedly find some of them to be helpful. I did. The list of publications with their publication numbers in parentheses follows:

- *Guide to Health Insurance for People with Medicare* **(518B), [A Must Read]**
- *Medicare: Coverage for Second Surgical Opinion* (521B)
- *Medicare: Hospice Benefits* (591B)
- *Medicare and Managed Care Plans* (592B)
- *Medicare and Other Health Benefits* (593B)
- *Medicare: Savings for Qualified Beneficiaries* (596B)
- *Medicare and Your Physician's Bill* (520B)
- *Medicare and Advance Directives* (519B)
- *Manual de Medicare* (595B) (Spanish Language)
- *Medicare Coverage of Kidney Dialysis and Kidney Transplant Services: A, Supplement to Your Medicare Handbook* (594B)
- *Continuous Improvement* (637A)

---

***From this point on you are going to gather information to make decisions. Let's take a look at the Medicare Decision Process.***

---

 ## The Medicare Decision Process

Medicare differs from commercial health care insurance and HMOs in a very significant way. With commercial insurance you have a very wide selection of types of policies and HMOs from which to select. And for each of them, there is also a wide variety of choices of coverages, pricing options, and costs. All of this combines to make decision making complex if you don't approach it in an organized, step by step manner. Hopefully, you found the "Decision Process" helpful as you were considering multiple variables of plan, coverage, pricing, and cost at the same time.

With Medicare, you will find a much more structured environment with fewer variables. Therefore, the decision process for Medicare is simpler. You start with a known factor, the coverage and costs of Medicare Part A and

Medicare Part B. The one variable you might have to make a judgment on would be Part B, if you had employer retirement insurance. Other than that, you are going to be evaluating options to find the one which best fills the gaps or extends the coverage of Medicare. Is it one of the ten standard Medigap plans or one of the Medicare HMOs in your community?

Sometime before you reach retirement age, you will need to develop a budget of some sort. Part of that budget will have to be some amount for medical costs, including the cost of Medicare and other insurance. You may already have a trial budget with medical expenses built into it. Whether you have a budget or not, you should determine what you need in the way of a health care plan. Then determine the best way to get it considering coverage, type of plan (fee-for-service or HMO), and cost. Evaluate your health care plan selection and cost against your budget, if you have one. You may have to redo your budget or your health care plan selection or both.

## Medicare Decision Process Questions

After a subset of "Decision Process" questions which we will use for Medicare, I will start you through the process. Let's get started on the modified "Decision Process" for Medicare.

**1. What were my spouse's and my medical procedures (e.g., office visits, surgery, physical, mammogram, physical therapy) last year?** Use the "Medical Expenses" form to list them. (See "The Health Insurance Decision Process" in Chapter 4, "The Decision Making Process.")

**2. What coverages do I need that I don't have now?** Medicare and its supplements are designed to fill the needs of people 65 and over. By completing your "Medical Expenses" form; going through the Medicare, Medigap, and Medicare HMO offerings; and being aware of the Medicare gaps which are not filled, this question should be answered for you.

**3. What's available?** You will see most of what's available in table format on the "Medicare–Medigap–HMO Coverage and Cost Tables" in Chapter 9. To get Medigap pricing, contact your Social Security Administration local office. Ask for the names of the Medicare-approved Medigap carriers and HMOs in your area. Call or write them to get their sales literature.

**4. Which plan meets my needs?** After gathering plan and pricing information from the Medicare-approved Medigap insurers and the Medicare HMOs, you will use evaluation techniques similar to the those used in evaluating employer and commercial health care plans and HMOs. The plan comparisons should be easier to make, because of the standardization of Medicare and Medigap. There are "Medicare–Medigap–HMO Coverage and Cost Worksheets" in the appendices to help you.

**5. Can I live with its rules?** Once again, asking the right questions will help. Use the "Medigap Carrier Questions," "Medicare HMO Questions," "Medigap Policyholder Questions," "Medicare HMO Member Questions," and "Questions to Ask Your Doctor." These questions are made up as forms for your use and can be found in the appendices.

**6. Is it worth the price?** Only you can answer this question and the next one.

**7. Can I afford it?**

---

Remember the lesson we learned from the "Sample Example."
"You don't know what your insurance covers,
until you know what it does not cover."
Let's see what Medicare does not cover and what we can do about it.

---

### Medicare Coverage Gaps

Medicare provides very good coverage at bargain rates. Hospitalization (Medicare Part A) is free. If you decide that you want Medicare Part B, its premium is $43.80, which will be deducted from your monthly Social Security check.

There are some things that Medicare does not cover. Both Part A and Part B have deductibles and copayments. Unless you have long-term hospital stays or require custodial nursing home confinement, the coverage Medicare provides may be as good as that provided by your employer, at lower cost to you.

Let's assume that you are basically healthy and occasionally go to a doctor who accepts assignment and usually orders blood tests and X rays. You have insurance coverage for $625.60/year, plus the cost of any prescriptions and 20% of your doctor's fees. If any serious health problem develops, you have some protection. [($43.80 × 12) = ($525.60) + $100.00 deductible = $625.60]

It's important to put Medicare coverage and cost in perspective, because the following analysis concentrates on its gaps, the "What happens if?" considerations. Let's look at the potential financial impact that prolonged hospitalization, a skilled nursing home stay, and custodial nursing home care could have.

Prolonged hospitalization is somewhat rare, but when it happens there is a big financial exposure under Medicare. Once checked in as an inpatient, you pay the first $760 in expenses in the calendar year. Other than that, the hospital portion of expenses are paid in full for the first 60 days. (You will still be responsible for physician copayments.) Beyond the first 60 days your portion of the bill mounts up fast, at $190 a day for the next 30 days. Stays beyond 60 days are unlikely, but can happen. I had a 76-day stay. Beyond 90 days, you can use your one-time reserve of 60 days so that your portion of the daily bill is cut to $380/day. Beyond that, you are on your own. Your expense for hospitalization costs are as follows:

| Days | 1–60 | $ 760 | (Annual Deductible) |
|------|------|-------|---------------------|
| Days | 61–90 | 5,700 | ($190/day Coverage) |
| Days | 91–150 | 22,800 | (If you use your 60 reserve days at $380/day) |
| Total | | $ 29,260 | |

Skilled nursing is another area of significant exposure. The first 20 days are free, but days 21–100 cost $95/day. That amounts to $7,600 for 100 days. Beyond the 100th day, there is no coverage. Once again, it may not happen to you, but I had a 45 day stay in 1994. My insurance was billed $21,207.58 at $471.28/day.

Medicare does not provide coverage for custodial nursing home care. Without Long-Term Care insurance, custodial care can deplete a family's financial assets in a hurry. *Consumer Reports* ran a series of three articles on nursing homes in their August, September, and October 1995 issues. *Consumer Reports* ranked 43 nursing home chains and reported nursing home costs for some of the homes they rated. Their monthly costs ranged from $3,500 to $5,550. To order a reprint write: Consumers Union, Bulk Reprints, 101 Truman Avenue, Yonkers, New York 10703-1057.

Medicare lacks in its coverage of preventive medicine costs. It either does not cover the preventive medicine procedure at all or does not provide coverage as frequently as recommended by organizations such as The American Cancer Society. It does not cover routine physical examinations, and flexible sigmoidoscopys for men are not covered annually. Instead of the recommended annual frequency, Pap Smears are only covered every 3 years and mammograms every 2 years.

*Your Medicare Handbook 1995* on page 18 mentioned the possibility of more frequent examinations under certain circumstances and gave a telephone number "For accurate up-to-date information on cancer prevention, detection, diagnosis, and treatment. . . ." The number is 1-800-4-CANCER. Talk to Medicare to get information for your specific situation.

 ## Filling the Medicare Gaps

There are a number of ways to close Medicare gaps. You could self-insure, use employer-provided insurance, buy Medigap insurance, enroll in a Medicare HMO plan, buy one or more supplemental insurance policies, or become a Medicaid patient if you meet a set of rigid means tests imposed by your state. Let's look at each of these options.

### Self-Insurance

This merely means that you pay any medical bills not covered by Medicare. If you remain healthy up to the day you die, you might be ahead financially with this approach, but you can't know if that will be the case. For those who are not *very* poor or *very* rich, self-insurance is the choice by default. Let me explain.

When you turn 65, you will have a 6-month open enrollment period in which to buy insurance designed to fill Medicare gaps and extend coverage. If you don't act within 6 months and you have a history of illness, you could be denied access to these insurance options. Although some insurers might have an open enrollment, inaction during the 6-month open enrollment period could result in your having to pay the bills Medicare doesn't pay. You would be self-insured for those coinsurance and other Medicare gaps by default.

### Employer Insurance

If you are fortunate enough to have employer-provided insurance available to you in retirement, you might want to use it as your Medicare secondary insurer. If coverage is good and the rates low, this decision might seem like a "no brainer." Why wouldn't you want to do this?

Given changes in today's corporate structures, there could be some risk. If your company is taken over, merges, or simply goes out of business, you could find your cost sharing going up and your coverage going down. Consider the possibility as you check out your employer's retirement health insurance offering against other available options.

*"Do we get the Medigap policy from the government or from someone else? If we buy it from an insurance company, how do we know what we're getting?"*

### Medigap

Medigap insurance is not available from the government. You purchase it from private insurers. A list of Medicare approved insurers offering Medigap policies in your area is available from your local Social Security Administration office. For a number of years, insurers developed and sold policies to fill the gaps in Medicare coverage. There were no standards for the policies being offered. In 1992, the National Association of Insurance Commissioners created ten standardized plans. By law, policies must conform to these standards if they are to be sold as Medigap policies.

There are ten standard coverage plans, Plan A through Plan J. Although all the plans within a plan type (e.g., Plan A, Plan C, Plan F) by law offer the same coverage, there can be differences in their prices and their price bases. I will discuss pricing later. Right now, let's concentrate on the gap filling coverages offered by these plans. A Medigap plan might pay deductibles for Medicare Plan A or Plan B. Another plan might pay copayments for Plan A (e.g., hospital per day copayments, extended hospital stays beyond 90 days). Some plans might provide coverage not offered by either Medicare plan (e.g., prescriptions, preventive care). **None of the Medigap plans offers coverage for custodial care.**

### Health Maintenance Organization (HMO)

There are Medicare approved HMOs. You can use an HMO membership to fill Medicare's gaps and extend its coverage. To do this, sign up for Medicare Plan B and join a Medicare-approved HMO. Medicare will pay the HMO, and you will receive your health care through the plan you selected. Any additional costs to you will depend on the HMO plan you select. It's possible to receive all the benefits of a Medigap policy and more. Costs will depend on the plan, the location and the HMO.

---

"When does Medicaid take over?"
Hopefully, for your sake, never!

---

## Medicaid

Let's start with some background on Medicaid. What is it? Who runs it? Where does it get its funding? Medicaid is a joint federal and state program. It provides health care to those members of our society who otherwise would not have access to any health care. Its funding comes from our tax payments to our federal and state governments. The federal budget includes money for Medicaid. The funds are given to the states to run the Medicaid program with federal guidelines. The states must augment the Medicaid funding with tax money collected in their states.

Medicaid provides complete medical and custodial care for its clients. There are 37 million Americans who receive their health care through Medicaid. Of those 37 million, 5 million are over age 65. Included in this number are 2 million who have their Medicare premiums, deductibles, copayments, and coinsurance paid by Medicaid. Two-thirds of the nation's nursing home residents have their bills paid by Medicaid.

An application for Medicaid demands complete financial disclosure. The applicant must have few, if any, assets. Bank accounts, income from pensions, alimony, real or personal property, even the deed to a cemetery plot are open to scrutiny. Each state has its own set of standards for measuring need. There are rules to prevent an individual from giving away assets to qualify for Medicaid and become a ward of the state. Those who have assets and try to give them away so that Medicaid will pay for their custodial care must do so 3 years before the need arises. Giving away your assets to qualify for Medicaid is probably going to be made more difficult to do.

It may be possible for the spouse of a long-term custodial resident to spend up to half of their assets for his or her spouse's custodial care and keep the other half for himself or herself. The ability to do this depends on the laws of the state and its rules for Medicaid qualification. If this splitting of assets is allowed, Medicaid would provide for the custodial resident's care after his or her half of the couple's assets have been spent. Your local Social Security office can answer questions regarding Medicaid but will refer you to your county social services office for personal guidance and help.

Many who qualify for Medicaid come from a tradition of poverty, with little or nothing in the way of education, money, or ability to break the so-called chain of poverty. Others are the newly impoverished, middle-class people of advanced age who may need long-term nursing home care before their deaths.

Traditionally, Medicaid health care has been provided by hospitals and clinics receiving public funding. That's changing. Some agencies now have HMOs provide health care to their Medicaid clients. A number of counties use HMOs to provide Medicaid services. The state of Tennessee was featured on *The Jim Lehrer News Hour* on public television in 1996. They had recently contracted with HMOs to provide Medicaid health care. HMOs provide cost containment and budget predictability to the state. Tennessee is also looking for improvement in the availability and quality of care for the poor.

Until recently the states ran Medicaid under strict guidelines dictated by the federal government. Although the states ran the program, the federal government was very involved in how the states implemented Medicaid. It tended to be a "one size fits all program." By that I mean that there was a degree of uniformity in its implementation from Alaska to Rhode Island, two states who would be likely to have dissimilar needs.

In 1995 and the first half of 1996, there was a move in Congress to relax or even cut the strings that are attached to federal funding for Welfare and, with it, Medicaid. There was a proposal to give "Block Grant" funding to the states, which they in turn would be expected to spend on Welfare, including Medicaid, at their discretion. A significant number of Senators and Representatives believed the states could run Welfare, including Medicaid, better than the way it was being run. Their arguments boiled down to the following:

- Each state has a unique set of social problems. One solution does not fit all.
- State government is closer to its residents and understands their needs better.

- Federal government staffs are no better or brighter than the state governments' staffs.
- The state governments couldn't make Welfare and Medicaid any worse.

Our Executive Branch had imposed strict guidelines for spending the federal funding contribution to Medicaid. The guidelines were put in place over time to make sure that our most vulnerable citizens (e.g., disabled children, nursing home residents), receive quality care, regardless of a state's budgetary problems or priorities. By way of example, Medicaid guidelines were put in place to make sure that nursing home residents were not unduly restrained or discharged when they ran out of money. The federal government has been able to impose standards of care at a national level and make them stick.

With the polarization of the positions taken by our Congress and our President, the nation's governors early in 1996, unanimously proposed a compromise solution to the Medicaid impasse. They proposed "Block Grants" with federal guidelines, but without federal bureaucratic participation in each state's implementation of Welfare. After 7 months of discussions and negotiations among parties, both Houses of Congress and the President, Congress passed a bill on August 2, 1996. President Clinton signed it on the same day. The individual states will implement welfare programs for their state, using federal and state funds, with some guidelines imposed by the Federal Government.

I went through this discussion of Welfare including Medicaid to let you know that there will undoubtedly be some changes in the way Medicaid is administered. The federal government will still impose some guidelines, but will not be as deeply involved in state level Medicaid management. Hopefully, the changes made to meet the particular needs of each state will enhance Medicaid for the residents of all states.

## Sources of Medicare, Medicaid, and Other Information

**The Eldercare Locator** (1-800-677-1116) is a national service that will point the caller to senior services in his or her county or region. The Older Americans Act of 1965 mandated that an Information and Referral Service must be provided to all senior Americans at the local level. How it is implemented is left up to the individual states and their counties. When you call the Eldercare Locator, you will be directed to the appropriate local agency or to your local Information and Referral Service. In Santa Clara County, California, this agency publishes a directory of services (136 pages for 1996) called "The Senior Handbook," which is very helpful. Your agency may take a very different approach based on the needs of your county or region and the funds available to the agency, but by law there must be someone to direct you to the right agency.

**Social Security Administration (SSA)** is the agency that will enroll you in the Medicare program. You will find the local office telephone number and address in the business pages section of the white pages of your phone book. This is the source for *Your Medicare Handbook* and a number of other publications and is the official source for current and detailed information.

Another point of some importance: If you are within 5 years of eligibility for Social Security Retirement, use the same telephone number to get information on your projected retirement income. You will have to provide your social security number and that of your spouse. In return, the agency will send you a projection of Social Securty payments you should expect to receive at retirement ages 62 through 65 for yourself and your spouse.

**Health Insurance Information and Counseling** offices are located in each state and territory. They can provide free information, assistance, and counseling on the Medicare, Medicaid, Medigap, long-term nursing care, and other health insurance benefits prior to your enrollment. After Medicare enrollment, they can help you understand your billing and insurance reimbursements. Their local telephone number is available from the Medicare Hotline (1-800-638-6833) and also is listed in *Your Medicare Handbook*.

**Health Insurance Counseling and Advocacy Program (HICAP)** is a source for counseling and information on other agencies and services available in your county. HICAP receives funding from both the government and from private donations. Look for their number in the business section of the white pages under the name "Council on Aging." Most counties have their own agencies, so if their number is not listed under this name, call your county's information number and ask them how to contact HICAP. Their services to you are free.

**American Association of Retired Persons (AARP)** is a good source of information on Medicare, Medicaid, Medigap, and supplemental policies. AARP's membership and general information telephone number is 1-800-424-3410. When you turn 50, you can become a member. Check on annual dues with AARP.

All of these organizations are at least partially funded by tax dollars. If you are nearing the date of your eligibility or if you are doing some retirement planning, use them. At a minimum, you should call the Social Security Administration and ask them to send you information on Medicare. Their publications will tell you how to get still more information. When you reach this transition point in your life, you need to make some important decisions. Base these decisions on as much information as you can get.

Other information is available to help you better manage the quality and cost of your health care. You will find names, addresses, telephone numbers, fax numbers, and internet access addresses in the "Information Directory" in the appendices. It lists all the organizations referenced so far and others not specifically mentioned. For example, you will find information about "Medical Databases" access. Similarly, "Doctor Information" is available from a variety of sources. The "Information Directory" lists information sources, including organizations not specifically mentioned in this text.

Next we will see how Medigap can help you enhance your Medicare coverage.

### ▼ KEY POINTS     Medicare and Medicaid

1. Medicare provides coverage for 38 million Americans:
   Over 65 and/or
   Disabled
2. Medicare Part A (Hospitalization) is automatic and free to beneficiaries.
3. Medicare Part B (Medical/Doctor) is optional at a monthly cost of $43.80 to beneficiaries in 1997.
4. Medicare has gaps which can be partially filled by:
   Medigap (10 Plans which must conform to Federal Government standards) or
   Medicare HMOs which must be approved by the Federal Government.
5. Medicaid provides health care to 37 million poor.
6. Medicare does not provide any coverage for long-term custodial care.
7. Long-Term Care (Custodial Care) policies are available in the marketplace.
8. Sources of additional information are listed in this chapter and in the "Information Directory" appendix.

# Medigap

---

You have been introduced to Medicare Part A and Part B.
You have seen some of their gaps and
general approaches to filling them.
It's time to look into the ten Medigap Plans.

---

 **Introduction to Medigap Plans**

In the last chapter you saw that Medicare needs to be enhanced with additional insurance, if you are going to have the coverage you want and need. There are ten standard Medigap plans. Insurance carriers may offer some or all of them. In some states they are prohibited from offering certain plans. In others, earlier versions of "Medigap Plans" are still in force and can still be sold. Nevertheless, if an insurance carrier offers any Medigap Plans, it must offer Plan A, sometimes referred to as the "Basic Plan." Any other coverages they offer must conform to one of the ten standard plans, Plan A through Plan J, except for the special allowable variances in some states.

You may be asking how you're going to know about special Medigap rules in certain states and, for that matter, other special considerations and rules. The best way I know is by taking advantage of the free information booklets that I will tell about throughout this book. If you don't read any others, make sure you get and read the most current edition of *Your Medicare Handbook* from Medicare and the *Guide to Health Insurance for People with Medicare* (518B), from the Consumer Information Center, Department 33, Pueblo, CO 81009.

As I mentioned in the first chapter, health care information often has to be pulled together to be understood. This is very true of Medicare. Information can be found in a number of federal government publications. In the last chapter you saw examples of public domain tables which I have enhanced for clarity. I have used the same technique in this chapter. I also have created very detailed tables and forms, so you don't have to look at multiple dissimilar data presentations as you make decisions.

In this chapter, I want to show you the range of coverage Medigap offers. You will go through an overview of Medicare vs. Medigap Plan A vs. Plan J. Then we'll discuss some things you need to consider when evaluating Medigap coverages. Next, we will go through the detailed coverages of Medicare vs. Medigap Plan A vs. Medigap Plan J. In later chapters, I build on these tables to create worksheets for your use in comparing the detailed coverages of Medicare, all ten Medigap Plans, and the Medicare HMOs available in your community.

## The "Medigap Overview" Table

The table on the next page will give you the big picture of Medicare coverages and those offered by the ten Medigap Plans. Let's look at the first line in the table to see what it shows us.

The first line refers to Medicare "Part A." Specifically, it refers to the copayment provision for days 61–90 of inpatient hospital confinement. It shows that without Medigap, you would have to pay $190 per day ($5,700 if you stayed for the full 30 days). Medigap "Plans A–J" would make that copayment for you.

As you go down the table, you will notice that Medicare "Part A" does not pay the "Skilled nursing home days 21–100 $95/day copay" ($7,600) for you. Medigap "Plan B" also does not pay this copayment. "Plans C–J" do pay this copayment amount for you. Generally speaking, as you go across the chart to the right, the Medigap Plans become more inclusive in their coverage and more expensive. None of the Medigap Plans pay for skilled nursing home stays beyond 100 days or custodial care coverage.

The columns from left to right are:

- Plan—"A" indicates Medicare Part A enhancement
    —"B" indicates Medicare Part B enhancement
    —A blank under a part column indicates an enhancement to Medicare.
- Medigap Coverage—describes the coverage area affected
- ABCDEFGHIJ—a "Y" at the juncture of a column and a line means Medicare coverage is enhanced by the Medigap Plan represented by the column.

**MEDIGAP OVERVIEW**

| Plan | Medigap Coverage* | A | B | C | D | E | F | G | H | I | J |
|---|---|---|---|---|---|---|---|---|---|---|---|
| A | Hospital days 61-90 $190/day copay | Y | Y | Y | Y | Y | Y | Y | Y | Y | Y |
| A | Reserve days 91-150** $380/day copay | Y | Y | Y | Y | Y | Y | Y | Y | Y | Y |
| A | 365 extra hospital days—all charges | Y | Y | Y | Y | Y | Y | Y | Y | Y | Y |
| A | Blood deductible first 3 pints | Y | Y | Y | Y | Y | Y | Y | Y | Y | Y |
| A | Physician charges 20% copay | Y | Y | Y | Y | Y | Y | Y | Y | Y | Y |
| A | Skilled nursing home days 21–100 $95/day copay | | | Y | Y | Y | Y | Y | Y | Y | Y |
| A | Annual deductible $760 | | Y | Y | Y | Y | Y | Y | Y | Y | Y |
|   | Foreign country emergency care 80% after $250 deductible | | | Y | Y | Y | Y | Y | Y | Y | Y |
| B | Annual deductible $100 | | | Y | | | Y | | | | Y |
| B | Excess physician charges allowed 15% | | | | | | Y | 80% | | Y | Y |
|   | At-home recovery care up to $1,600/year | | | | Y | | | Y | | Y | Y |
|   | Prescriptions—50% after $250 deductible: next $2,500 drugs | | | | | | | | Y | Y | |
|   | Prescriptions—50% after $250 deductible: next $6,000 drugs | | | | | | | | | | Y |
|   | Preventive care up to $120/year | | | | | Y | | | | | Y |

\* Based on Medicare-Approved charge amounts
\*\* One-time 60 reserve days

**Evaluating Medigap Options**

Plan A is the basic or core benefit package and is the basis for all the plans. With the possible exception of the skilled nursing coverage for days 21–100 at $95/day, Plan A takes care of most big financial exposure items. The skilled nursing benefit range is between $0 and $7,600 (80 days × $95/day). After 100 days there is no Medicare or Medigap coverage.

You might select the most inclusive plan just because you can afford it or you want to be fully covered. Before making that choice, ask yourself whether the coverage is worth the cost. The coverages for deductibles, at-home recovery care, preventive care, and even prescriptions are capped. By that I mean the financial exposure of not having the insurance can be determined because there are limits on how much Medigap insurance will pay. Let me explain by example. Your annual deductible exposure for Part B (medical insurance) is $100. Ask yourself whether you want to protect yourself from a $100 exposure. Then ask how much that coverage costs. Is it worth it to you?

You may find that the plans that are sold in your area refer to Medigap Plans A–J in "Good, Better, Best" type terminology. The brochures will probably refer to Plan A with "A" or "Basic" somewhere in the name of their Medigap Plan A. There will also be some consistency in terminology and a checklist that will relate to the table on the preceding page. You can determine which plan it is in this way. Pricing options will undoubtedly be handled differently by each insurer. All Medigap insurers must offer a "Medigap Plan A" policy. They may or may not offer all the other plans.

When you first receive information from the Medicare-approved Medigap insurers, it may seem overwhelming. To make the brochure information more useable, compare the coverages offered for each plan to the Medigap plans on the Medigap Coverage table. As you do, use a magic marker to rename the policies in the brochure: "Plan A, B, . . . J." Then write down the insurer's cost(s) for each plan or use the cost table provided in the brochure after you have renamed it as "Plan A, B, . . . J." You should be better able to compare the policies on an "apples-to-apples" coverage and cost basis.

You can sign up for Part B and a Medigap plan during the 6-month open enrollment, regardless of your health status. That does not mean, however, that all coverages of a particular Medigap plan will be made available to you. For example, you may be refused prescription coverage if you take too many prescription medications. Medigap insurers may or may not be allowed to refuse any coverage they offer during the 6-month Medicare open enrollment. Individual states have rules governing Medigap policies, including rules for coverage availability beyond the core benefits (Medigap Plan A). Before you look into Medigap plans, consult your state Insurance Commissioner's Office to get information and assistance in understanding the rules that apply to you.

The August '94 and September '94 issues of *Consumer Reports* featured excellent articles about Medigap policies, which explain Medicare, Medigap, and some things to consider in your evaluation of Medigap options. The articles cite Consumers Union studies that rate Medigap policies and insurers. Although these articles are dated, they are still worth reading. The August '94 issue gives the names and telephone numbers of the carriers having the policies Consumers Union rated best by state or by region within a state. If you do not have your own *Consumer Reports* library, I recommend that you get a copy of these issues for your reference by writing to Consumers Union at: Back Issues, Consumer Reports, P.O. Box 53016, Boulder, CO 80322-3016.

Medigap policies have been standardized; their prices have not. Compare prices as part of the buying process. The prices for Medigap Plan C policies, rated best in the *Consumer Reports* articles referenced, ranged between $501/year and $1182/year. The variance in prices is accounted for by cost differences among buying areas in 1994. The policy rating system that was used also accounts for cost differentials.

Policies are offered based on "community rates," "issue-age rates," or "attained-age rates." All three rating systems allow for rate increases based on inflation. If you have a "community rates" policy, you will pay the same rate as everyone else having that policy regardless of age. With "issue-age rates," you will pay the same amount as everyone else who is your age. With both of these rating systems, your rates go up based on inflation. The "attained-age" policies are generally less expensive than "community" or "issue-age" policies for a 65-year-old at time of issue, but go up in price with age and inflation. Make sure you know what you are getting and what the implications are for you as you get older. Fewer and fewer "community rates" and "issue-age rates" policies are being offered.

I caution you that the Medigap Plan C price range, which *Consumer Reports* cited in their 1994 articles, may not be representative today. Some states have seen sharp premium increases in 1995 and 1996. You need to get current costs from your local Medigap insurers before doing any financial planning for retirement health care costs.

You also need to check out the insurer you're considering before signing up for their Medigap policy. Call your local Better Business Bureau to see if there have been any complaints against them. Talk to people who already are Medicare beneficiaries. Find out if they have a Medigap policy. If so, who is the insurer? Have they had any claims? How were they handled? Does the insurer make it easy to do business with them? Do they bog people down in bureaucratic detail? Take the time to check their reputation, because, if all goes well, you're going to be doing business with the insurer for a long time. You will be provided some questions to ask in Chapter 8, "A System for Evaluating Local Medigap Insurers and Medicare HMOs."

If you are a Medicare beneficiary under age 65 by reason of disability, you may be offered "supplemental insurance" resembling a Medigap policy, which does not conform to any of the plans. It is not a Medigap policy. Nevertheless, this type plan might be of some interest to you if you are in this situation. It might provide some protection from catastrophic costs. You would have to evaluate it on a cost/benefit basis. Remember, when you reach age 65, you have access to the regular Medigap policies regardless of how you initially became a Medicare beneficiary.

Before wrapping up the discussion on Medigap, I want to mention another very good source for Medigap and related information. The American Association of Retired Persons (AARP) has a number of informative publications, as those of you who are members undoubtedly know. Their booklet on Medigap is particularly helpful and well written. If you or your spouse are 50 or older, AARP membership is available to you. As a member you can order publications on their easy to use automated phone system. The AARP membership and information telephone number is 1-800-424-3210.

*So much for the overview of Medicare and Medigap. Remember the "Sample Example?" Let's get into the details of coverage and non-coverage.*

 **Detailed Medicare—Medigap Tables**

Let's look at seven tables which show Medicare coverages and the gap filling and Medicare extensions of two Medigap Plans. I showed the basic coverage of Medigap Plan A and the most inclusive of the Medigap offerings Plan J. I took this approach to give you an uncluttered view of the details of Medicare coverage and the range of Medigap options available. As you scan down through the coverages offered by Medigap Plans A and J, you might want to highlight the coverages that are of interest to you. Later in this chapter, you will review detailed coverage information for all ten Medigap policies.

Before reviewing the "Medicare—Medigap Tables" shown on the next few pages, I caution you that the information for these tables was pulled from various sources and cross-checked. Before making any decisions, however, you will need to get current and accurate information from your Medicare carrier and the Medigap insurers in your area. The tables are arranged by Medicare coverage and cost groupings as follows:

- Hospital Inpatient
- Skilled Nursing Facility Inpatient
- Home Health Services,
- Hospice Services
- Doctor's Services

- Hospital Outpatient Services
- Other Part B Provisions

Let's go through the heading and first line of the first table—"Hospital Inpatient." On the left side of the chart, you will see the heading "Hospital Inpatient." This heading has the coverage and cost categories listed beneath it. The three columns to the right indicate whether the costs or percentages of cost listed beneath them are Medicare (A or B), Medigap Plan A, or Medigap Plan J. The heading above these three columns indicates that the columns contain the costs or percentage of cost that the patient pays.

The first line is "Part A annual deductible." As you read across the line, it indicates that the Medicare patient must pay up to a deductible amount ($760 in 1997) each year that he or she is a hospital inpatient. The patient with Medigap Plan A coverage would still be responsible for an annual inpatient hospitalization deductible. If the patient has Medigap Plan J coverage, the patient does not have to pay this expense. Let's look at the tables.

| Hospital Inpatient | Percentages or Dollar Amounts You Pay | | |
|---|---|---|---|
| | Medicare A | Medigap A | Medigap J |
| Part A annual deductible | $760 | $760 | $0 |
| Semiprivate room days 1–60 | $0 | $0 | $0 |
| Semiprivate room days 61–90 | $190/day | $0 | $0 |
| Reserve days (60) 91–150 | $380/day | $0 | $0 |
| Extra 365 days | 100% | $0 | $0 |
| All meals | $0 | $0 | $0 |
| Special diets | $0 | $0 | $0 |
| Regular nursing services | $0 | $0 | $0 |
| Special care units | $0 | $0 | $0 |
| Drugs | $0 | $0 | $0 |
| Blood—first 3 pints | 100% | $0 | $0 |
| Blood—after first 3 pints | $0 | $0 | $0 |
| Lab tests | $0 | $0 | $0 |
| X rays other radiology | $0 | $0 | $0 |
| Radiation therapy | $0 | $0 | $0 |
| Medical supplies | $0 | $0 | $0 |
| Wheelchairs & appliances | $0 | $0 | $0 |
| Operating room | $0 | $0 | $0 |
| Recovery room | $0 | $0 | $0 |
| Rehabilitation services | $0 | $0 | $0 |
| Private room required | $0 | $0 | $0 |
| Private room not required | 100% | 100% | 100% |
| Private duty nurses | 100% | 100% | 100% |
| Personal items | 100% | 100% | 100% |

| **Skilled Nursing Facility Inpatient** | **Percentages or Dollar Amounts You Pay** | | |
|---|---|---|---|
| | **Medicare A** | **Medigap A** | **Medigap J** |
| Semiprivate room days 1–20 | $0 | $0 | $0 |
| Semiprivate room days 21–100 | $95/day | $95/day | $0 |
| All meals | $0 | $0 | $0 |
| Special diets | $0 | $0 | $0 |
| Regular nursing services | $0 | $0 | $0 |
| Therapy | $0 | $0 | $0 |
| Drugs | $0 | $0 | $0 |
| Blood transfusions | $0 | $0 | $0 |
| Medical supplies | $0 | $0 | $0 |
| Wheelchair & other appliances | $0 | $0 | $0 |
| Private room medically required | $0 | $0 | $0 |
| Private room not required | 100% | 100% | 100% |
| Private duty nurses | 100% | 100% | 100% |
| Personal items (e.g., phone, TV) | 100% | 100% | 100% |
| Any other billed services | 100% | 100% | 100% |

| **Home Health Services** | **Percentages or Dollar Amounts You Pay** | | |
|---|---|---|---|
| | **Medicare A** | **Medigap A** | **Medigap J** |
| Part-time & Intermittent nursing | $0 | $0 | $0 |
| Home health aide services | $0 | $0 | $0 |
| Home health care extension* | 100% | 100% | $0 |
| Physical therapy | $0 | $0 | $0 |
| Speech therapy | $0 | $0 | $0 |
| Occupational therapy | $0 | $0 | $0 |
| Medical social services | $0 | $0 | $0 |
| Medical supplies | $0 | $0 | $0 |
| Durable medical equipment | 20% | 20% | 20% |
| 24-hour nursing | 100% | 100% | 100% |
| Drugs & biologicals | 100% | 100% | 100% |
| Meals delivered to home | 100% | 100% | 100% |
| Homemaker services | 100% | 100% | 100% |
| Blood transfusions | 100% | 100% | 100% |

* Medigap "Home Health Care Extension" benefit extends coverage by up to 8 weeks after Medicare coverage ends, with up to $1,600 per year at $40 per visit for activities of daily living (e.g., bathing, dressing, hygiene).

MEDIGAP ■ 113

| Hospice Services (At Home) | Percentages or Dollar Amounts You Pay | | |
|---|---|---|---|
| | **Medicare A** | **Medigap A** | **Medigap J** |
| Nursing services | $0 | $0 | $0 |
| Doctor services | $0 | $0 | $0 |
| Inpatient drugs * | $0 | $0 | $0 |
| Outpatient pain & symptom drugs * | $0 | $0 | $0 |
| Physical therapy | $0 | $0 | $0 |
| Occupational therapy | $0 | $0 | $0 |
| Speech-language therapy | $0 | $0 | $0 |
| Medical social services | $0 | $0 | $0 |
| Medical supplies | $0 | $0 | $0 |
| Medical appliances | $0 | $0 | $0 |
| Short-term inpatient care | $0 | $0 | $0 |
| Inpatient respite care** | $0 | $0 | $0 |
| Counseling | $0 | $0 | $0 |
| Non-terminal pain treatment | $0 | $0 | $0 |
| Non-terminal symptom treatment | 100% | 100% | 100% |

\* You may have to pay up to $5.00 for each prescription drug.
\*\* You may have to pay about $5.00 a day.

| Doctor Services* | Percentages or Dollar Amounts You Pay | | |
|---|---|---|---|
| | **Medicare B** | **Medigap A** | **Medigap J** |
| Part B deductible | $100 | $100 | $0 |
| Medical & surgical services | 20% | $0 | $0 |
| Anesthesia | 20% | $0 | $0 |
| Diagnostic tests & procedures | 20% | $0 | $0 |
| Inpatient Radiologist services | 20% | $0 | $0 |
| Outpatient Radiologist services | 20% | $0 | $0 |
| Inpatient Pathologist services | 20% | $0 | $0 |
| Outpatient Pathologist services | 20% | $0 | $0 |
| Outpatient mental illness treatment | 20% | $0 | $0 |
| X rays including at home | 20% | $0 | $0 |
| Doctor's office nurse services | 20% | $0 | $0 |
| Professional only drugs | 20% | $0 | $0 |
| Professional only biologicals | 20% | $0 | $0 |
| Blood-first 3 pints | 100% | $0 | $0 |
| Blood-after first 3 pints | $0 | $0 | $0 |
| Medical supplies | 20% | $0 | $0 |
| Physical therapy | 20% | $0 | $0 |
| Occupational therapy | 20% | $0 | $0 |
| Speech pathology services | 20% | $0 | $0 |
| Physical examination | | | |
|   First $120/year | $120 | $120 | $0 |
|   Over $120/year | 100% | 100% | 100% |
| Routine foot care | 100% | 100% | 100% |
| Routine dental care | 100% | 100% | 100% |

*(continued next page)*

| Doctor Services* | Percentages or Dollar Amounts You Pay | | |
|---|---|---|---|
| | Medicare B | Medigap A | Medigap J |
| Eye examinations for glasses | 100% | 100% | 100% |
| Hearing aid examinations | 100% | 100% | 100% |
| Hearing aids | 100% | 100% | 100% |
| Most immunizations | 100% | 100% | 100% |
| Most prescription drugs | | | |
| First $250 per year | $250 | $250 | $250 |
| Next $6,000 of drugs ($3,000 benefit limit) | 100% | 100% | 50% |
| Beyond $6,250 per year | 100% | 100% | 100% |
| Elective cosmetic surgery | 100% | 100% | 100% |

\* The following footnote applies to this table ("Doctor Services") and the two tables that follow: "Hospital Outpatient Services" and "Other Part B Provisions." The 20% copay shown for some benefits indicates that Medicare pays 80% of the Medicare approved rate. The beneficiary is responsible for up to an additional 15% if the services are rendered by a provider who does not accept assignment or is not an approved Medicare facility. The "$0" reference in the Medigap column indicates that Medigap pays for that 20%. Any excess charges are still your responsibility, unless you have "Excess Charges Coverage." Plan J excess charges coverage pays up to 15% over the Medicare allowed charge amount.

| Hospital Outpatient Services* | Percentages or Dollar Amounts You Pay | | |
|---|---|---|---|
| | Medicare B | Medigap A | Medigap J |
| Emergency room services | 20%+ | $0+ | $0+ |
| Outpatient clinic services | 20%+ | $0+ | $0+ |
| Same day surgery (ER & Clinic) | 20%+ | $0+ | $0+ |
| Hospital laboratory tests | $0+ | $0+ | $0+ |
| Outpatient mental health services** | 50%+ | 30%+ | 30%+ |
| Hospital X rays & other radiology | 20%+ | $0+ | $0+ |
| Medical supplies | 20%+ | $0+ | $0+ |
| Professional only drugs | 20%+ | $0+ | $0+ |
| Professional only biologicals | 20%+ | $0+ | $0+ |
| Physical examination | | | |
| First $120/year | $120 | $120 | $0 |
| Over $120/year | 100% | 100% | 100% |
| Eye examinations for glasses | 100% | 100% | 100% |
| Ear examinations for hearing aid | 100% | 100% | 100% |
| Most prescription drugs | | | |
| First $250 per year | $250 | $250 | $250 |
| Next $6,000 of drugs ($3,000 benefit limit) | 100% | 100% | 50% |
| Beyond $6,250 per year | 100% | 100% | 100% |
| Most routine foot care | 100% | 100% | 100% |
| Outpatient blood transfusions | 100% | 100% | 100% |

\*\* "Outpatient mental health services require you to pay a 50% copayment. Medigap policies provide for a 20% copayment. Check with your Medigap carrier for the coverage they offer for this 50% copayment.

\+ Medicare pays 80% of Approved; Medigap pays 20% of Approved; You pay 20% of Billed.

| Other Part B Provisions* | Percentages or Dollar Amounts You Pay | | |
|---|---|---|---|
| | **Medicare** | **Medigap A** | **Medigap J** |
| Excess charges | 15% | 15% | $0 |
| Foreign travel emergency | | | |
|   First $250 in expenses | $250 | $250 | $250 |
|   Charges over $250 | 100% | 100% | $0 |
| Durable medical equipment | 20% | $0 | $0 |
| Pap smear every 3 years | 20% | $0 | $0 |
| Mammogram every 2 years | 20% | $0 | $0 |
| **Medicare "Helps Pay" the Following**\*\* | | | |
| Kidney dialysis | 20% | $0 | $0 |
| Kidney transplants | 20% | $0 | $0 |
| Heart transplants | 20% | $0 | $0 |
| Liver transplants | 20% | $0 | $0 |
| Ambulance between home & | | | |
|   skilled nursing facility | 20% | $0 | $0 |
|   hospital | 20% | $0 | $0 |
| Prosthetic devices | 20% | $0 | $0 |
| Therapeutic shoes for diabetics | 20% | $0 | $0 |
| Certain drugs & biologicals | 20% | $0 | $0 |

\* The 20% copay shown for some benefits indicates that Medicare pays 80% of the Medicare-approved rate. The beneficiary is responsible for up to an additional 15% if the services are rendered by a provider who does not accept assignment or is not an approved Medicare facility. The "$0" reference in the Medigap column indicates that Medigap pays for that 20%. Any excess charges are still the beneficiary's responsibility, except for Medigap Plan J, which pays up to the 15% limit on excess charges.

\*\* In *Your Medicare Handbook 1995*, when referring to the coverage for all of the "Other Part B Benefits" listed from the entry "Kidney Dialysis" through the end of the chart, states that Medicare "helps pay." When I called the Medicare carrier for my area, I was told this means Medicare covers 80% of the approved amount. Presumably, Medigap would pay the remaining 20%.

+ Medicare pays 80% of Medicare-approved amount and Medigap pays 20%. You pay 20% of billed amount, which can be more than 80% of approved amount. There is no cap on amount.

If any of these benefits could apply to you, call your Medicare carrier to see if you meet the qualifications for coverage. Get a detailed understanding about how these provisions apply specifically to your situation. The Medicare carrier for your area is listed in *Your Medicare Handbook 1996*. Their number is also available from your local Social Security Administration office, whose number can be found in the business section of the white pages of your telephone directory. You need to check with the Medigap insurers for your community to find out what portion of these expenses each of them will pay.

*If you saw a coverage item at 100% in all three columns, it does not exist. If there is a treatment you periodically receive, and you did not see it listed, it may still be covered for some patients with special considerations. Call your local Medicare carrier to find out if that's the case, and to see if you qualify for coverage.*

### ▼ KEY POINTS                                        Medigap

1. There are ten standard Medigap Plans (A–J).
2. The names of approved Medigap providers in your community are available from:
   The Medicare Hotline (1-800-638-6833) and
   Your local Social Security Administration office.
3. If an insurer sells any Medigap Plans, it must sell Plan A.
4. An insurer does not have to sell all ten plans.
5. Evaluate a plan's benefits against the plan's premium amount.
6. Make sure you know your projected premium cost at age 65, 70, 75, etc.
7. Compare all the plans available in your community.

# Medicare HMOs

> "My husband and I have been members of an HMO for years.
> We would like to stay in it for Medicare coverage.
> Is that possible?
> How would that work?"
> You can get Medicare coverage through an HMO,
> possibly an affiliate of yours.
> We will discuss how it works in this chapter.

 **Medicare HMOs Introduction**

HMOs provide health care to Medicare beneficiaries through "Medicare HMOs," often referred to by HMOs as their "Senior Plans." They emphasize preventive care and health maintenance. If you become a Medicare "Part A" and "Part B" beneficiary and sign up as a member of a Medicare approved HMO, Medicare pays the HMO to provide for your health care needs. They pay the HMO 95% of Medicare's 5-year average cost per fee-for-service beneficiary in your county. Nothing changes in your relationship with Medicare. The monthly fee for Part B is still deducted from your monthly Social Security check.

The Social Security Administration in their publication, *Your Medicare Handbook 1995* states

> Many Medicare beneficiaries join managed care plans. These plans are prepaid, coordinated care plans, most of which are health maintenance organizations (HMOs).... Managed care plans may also offer benefits not covered by Medicare for little or no additional cost. Benefits may include preventive care, prescription drugs, dental care, hearing aids, and eyeglasses.

The HMOs who offer coverage in your county will tailor their plans based upon the amount of money they expect to receive from Medicare and the costs they will incur. As with individual and employer provided HMO plans, there are a number of HMO types (e.g., IPA, Group, Staff) offering "Senior Plans." The HMOs can be local, regional, or national. Check with your local Social Security Administration office for a list of the Medicare-approved HMOs in your county.

Call the HMOs to have them send you information about their Medicare HMO plans with a word of caution. When my wife called insurance companies to get Medigap brochures, and HMOs to get Medicare HMO plans information, they sent us very detailed information on the coverages provided and the costs. All companies replied in 2–4 days. Their representatives were aggressively polite for the most part, but my wife was asked unnecessary questions. Be prepared to give only the information the companies need; don't volunteer more. They need your name, address, telephone number, and your age group (under 65 or 65 and older) to send you the correct information. Insurance companies and HMOs do not need your Social Security Number, health status, or the names of your current insurance policies.

Depending on the Medicare HMO plan you select, you might not need Medigap insurance. To repeat a point made earlier, the Medicare funding for your premium-free Medicare Part A coverage and your Medicare Part B monthly deduction ($43.80 in 1997) are paid to the Medicare-approved HMO plan you select. The Medicare HMO might offer a "no premium plan." You would undoubtedly have to pay on some sort of cost sharing basis, such as copayments for selected benefits. With this type plan, you would pay relatively small amounts as you receive medical care, instead of being obligated to pay a monthly premium.

As part of your investigation of Medicare HMO plan coverages, consider the benefits that are not part of the Medicare program, but that are often part of Medicare HMO coverage. Typically, HMOs will offer dental coverage, prescriptions, and eye examinations and glasses. They may also have exercise facilities, interest group activities, member magazines, and health care related classes. You may even get paid to attend a class. There could also be Medicare covered items which are not part of an HMO plan. Compare the coverage item by item to the "Detailed Medicare–Medigap Tables" or the upcoming "Medicare–Medigap–HMO Coverage and Cost Tables."

Both coverages and pricing will differ from one Medicare HMO plan to the next. Some plans might include other benefits (e.g., eyeglasses, dental care). You might have to pay deductibles, copayments, or premiums for these enhanced coverage plans. Medicare HMOs might offer "Point of Service" (POS) plans, which include fee-for-service features. These plans offer you access and flexibility not normally found in an HMO environment, at an increased cost.

If you have a Medigap policy and decide to join a Medicare HMO, you may want to consider keeping the Medigap policy for a while as a safety valve. Keep in mind that if you decide that you don't care for your Medicare HMO and want to go back to Medicare with Medigap, you may not be able to get the Medigap policy you want, particularly if you have a health problem.

In your deliberations, you may also want to consider the fact that HMOs play a prominent role in the plans our federal government is making to keep Medicare affordable in the future. The estimates of Americans receiving health care from managed care plans is somewhere between 65 and 100 million people, depending upon the article you read. Recently, I saw an estimate of 150 million. States and individual counties are starting to look to managed care as their vehicle for providing medical care to the needy. Clearly, managed care is no longer in the future. It is here and now.

*Three factors influence Medicare HMO contracts, costs, and coverage:*
*HMO Model*
*HMO Rating Systems*
*HMO/Medicare Agreement*

 **Medicare HMO Contracts**

### The HMO Model

The HMO Model (e.g., Staff, IPA, Group) influences the HMO Plan's coverage and pricing in the same way it does for commercial HMOs. You have been through this in detail in Chapter 3 "Insurance Plan Options." We will not go through those discussions here.

### HMO Rating Systems

The rating system, which is used to price your Medicare HMO Plan, is an important consideration for you. It is not very complicated. There are three approaches to rating a Medicare HMO Plan: "Attained-Age Rates," "Issue-Age Rates," and "Community Rates." The choice of rate structure used has an effect on the price of the HMO Plan when issued and as you grow older. Let's go through the three rate structures.

The "Attained Age Rates" plans have the lowest priced plan for you, when you buy the plan at age 65. As you grow older its price goes up based on inflation and on your age. It can be quite expensive in your advanced years. If you are offered one of these plans, get a written projection of the "Attained Age" cost increases planned for you through age 100. Also get a written table of what people, ages 65 to 100, are paying today under an "Attained Age" plan.

A Medicare HMO Plan priced on an "Issue-Age Rate" is more expensive than an "Attained-Age Policy" would be at an issue age of 65. It is less expensive, however, as you advance in age. Your premium can be increased only for inflation. It will go up as you get older, assuming that inflation continues.

If you have a Medicare HMO Plan that was priced on "Community Rates," you will pay the same amount for the policy as all others who have the same plan regardless of age. This policy will be more expensive at the time you buy it at age 65. As you grow older, however, it will only increase based on inflation. If people stopped buying this plan, your costs could go up because you could be one of the youngest of a group that has lived through more years of inflation.

You may not have much choice on these plans. More and more companies are selling "Attained Age" plans. If you have a choice, there are a number of factors to consider, including

- your health status
- longevity in your family
- the projected rates for "Attained Age" plans as you get older
- whether you could better afford the higher expense now or later
- projected total cost over the term of the plan at ages 65 through 100

### Medicare/HMO Agreement

The agreement between a Medicare HMO and Medicare determines the basis upon which the HMO can build its Plans. Let me explain. There are five types of agreements:

- Traditional Medicare-supplement policy (Medigap)
- Medicare Select plan (Managed care versions of Medigap Plans)
- "Medicare Cost" plan
- "Medicare Risk" plan
- "Health Care Prepayment Plan" (HCPP)

I don't think that we need to discuss Medigap. Rather we should spend a few minutes on the "Medicare Select" plan. You may be offered a "Select Plan" if you live in one of the states where this plan can be sold (20 states in 1996). Select plans are managed care plans that conform to the standard Medigap Plans A–J with a couple of exceptions:

- They may offer additional benefits that their corresponding Medigap Plan does not offer.
- Minnesota and Wisconsin had standardized Medigap plans before the federal government did. Their Medigap and Select Plans are allowed to differ from the standard federal plans.

Select Plans may offer lower premiums because of their ability to better control their risks, just as in other managed care plans. If you receive information on one of these plans, consider it along with the other Medigap and HMO plans.

The "Medicare Select" plan was approved by Congress as an experimental plan to extend through June 30, 1995. It includes provisions for continuation of the plan for those who have them, if the "experiment" were to be terminated. There is also provision for the "Select" plan policyholders to switch to another plan without regard to health status, if the "experiment" ends. These plans are still being offered in my state.

The 20 states authorized to offer "Select Plans" in 1996 were:

| | | | |
|---|---|---|---|
| Alabama | Arizona | California | Florida |
| Illinois | Indiana | Iowa | Kansas |
| Kentucky | Michigan | Minnesota | Missouri |
| North Dakota | Ohio | Oklahoma | Rhode Island |
| Texas | Washington | Wisconsin | Wyoming |

The other three plans, "Cost," "Risk," and "Health Care Prepayment Plan," impact the coverage and pricing of Medicare HMOs. Let's look at the main points of each of them.

### Cost
- HMO cannot provide extra benefits without additional cost to you.
- HMO cannot require you to buy extra benefits.
- You can go to providers affiliated with the plan and pay copayments.
- You can go to providers not affiliated with the plan. Medicare will pay for its coverage, and you will be responsible for deductibles and copayments.

### Risk
- Can provide extra benefits at no extra cost to you.
- May require you to buy extra benefits as a condition of enrollment.
- Can lock you into getting all your covered care through the plan and its referrals.
- Must have one 30-day open enrollment period a year for all Medicare Part B beneficiaries, except kidney dialysis patients, but including disabled patients.

### Health Care Prepayment Plan (HCPP)
- HMO cannot provide extra benefits without additional cost to you.
- HMO cannot require you to buy extra benefits.
- You can go to providers affiliated with the plan and pay copayments.
- You can go to providers not affiliated with the plan. Medicare will pay for its coverage, and you will be responsible for deductibles and copayments.
- Do not have to offer all Medicare coverages.
- Do not have to have an open enrollment period.
- May refuse to enroll you based on your health conditions.
- Medicare rules for payment only apply to Medicare Plan B services.
- May offer to provide Plan A services if you prepay an amount to cover deductibles and coinsurance. If they do, these services are not governed by Medicare rules.

As part of an evaluation of HMOs, I would want to know which rate system was used in pricing my policy and which one of the agreement types that the HMO had with Medicare. I realize that we are getting into some depth on the subject of Medicare HMOs, but I think you need to have this information to make an informed judgment. You will better know what membership prices to expect in future years, and you will have some understanding of what the Medicare HMO can and cannot do. Ask Medicare HMOs which Medicare agreement type and which rate structure they used for the plans they are offering to you.

---

The financial part of the Medicare–Medigap–HMO decision may be more important to you in retirement than it was while you were working.
By studying your options, you can have quality health care as a Medicare beneficiary, at relatively low cost.

---

### ▼ KEY POINTS                    Medicare HMOs

1. Medicare approves some HMOs as health care providers for Medicare beneficiaries.

2. The names of approved Medicare HMOs in your community are available from:
   The Medicare Hotline (1-800-638-6833) and
   Your local Social Security Administration office.

3. Your financial relationship with Medicare does not change.

4. Some HMOs offer Medicare "no premium" managed care plans which also provide additional benefits.

5. Additional benefits and services are available from some Medicare HMOs.

6. Make sure you know your projected membership fees at age 65, 70, 75, etc.

7. Compare all the Medicare HMOs offerings available in your community.

# A System for Evaluating Local Medigap Insurers and Medicare HMOs

Once again, you are going to rely on the six honest serving men, left to all of us by Rudyard Kipling. This time they will help find the best Medigap Carrier or Medicare HMO for you.

 **Narrow Down Your Options**

Look through the Medigap Plans that you received from the local Medigap insurers. Set aside the plans that hold some interest for you from a coverage and price basis. Do the same with the HMO Plans from the local Medicare HMOs. Then check them all out with the Better Business Bureau. See if there have been any complaints about them, what the nature of the complaints were, and whether they have been resolved.

From this point on, you will be working with the Medigap insurers and the Medicare HMOs, who made it through the Better Business Bureau check. The next step is to ask questions about them, as we did in an earlier chapter about commercial health insurance and HMOs. Except for the questions of your doctor, the questions will be a little different this time. They will be directed to the Medigap insurers and their policyholders, the Medicare HMOs and their members, and your doctor.

Make sure that the Medicare HMOs and the Medigap insurers who offer prescription coverage send you a copy of their "Formularies" (the list of the prescription drugs included in their coverage) to check your family's needs against it.

The "Sample Example" pointed out what can happen if you don't know what your coverage is before you sign up for a Medigap Plan or a Medicare HMO plan, but there's more than coverage to ask about. The questions I would ask of the Medigap insurers, Medicare HMOs, and the people who are their policyholders or members follow. These questions, and others which you add, should give you the answers you need before making a decision. You will find a blank question form in the Appendices for your other questions.

### Get Ready to Ask the Right Questions

At this point you should have evaluated the plan you have today, using your "Medical Expenses." You should have asked yourself some questions about what you can afford and what you need. You should have gathered coverage and cost information from the Medigap insurers and Medicare HMO plans. Now I'm going to give you some questions to help determine the value the plans might hold for you. Add to the list and reword it to meet your needs. Go through the list of questions before asking them, making prompting notes on the question lines as needed. You will need to do some homework on three of the questions.

1. Preexisting conditions. Write your preexisting conditions on the line for that question to make sure you don't forget to mention them.

2. List your special needs. There is a question about special needs. Either write the needs on its question line or keep the list handy when you ask that question.

3. List your prescription medications. Have the list handy when you ask the prescription coverage questions. Check it against the "Formularies" you received from the Medicare HMOs and Medigap Plans if you're considering Medigap Plans H, I, or J.

Determine whether each of the plans you are investigating has exactly the same drugs. If not, you will need to ask if they have a generic of each drug, a substitute (different medication to treat the same symptom or malady), or nothing to meet your needs. Ask your doctor about any generic or substitute offered by the Medicare HMO or Medigap carrier before you make your decision about the coverage you are considering.

### Use Questions to Grade and Compare

You are going to use the answers you get to your questions to arrive at a numerical grade for each question and for the interview as a whole. By using the same system with all the local Medigap carriers and Medicare HMOs, you will have a basis for comparing the plans. There are sets of questions to ask various types of health care coverage plans. I have tried to put the questions in a priority sequence, at least for the first few questions. If you get the wrong answers early in the questioning, you can save some time by dropping the plan from consideration quickly.

As you get answers to your questions, you will grade the plan. Let me explain how it works. There is a line above each question. Before you start your interview process, you will assign an "Importance" level to each question you intend to ask. As the respondent answers a question, you give the answer a "Score." Sometime after the interview, multiply the "Score" for each answer by its "Importance" to develop a "Weighted Score." Add up the weighted scores and divide by the number of questions you asked. You will have reduced the answers to a numeric value, which can easily be used for comparison to the values from others that you interviewed. Use the system as follows.

**Plans** will show for whom the question is intended. In the first set of questions, the word "Plans" will be followed by "HMO," "Medigap," or "All."

**Importance** has a line for your entry of the question's importance in your decision process. I suggest that you use a scale of 1 to 5, with 5 being very important. If it has no importance to you, don't ask the question. After assigning an importance level to each question, make copies of the forms for your use.

**Score** has a line for your entry. I suggest that you use a scale of 0 to 10, with 10 being the best score. If you heard exactly the right answer and you really liked the way the respondent answered it (e.g., with enthusiastic understanding of its importance), write in a 10 as soon as you have your answer. If the plan does not have the coverage, put down a 0 for their the score. (If they don't have the coverage, it doesn't matter how the question was answered.) Don't at any time tell the person who answers the questions that you have assigned importance levels to the questions or the relative level assigned to any of them.

It's important that you write in the score before you go to your next question. The score will show how you felt about the answer at that moment and will have the least chance of being contaminated by your impressions of answers to other questions.

**Weighted Score** has a line for your entry. When you finish with all your questions, multiply the "Score" for each question by its "Importance," and write in its "Weighted Score." When you have all the "Weighted Scores," add them up and divide by the number of questions you asked. You will now have a numeric evaluation based on the questions you asked. It should be interesting to compare a weighted score of your current plan to these other plans.

*All the following questions are provided in Appendix D as forms with more room for your use.*

*From the Medigap carriers and the HMOs, we will get answers to: "What" and "Why" and "When" and "Where" and "Who."*

### Medigap Carrier and Medicare HMO Questions

I have started with nine questions which apply only to Medigap carriers. They are intended to give you a feel for how it would be to work with the carrier, particularly with regard to customer service (e.g., claims processing). These are not the highest priority questions. Nevertheless, it is important to have a carrier who places emphasis on claim accuracy and who takes responsibility to resolve the problems that result from an error's entering the billing system. Questions pertaining to Medicare HMOs or both Medigap carriers and Medicare HMOs follow the first nine questions for Medigap only.

### MEDIGAP CARRIER AND MEDICARE HMO QUESTIONS

| | | | |
|---|---|---|---|
| Plans: Medigap | Importance: _____ | Score: _____ | Weighted Score: _____ |
| How quickly do you turn around claims? <br> How do you measure claim turnaround? <br> What are your statistics on claim turnaround? ||||
| Plans: Medigap | Importance: _____ | Score: _____ | Weighted Score: _____ |
| If you make an error on a claim, how do you handle making the correction? <br> Who is responsible for the making the correction? ||||
| Plans: Medigap | Importance: _____ | Score: _____ | Weighted Score: _____ |
| What is your claim error rate? ||||
| Plans: Medigap | Importance: _____ | Score: _____ | Weighted Score: _____ |
| How do you measure and manage the quality of your claim processing? <br> What are your statistics on errors in claim processing? ||||
| Plans: Medigap | Importance: _____ | Score: _____ | Weighted Score: _____ |
| If a client tells you that he or she is being billed by a provider, who sent in a claim months ago and was never reimbursed, what action do you take? ||||

## MEDIGAP CARRIER AND MEDICARE HMO QUESTIONS

| Plans: Medigap | Importance: _____ | Score: _____ | Weighted Score: _____ |
|---|---|---|---|
| What will the providers tell me when I ask them about your claim processing? ||||

| Plans: Medigap | Importance: _____ | Score: _____ | Weighted Score: _____ |
|---|---|---|---|
| What will the providers tell me when I ask them whether they enjoy working with you? ||||

| Plans: Medigap | Importance: _____ | Score: _____ | Weighted Score: _____ |
|---|---|---|---|
| Do you have an advocacy system for clients? <br> How does it work? <br> Where does the advocate report in your organization? <br> What is the level of the reporting executive? ||||

| Plans: Medigap | Importance: _____ | Score: _____ | Weighted Score: _____ |
|---|---|---|---|
| How do you like working here? ||||

| Plans: Both | Importance: _____ | Score: _____ | Weighted Score: _____ |
|---|---|---|---|
| Is there a maximum lifetime benefit? <br> If yes, how much is it? ||||

| Plans: Both | Importance: _____ | Score: _____ | Weighted Score: _____ |
|---|---|---|---|
| Do you have disease or procedural limits? <br> If yes, what are they? <br> How much are they by disease or procedure? ||||

| Plans: Both | Importance: _____ | Score: _____ | Weighted Score: _____ |
|---|---|---|---|
| What procedures are considered "experimental"? ||||

| Plans: HMO | Importance: _____ | Score: _____ | Weighted Score: _____ |
|---|---|---|---|
| Do you have carve-outs for certain diseases? <br> If yes, what are they? <br> Where do you send the patients for each disease? ||||

| Plans: Both | Importance: _____ | Score: _____ | Weighted Score: _____ |
|---|---|---|---|
| Is this a national HMO or Medigap plan? <br> If not, do I have coverage outside of your region? <br> How does that coverage work? ||||

**128** ■ THE MCNALLY METHOD FOR MANAGING YOUR HEALTH CARE

## MEDIGAP CARRIER AND MEDICARE HMO QUESTIONS

| | | | |
|---|---|---|---|
| Plans: Both | Importance: _____ | Score: _____ | Weighted Score: _____ |

Will I have worldwide health care coverage?

If yes, how does it work?

Does it have deductibles, copays, and limits?

If I am not covered, what happens to my family or me if we need care while abroad?

| | | | |
|---|---|---|---|
| Plans: HMO | Importance: _____ | Score: _____ | Weighted Score: _____ |

May I have a list of your providers?

If not, why not?

| | | | |
|---|---|---|---|
| Plans: HMO | Importance: _____ | Score: _____ | Weighted Score: _____ |

What percentage of your providers out of residency for 5 years are Board Certified?

What percentage passed their Boards on the first try?

What percentage failed and are not Board Certified?

| | | | |
|---|---|---|---|
| Plans: HMO | Importance: _____ | Score: _____ | Weighted Score: _____ |

May I select my own Primary Care Physician?

Is the one I want available? (A follow-up question before you sign up)

| | | | |
|---|---|---|---|
| Plans: HMO | Importance: _____ | Score: _____ | Weighted Score: _____ |

From what fields do you draw your Primary Care Providers?

| | | | |
|---|---|---|---|
| Plans: All | Importance: _____ | Score: _____ | Weighted Score: _____ |

Can women have a gynecologist as their PCP?

| | | | |
|---|---|---|---|
| Plans: HMO | Importance: _____ | Score: _____ | Weighted Score: _____ |

Are patients with chronic problems allowed to have a specialist as their PCP?

| | | | |
|---|---|---|---|
| Plans: HMO | Importance: _____ | Score: _____ | Weighted Score: _____ |

If being treated by a specialist for a problem that requires follow-up or continuing care, can my specialist become my PCP, either temporarily or permanently?

| | | | |
|---|---|---|---|
| Plans: HMO | Importance: _____ | Score: _____ | Weighted Score: _____ |

If being treated by a specialist for a problem that requires follow-up or continuing care, do I have to have a PCP referral for each follow-up visit?

| | | | |
|---|---|---|---|
| Plans: All | Importance: _____ | Score: _____ | Weighted Score: _____ |

Are women allowed to have annual mammograms in this plan?

## MEDIGAP CARRIER AND MEDICARE HMO QUESTIONS

| Plans: All | Importance: _____ | Score: _____ | Weighted Score: _____ |
|---|---|---|---|
| Are women allowed to have annual Pap smears in this plan? | | | |

| Plans: All | Importance: _____ | Score: _____ | Weighted Score: _____ |
|---|---|---|---|
| Are men allowed to have an annual sigmoidoscopy in this plan? | | | |

| Plans: HMO | Importance: _____ | Score: _____ | Weighted Score: _____ |
|---|---|---|---|
| Are annual gynecological examinations and mammograms allowed without referral? If not, why not? | | | |

| Plans: HMO | Importance: _____ | Score: _____ | Weighted Score: _____ |
|---|---|---|---|
| What is the average wait (days) for a PCP appointment? | | | |

| Plans: HMO | Importance: _____ | Score: _____ | Weighted Score: _____ |
|---|---|---|---|
| What is the average length (minutes) of PCP office visits? | | | |

| Plans: HMO | Importance: _____ | Score: _____ | Weighted Score: _____ |
|---|---|---|---|
| When a referral to a specialist occurs, what is the average length of wait (days) between being seen by the PCP and a specialist? | | | |

| Plans: HMO | Importance: _____ | Score: _____ | Weighted Score: _____ |
|---|---|---|---|
| What is the average length (minutes) of specialist office visits? | | | |

| Plans: All | Importance: _____ | Score: _____ | Weighted Score: _____ |
|---|---|---|---|
| Does this plan provide allergy treatment? If yes, how does it work. If no, how would I go about getting allergy treatment? | | | |

| Plans: HMO | Importance: _____ | Score: _____ | Weighted Score: _____ |
|---|---|---|---|
| What specialties participate in your plan? What specialties do not participate in your plan? | | | |

| Plans: HMO | Importance: _____ | Score: _____ | Weighted Score: _____ |
|---|---|---|---|
| What percentage of your specialists are Board Certified in their specialty? What percentage passed on their first try? What percentage failed and never have been Board Certified? | | | |

| Plans: HMO | Importance: _____ | Score: _____ | Weighted Score: _____ |
|---|---|---|---|
| Where will I be referred if I need highly specialized medical care (e.g., rare disease treatment, transplant)? | | | |

## MEDIGAP CARRIER AND MEDICARE HMO QUESTIONS

| Plans: HMO | Importance: _____ | Score: _____ | Weighted Score: _____ |

May I request and receive a second opinion?

If yes, how would I go about getting the second opinion?

| Plans: All | Importance: _____ | Score: _____ | Weighted Score: _____ |

What is the prescription drug benefit?

| Plans: All | Importance: _____ | Score: _____ | Weighted Score: _____ |

I have a list of my current prescriptions and need to know which of my medications are not in your formulary?

| Plans: All | Importance: _____ | Score: _____ | Weighted Score: _____ |

Do you have other brands of the same drug?

If so what are they?

| Plans: All | Importance: _____ | Score: _____ | Weighted Score: _____ |

Do you have substitute drugs?

If so, what are they?

| Plans: All | Importance: _____ | Score: _____ | Weighted Score: _____ |

What are the caps on your prescription benefits?

| Plans: All | Importance: _____ | Score: _____ | Weighted Score: _____ |

Does your prescription benefit have a copayment or coinsurance provision?

If yes, what is it?

Is that all I have to pay?

| Plans: All | Importance: _____ | Score: _____ | Weighted Score: _____ |

Do you have a formal complaint program?

If yes, please describe it.

| Plans: All | Importance: _____ | Score: _____ | Weighted Score: _____ |

Do your patients have an Advocate to whom they can appeal?

If yes, please describe how that function works.

| Plans: All | Importance: _____ | Score: _____ | Weighted Score: _____ |

If after going through your advocacy or grievance program I am not satisfied with the answer, to whom do I go in your management?

To whom do I go for outside advocacy or arbitration?

## MEDIGAP CARRIER AND MEDICARE HMO QUESTIONS

| Plans: All | Importance: _____ | Score: _____ | Weighted Score: _____ |
|---|---|---|---|

What measurement criteria are used in the evaluation of your doctors?

What is the weighting for each of the measurement criteria?

| Plans: HMO | Importance: _____ | Score: _____ | Weighted Score: _____ |
|---|---|---|---|

What was the NCQA rating by your HMO membership for each of the last 3 years?

| Plans: HMO | Importance: _____ | Score: _____ | Weighted Score: _____ |
|---|---|---|---|

What was your overall NCQA rating for each of the last 3 years?

| Plans: | Importance: _____ | Score: _____ | Weighted Score: _____ |
|---|---|---|---|

| Plans: | Importance: _____ | Score: _____ | Weighted Score: _____ |
|---|---|---|---|

| Plans: | Importance: _____ | Score: _____ | Weighted Score: _____ |
|---|---|---|---|

| Plans: | Importance: _____ | Score: _____ | Weighted Score: _____ |
|---|---|---|---|

| Plans: | Importance: _____ | Score: _____ | Weighted Score: _____ |
|---|---|---|---|

*To find out whether you might like a particular Medigap Carrier or Medicare HMO, you must get their clients and associates to answer the quality question:*
*How?*

### Health Care Plan Enrollee Questions

The questions you asked the Medigap carriers and the Medicare HMOs should help you to find out the "What" and "Why" and "When" and "Where" and "Who." If you want to find out the quality with which they do things, you have to ask questions, which when answered will tell you "How." How do they treat people? How do they discharge their responsibilities? We have to ask someone other than the Medigap carrier or the Medicare HMO. For that answer we have to ask the Medigap policyholder, Medicare HMO member, patient, or your doctor if he or she works with Medicare HMOs. And that's what we are going to do next.

### Medigap Policyholder Questions

**MEDIGAP POLICYHOLDER QUESTIONS**

| | | | |
|---|---|---|---|
| Plans: Medigap | Importance: _____ | Score: _____ | Weighted Score: _____ |
| Who is your Medigap carrier? | | | |
| Plans: Medigap | Importance: _____ | Score: _____ | Weighted Score: _____ |
| How long have you been with this carrier? | | | |
| Plans: Medigap | Importance: _____ | Score: _____ | Weighted Score: _____ |
| Which Medigap Plan do you have (A–J)? <br> Do you like it? | | | |
| Plans: Medigap | Importance: _____ | Score: _____ | Weighted Score: _____ |
| Have you had any Medigap claims? <br> (If yes, go to the next questions.) | | | |
| Plans: Medigap | Importance: _____ | Score: _____ | Weighted Score: _____ |
| How long does it take to get claims processed? | | | |
| Plans: Medigap | Importance: _____ | Score: _____ | Weighted Score: _____ |
| Have you had to deal with many claims errors? | | | |
| Plans: Medigap | Importance: _____ | Score: _____ | Weighted Score: _____ |
| Have you been able to make one phone call to your Medigap carrier to get errors resolved? <br> If not, what usually happens? | | | |
| Plans: Medigap | Importance: _____ | Score: _____ | Weighted Score: _____ |
| Have you ever had to manage communications between the Claims Office and the Provider? | | | |

## MEDIGAP POLICYHOLDER QUESTIONS

| Plans: Medigap | Importance: _____ | Score: _____ | Weighted Score: _____ |
|---|---|---|---|
| Do you find it pleasant to work with your Medigap carrier? <br> Do they take responsibility for their errors and fix them? <br> Are they polite? ||||
| Plans: Medigap | Importance: _____ | Score: _____ | Weighted Score: _____ |
| I'm considering Medigap, would you recommend your carrier? <br> Why or why not? ||||

## Medicare HMO Member Questions

## MEDICARE HMO MEMBER QUESTIONS

| Plans: HMO | Importance: _____ | Score: _____ | Weighted Score: _____ |
|---|---|---|---|
| How do you like your Medicare HMO plan? ||||
| Plans: HMO | Importance: _____ | Score: _____ | Weighted Score: _____ |
| How long have you been receiving care under this Medicare HMO plan? ||||
| Plans: HMO | Importance: _____ | Score: _____ | Weighted Score: _____ |
| What plan did you have before this one? <br> Was it another Medicare HMO? <br> Another plan with the same Medicare HMO? ||||
| Plans: HMO | Importance: _____ | Score: _____ | Weighted Score: _____ |
| Have you had a Medigap plan? <br> If yes, which plan (A–J)? <br> Who was the carrier? <br> Why did you leave that plan? ||||
| Plans: HMO | Importance: _____ | Score: _____ | Weighted Score: _____ |
| Why did you change over to this plan? ||||

## MEDICARE HMO MEMBER QUESTIONS

| Plans: HMO | Importance: _____ | Score: _____ | Weighted Score: _____ |
|---|---|---|---|
| How do you like your Primary Care Physician? | | | |
| Plans: HMO | Importance: _____ | Score: _____ | Weighted Score: _____ |
| How long do you have to wait to get an appointment with your Primary Care Physician? | | | |
| Plans: HMO | Importance: _____ | Score: _____ | Weighted Score: _____ |
| How are you treated on the phone when you call in to get an appointment? | | | |
| Plans: HMO | Importance: _____ | Score: _____ | Weighted Score: _____ |
| Have you ever had any problems which required help from a specialist? <br> If yes, how long did it take to get to see the specialist? | | | |
| Plans: HMO | Importance: _____ | Score: _____ | Weighted Score: _____ |
| Does your doctor listen to you? | | | |
| Plans: HMO | Importance: _____ | Score: _____ | Weighted Score: _____ |
| Have you ever been sent a bill that you should not have received? <br> If yes, how did your Medicare HMO deal with it? <br> Was it a problem? Or did one phone call take care of it? | | | |
| Plans: HMO | Importance: _____ | Score: _____ | Weighted Score: _____ |
| What do you like most about the plan? | | | |
| Plans: HMO | Importance: _____ | Score: _____ | Weighted Score: _____ |
| What do you like least about the plan? | | | |
| Plans: HMO | Importance: _____ | Score: _____ | Weighted Score: _____ |
| I'm thinking of signing up for this plan; do you recommend it? <br> If yes, who is your PCP? | | | |

## Questions to Ask Your Doctor

Your doctor is an excellent source of information about Medicare HMOs, if he or she treats Medicare HMO patients. If your physician has worked under contract with several Medicare HMOs, that's even better. Tell your doctor that you are considering joining a Medicare HMO and ask the following questions. Some of the questions for your doctor can be answered by his or her staff. Get as many answers as you can from them to save your doctor's time.

## QUESTIONS TO ASK YOUR DOCTOR

| Plans: HMO | Importance: _____ | Score: _____ | Weighted Score: _____ |
|---|---|---|---|
| Do you have Medicare HMO patients? <br> If yes, from which Medicare HMOs? ||||
| Plans: HMO | Importance: _____ | Score: _____ | Weighted Score: _____ |
| Are you a Primary Care Physician for any Medicare HMOs? <br> If yes, which ones? ||||
| Plans: HMO | Importance: _____ | Score: _____ | Weighted Score: _____ |
| In your opinion, which Medicare HMOs do the best job on utilization reviews? ||||
| Plans: HMO | Importance: _____ | Score: _____ | Weighted Score: _____ |
| Do you feel that any of the Medicare HMOs intrude on your professional judgment? ||||
| Plans: HMO | Importance: _____ | Score: _____ | Weighted Score: _____ |
| With which Medicare HMOs are you able to refer patients to specialists by name? <br> Do you or your staff arrange for the appointment? <br> If not, does the Medicare HMO let you know when they have set it up? ||||
| Plans: HMO | Importance: _____ | Score: _____ | Weighted Score: _____ |
| If you were running a Medicare HMO and had a choice of how to pay physicians (e.g., capitation, hold backs, fees, salary), how would you do it? <br> Why? ||||
| Plans: HMO | Importance: _____ | Score: _____ | Weighted Score: _____ |
| How are you compensated by the Medicare HMOs with whom you work? ||||
| Plans: HMO | Importance: _____ | Score: _____ | Weighted Score: _____ |
| With which of the Medicare HMOs do you have the best working relationship? ||||
| Plans: HMO | Importance: _____ | Score: _____ | Weighted Score: _____ |
| With which of the Medicare HMOs do you not have a good working relationship? ||||
| Plans: HMO | Importance: _____ | Score: _____ | Weighted Score: _____ |
| If you were going to recommend a Medicare HMO to a family member, which one would you recommend? ||||

By asking these questions, you might be able to eliminate some of the local Medigap Carriers and Medicare HMOs. Compare the remaining Medigap and Medicare HMO candidates against each other and the detailed coverages for all Medigap Plans A–J, using "Medicare—Medigap—HMO Coverage and Cost Worksheets." We will look at table versions of the "Medicare—Medigap—HMO Coverage and Cost Worksheets" in the next chapter.

▼ **KEY POINTS**  **A System for Evaluating Medigap Insurers and Medicare HMOs**

1. Prepare to ask the right questions for your situation.
2. Draw from the questions provided for:
   Medigap carriers & Medicare HMOs,
   Policyholders & members, and
   Your doctor & his or her staff.
3. Prioritize the questions you will ask.
4. Score the answers you receive by phone or in person.
5. Divide the sum of weighted scores by the number of questions you asked to arrive at a grade for each insurer and HMO.

# Making Your Medicare Decisions

*Your government is here to help.*
*What form do you want the help to take?*

 **Completing the Medicare Decision Process**

### Medicare—Medigap—HMO Coverage and Cost Tables

You will find forms to help you compare your Medicare, Medigap and HMO offerings in the appendices. They show the coverages of Medicare and each of the Medigap plans (A–J) in detail. These "Medicare—Medigap—HMO Coverage and Cost Worksheets" can be used for comparing the detailed offerings of HMOs with Medicare and each of the Medigap plans. They have blank columns on their right side for entry of HMO coverages.

You will find table versions of the "Medicare—Medigap—HMO Coverage and Cost Worksheets" for your review on the next few pages. The information for these charts and the worksheets was pulled from various sources and cross-checked. Nevertheless, as with all the tables and forms contained in this book, they are intended for instruction and general guidance purposes only. They are not your source for official information about Medicare, Medigap, and Medicare HMO coverage in all the states and territories of the United States. Before making any decisions, get current and accurate information from your community's Medicare carrier, Medigap carriers, and Medicare HMOs.

From my experience, the level of detail shown on the following tables is what you can expect to find in the Medicare HMO ("Senior Plan") brochures. The tables included are:

**Medicare A**
- Hospital Inpatient
- Skilled Nursing Facility
- Home Health Services
- Hospice Services

**Medicare B**
- Doctors' Services
- Hospital Outpatient Services
- Other Part B Provisions

*Medicare coverages are shown on the following tables in regular typeface. Medigap coverage enhancements are in bold typeface against a tinted background.*

### About the "Medicare—Medigap—HMO Coverage and Cost Worksheets"

The "Medicare—Medigap—HMO Coverage and Cost Worksheets" have blank columns. Use these columns for the Medigap plans and the Medicare HMOs you want to evaluate. If you are down to one or two HMOs, you might highlight the Medigap Plan which most closely resembles each HMO's coverage. Note any extra coverages. Compare the costs. Or you might note the names of the finalist HMO Plan(s) at the top of a column. Then indicate the coverages and costs by putting entries in its column on the lines opposite the comparable coverage items shown on the left of the sheet. Then compare your Medigap and Medicare HMO options to Medigap Plans A–J and Medicare coverages.

*After your review of the following tables, I'll step you through a review of your "Medicare Decision Process"*

### Medicare Decision Process Status

We will go through the "Medicare Decision Process" point by point. Following the table, I'll repeat each of the seven steps, as originally presented. Then I will comment about our status, as though you had actually been going through the process.

## MEDICARE—MEDIGAP—HMO COVERAGE AND COST TABLE

| Hospital Inpatient | Mdcr A You Pay | "A" You Pay | "B" You Pay | "C" You Pay | "D" You Pay | "E" You Pay | "F" You Pay | "G" You Pay | "H" You Pay | "I" You Pay | "J" You Pay |
|---|---|---|---|---|---|---|---|---|---|---|---|
| Part A annual deductible | $760 | $760 | $0 | $0 | $0 | $0 | $0 | $0 | $0 | $0 | $0 |
| Semiprivate room days 1–60 | $0 | $0 | $0 | $0 | $0 | $0 | $0 | $0 | $0 | $0 | $0 |
| Semiprivate room days 61–90 | $190/day | $0 | $0 | $0 | $0 | $0 | $0 | $0 | $0 | $0 | $0 |
| Reserve days (60) 91–150* | $380/day | $0 | $0 | $0 | $0 | $0 | $0 | $0 | $0 | $0 | $0 |
| Extra 365 days | 100% | $0 | $0 | $0 | $0 | $0 | $0 | $0 | $0 | $0 | $0 |
| All meals | $0 | $0 | $0 | $0 | $0 | $0 | $0 | $0 | $0 | $0 | $0 |
| Special diets | $0 | $0 | $0 | $0 | $0 | $0 | $0 | $0 | $0 | $0 | $0 |
| Regular nursing services | $0 | $0 | $0 | $0 | $0 | $0 | $0 | $0 | $0 | $0 | $0 |
| Special care units | $0 | $0 | $0 | $0 | $0 | $0 | $0 | $0 | $0 | $0 | $0 |
| Drugs | $0 | $0 | $0 | $0 | $0 | $0 | $0 | $0 | $0 | $0 | $0 |
| Blood—first 3 pints | 100% | $0 | $0 | $0 | $0 | $0 | $0 | $0 | $0 | $0 | $0 |
| Blood—after first 3 pints | $0 | $0 | $0 | $0 | $0 | $0 | $0 | $0 | $0 | $0 | $0 |
| Lab tests | $0 | $0 | $0 | $0 | $0 | $0 | $0 | $0 | $0 | $0 | $0 |
| X rays other radiology | $0 | $0 | $0 | $0 | $0 | $0 | $0 | $0 | $0 | $0 | $0 |
| Radiation therapy | $0 | $0 | $0 | $0 | $0 | $0 | $0 | $0 | $0 | $0 | $0 |
| Medical supplies | $0 | $0 | $0 | $0 | $0 | $0 | $0 | $0 | $0 | $0 | $0 |
| Wheelchairs & appliances | $0 | $0 | $0 | $0 | $0 | $0 | $0 | $0 | $0 | $0 | $0 |
| Operating room | $0 | $0 | $0 | $0 | $0 | $0 | $0 | $0 | $0 | $0 | $0 |
| Recovery room | $0 | $0 | $0 | $0 | $0 | $0 | $0 | $0 | $0 | $0 | $0 |
| Rehabilitation services | $0 | $0 | $0 | $0 | $0 | $0 | $0 | $0 | $0 | $0 | $0 |
| Private room required | $0 | $0 | $0 | $0 | $0 | $0 | $0 | $0 | $0 | $0 | $0 |
| Private room not required | 100% | 100% | 100% | 100% | 100% | 100% | 100% | 100% | 100% | 100% | 100% |
| Private duty nurses | 100% | 100% | 100% | 100% | 100% | 100% | 100% | 100% | 100% | 100% | 100% |
| Personal items | 100% | 100% | 100% | 100% | 100% | 100% | 100% | 100% | 100% | 100% | 100% |

\* **One-time 60 reserve days are used in this example to extend coverage from 90 days to 150 days.**

## MEDICARE—MEDIGAP—HMO COVERAGE AND COST TABLE

| Skilled Nursing Facility Inpatient | Mdcr A You Pay | "A" You Pay | "B" You Pay | "C" You Pay | "D" You Pay | "E" You Pay | "F" You Pay | "G" You Pay | "H" You Pay | "I" You Pay | "J" You Pay |
|---|---|---|---|---|---|---|---|---|---|---|---|
| Semiprivate room days 1–20 | $0 | $0 | $0 | $0 | $0 | $0 | $0 | $0 | $0 | $0 | $0 |
| Semiprivate room days 21–100 | $95/day | $95/day | $95/day | $0 | $0 | $0 | $0 | $0 | $0 | $0 | $0 |
| All meals | $0 | $0 | $0 | $0 | $0 | $0 | $0 | $0 | $0 | $0 | $0 |
| Special diets | $0 | $0 | $0 | $0 | $0 | $0 | $0 | $0 | $0 | $0 | $0 |
| Regular nursing services | $0 | $0 | $0 | $0 | $0 | $0 | $0 | $0 | $0 | $0 | $0 |
| Therapy | $0 | $0 | $0 | $0 | $0 | $0 | $0 | $0 | $0 | $0 | $0 |
| Drugs | $0 | $0 | $0 | $0 | $0 | $0 | $0 | $0 | $0 | $0 | $0 |
| Blood transfusions | $0 | $0 | $0 | $0 | $0 | $0 | $0 | $0 | $0 | $0 | $0 |
| Medical supplies | $0 | $0 | $0 | $0 | $0 | $0 | $0 | $0 | $0 | $0 | $0 |
| Wheelchair & other appliances | $0 | $0 | $0 | $0 | $0 | $0 | $0 | $0 | $0 | $0 | $0 |
| Private room medically required | $0 | $0 | $0 | $0 | $0 | $0 | $0 | $0 | $0 | $0 | $0 |
| Private room (not required) | 100% | 100% | 100% | 100% | 100% | 100% | 100% | 100% | 100% | 100% | 100% |
| Private duty nurses | 100% | 100% | 100% | 100% | 100% | 100% | 100% | 100% | 100% | 100% | 100% |
| Personal items (e.g., phone, TV) | 100% | 100% | 100% | 100% | 100% | 100% | 100% | 100% | 100% | 100% | 100% |
| Any other billed services | 100% | 100% | 100% | 100% | 100% | 100% | 100% | 100% | 100% | 100% | 100% |

### Home Health Services

| | Mdcr A You Pay | "A" You Pay | "B" You Pay | "C" You Pay | "D" You Pay | "E" You Pay | "F" You Pay | "G" You Pay | "H" You Pay | "I" You Pay | "J" You Pay |
|---|---|---|---|---|---|---|---|---|---|---|---|
| Part-time & Intermittent nursing | $0 | $0 | $0 | $0 | $0 | $0 | $0 | $0 | $0 | $0 | $0 |
| Home health aide services | $0 | $0 | $0 | $0 | $0 | $0 | $0 | $0 | $0 | $0 | $0 |
| Home health care extensions 8 wks.; at $40/visit; $1,600 maximum | 100% | 100% | 100% | 100% | $0 | 100% | 100% | $0 | 100% | $0 | $0 |
| Physical therapy | $0 | $0 | $0 | $0 | $0 | $0 | $0 | $0 | $0 | $0 | $0 |
| Speech therapy | $0 | $0 | $0 | $0 | $0 | $0 | $0 | $0 | $0 | $0 | $0 |

| Service | | | | | | | | |
|---|---|---|---|---|---|---|---|---|
| Occupational therapy | $0 | $0 | $0 | $0 | $0 | $0 | $0 | $0 |
| Medical social services | $0 | $0 | $0 | $0 | $0 | $0 | $0 | $0 |
| Medical supplies | $0 | $0 | $0 | $0 | $0 | $0 | $0 | $0 |
| Durable medical equipment | 20% | 20% | 20% | 20% | 20% | 20% | 20% | 20% |
| 24-hour nursing | 100% | 100% | 100% | 100% | 100% | 100% | 100% | 100% |
| Drugs & biologicals | 100% | 100% | 100% | 100% | 100% | 100% | 100% | 100% |
| Meals delivered to home | 100% | 100% | 100% | 100% | 100% | 100% | 100% | 100% |
| Homemaker services | 100% | 100% | 100% | 100% | 100% | 100% | 100% | 100% |
| Blood transfusions | 100% | 100% | 100% | 100% | 100% | 100% | 100% | 100% |
| **Hospice Services (At Home)** | | | | | | | | |
| Nursing services | $0 | $0 | $0 | $0 | $0 | $0 | $0 | $0 |
| Doctor services | $0 | $0 | $0 | $0 | $0 | $0 | $0 | $0 |
| Inpatient drugs | $0 | $0 | $0 | $0 | $0 | $0 | $0 | $0 |
| Outpatient pain & symptom drugs up to $5 each | ≥$5 | ≥$5 | ≥$5 | ≥$5 | ≥$5 | ≥$5 | ≥$5 | ≥$5 |
| Physical therapy | $0 | $0 | $0 | $0 | $0 | $0 | $0 | $0 |
| Occupational therapy | $0 | $0 | $0 | $0 | $0 | $0 | $0 | $0 |
| Speech-language therapy | $0 | $0 | $0 | $0 | $0 | $0 | $0 | $0 |
| Medical social services | $0 | $0 | $0 | $0 | $0 | $0 | $0 | $0 |
| Medical supplies | $0 | $0 | $0 | $0 | $0 | $0 | $0 | $0 |
| Medical appliances | $0 | $0 | $0 | $0 | $0 | $0 | $0 | $0 |
| Inpatient respite care—up to 5 days Mdcre allowed rate (approx. $5/day) | ~$5 | ~$5 | ~$5 | ~$5 | ~$5 | ~$5 | ~$5 | ~$5 |
| Counseling | $0 | $0 | $0 | $0 | $0 | $0 | $0 | $0 |
| Non-terminal pain treatment | $0 | $0 | $0 | $0 | $0 | $0 | $0 | $0 |
| Non-terminal symptom treatment | 100% | 100% | 100% | 100% | 100% | 100% | 100% | 100% |

## MEDICARE—MEDIGAP—HMO COVERAGE AND COST TABLE

| Doctor Services* | Mdcr B You Pay | "A" You Pay | "B" You Pay | "C" You Pay | "D" You Pay | "E" You Pay | "F" You Pay | "G" You Pay | "H" You Pay | "I" You Pay | "J" You Pay |
|---|---|---|---|---|---|---|---|---|---|---|---|
| Part B deductible | $100 | $100 | $100 | $0 | $100 | $100 | $0 | $100 | $100 | $100 | $0 |
| Medical & surgical services | 20% | $0 | $0 | $0 | $0 | $0 | $0 | $0 | $0 | $0 | $0 |
| Anesthesia | 20% | $0 | $0 | $0 | $0 | $0 | $0 | $0 | $0 | $0 | $0 |
| Diagnostic tests & procedures | 20% | $0 | $0 | $0 | $0 | $0 | $0 | $0 | $0 | $0 | $0 |
| Inpatient radiologist services | 20% | $0 | $0 | $0 | $0 | $0 | $0 | $0 | $0 | $0 | $0 |
| Outpatient radiologist services | 20% | $0 | $0 | $0 | $0 | $0 | $0 | $0 | $0 | $0 | $0 |
| Inpatient pathologist services | 20% | $0 | $0 | $0 | $0 | $0 | $0 | $0 | $0 | $0 | $0 |
| Outpatient pathologist services | 20% | $0 | $0 | $0 | $0 | $0 | $0 | $0 | $0 | $0 | $0 |
| Inpatient mental illness treatment | 20% | $0 | $0 | $0 | $0 | $0 | $0 | $0 | $0 | $0 | $0 |
| X rays including at home | 20% | $0 | $0 | $0 | $0 | $0 | $0 | $0 | $0 | $0 | $0 |
| Doctor's office nurse services | 20% | $0 | $0 | $0 | $0 | $0 | $0 | $0 | $0 | $0 | $0 |
| Professional only drugs | 20% | $0 | $0 | $0 | $0 | $0 | $0 | $0 | $0 | $0 | $0 |
| Professional only biologicals | 20% | $0 | $0 | $0 | $0 | $0 | $0 | $0 | $0 | $0 | $0 |
| Blood—1st 3 pints | 100% | $0 | $0 | $0 | $0 | $0 | $0 | $0 | $0 | $0 | $0 |
| Blood—after 1st 3 pints | $0 | $0 | $0 | $0 | $0 | $0 | $0 | $0 | $0 | $0 | $0 |
| Medical supplies | 20% | $0 | $0 | $0 | $0 | $0 | $0 | $0 | $0 | $0 | $0 |
| Physical therapy | 20% | $0 | $0 | $0 | $0 | $0 | $0 | $0 | $0 | $0 | $0 |
| Occupational therapy | 20% | $0 | $0 | $0 | $0 | $0 | $0 | $0 | $0 | $0 | $0 |
| Speech pathology services | 20% | $0 | $0 | $0 | $0 | $0 | $0 | $0 | $0 | $0 | $0 |
| Physical examinations: | | | | | | | | | | | |
| 1st $120/year | $120 | $120 | $120 | $120 | $120 | $0 | $120 | $120 | $120 | $120 | $0 |
| Over $120/year | 100% | 100% | 100% | 100% | 100% | 100% | 100% | 100% | 100% | 100% | 100% |
| Routine foot care | 100% | 100% | 100% | 100% | 100% | 100% | 100% | 100% | 100% | 100% | 100% |
| Routine dental care | 100% | 100% | 100% | 100% | 100% | 100% | 100% | 100% | 100% | 100% | 100% |
| Eye examinations for glasses | 100% | 100% | 100% | 100% | 100% | 100% | 100% | 100% | 100% | 100% | 100% |

| | Mdcr B You Pay | "A" You Pay | "B" You Pay | "C" You Pay | "D" You Pay | "E" You Pay | "F" You Pay | "G" You Pay | "H" You Pay | "I" You Pay | "J" You Pay |
|---|---|---|---|---|---|---|---|---|---|---|---|
| Hearing aid examinations | 100% | 100% | 100% | 100% | 100% | 100% | 100% | 100% | 100% | 100% | 100% |
| Hearing aids | 100% | 100% | 100% | 100% | 100% | 100% | 100% | 100% | 100% | 100% | 100% |
| Most immunizations | 100% | 100% | 100% | 100% | 100% | 100% | 100% | 100% | 100% | 100% | 100% |
| Most prescription drugs: | | | | | | | | | | | |
| First $250 per year | $250 | $250 | $250 | $250 | $250 | $250 | $250 | $250 | $250 | $250 | $250 |
| $1,250 maximum benefit for $2,500 in additional drugs | 100% | 100% | 100% | 100% | 100% | 100% | 100% | 100% | 50% | 50% | 50% |
| $3,000 maximum benefit for $6,000 in additional drugs | 100% | 100% | 100% | 100% | 100% | 100% | 100% | 100% | 100% | 100% | 50% |
| Beyond $6,250 per year | 100% | 100% | 100% | 100% | 100% | 100% | 100% | 100% | 100% | 100% | 100% |
| Elective cosmetic surgery | 100% | 100% | 100% | 100% | 100% | 100% | 100% | 100% | 100% | 100% | 100% |

\* The 20% copay shown for some benefits indicates that Medicare pays 80% of the Medicare approved rate. The beneficiary is responsible for up to an additional 15%, if the services are rendered by a provider who does not accept assignment or is not a Medicare approved facility. The "$0" reference in the Medigap columns indicates that Medigap pays for the 20% copayment. See Medicare–Medigap–HMO Coverage and Cost Table for "Other Part B Provisions"

Prescription Drug Benefit of Medigap Plans H, I, J
You pay the first $250 of prescription drugs each year.
Medigap H & I pays 50% of the next $2,500 of prescription drugs you buy each year. ($1,250 is the maximum benefit.)
Medigap J pays 50% of the next $6,000 of prescription drugs you buy each year. ($3,000 is the maximum benefit.)

| Hospital Outpatient Services* | Mdcr B You Pay | "A" You Pay | "B" You Pay | "C" You Pay | "D" You Pay | "E" You Pay | "F" You Pay | "G" You Pay | "H" You Pay | "I" You Pay | "J" You Pay |
|---|---|---|---|---|---|---|---|---|---|---|---|
| Emergency room services | 20%+ | $0+ | $0+ | $0+ | $0+ | $0+ | $0+ | $0+ | $0+ | $0+ | $0+ |
| Outpatient clinic services | 20%+ | $0+ | $0+ | $0+ | $0+ | $0+ | $0+ | $0+ | $0+ | $0+ | $0+ |
| Same day surgery (ER & clinic) | 20%+ | $0+ | $0+ | $0+ | $0+ | $0+ | $0+ | $0+ | $0+ | $0+ | $0+ |
| Hospital laboratory tests | $0+ | $0+ | $0+ | $0+ | $0+ | $0+ | $0+ | $0+ | $0+ | $0+ | $0+ |
| Outpatient mental health services** | 50%+ | 30%+ | 30%+ | 30%+ | 30%+ | 30%+ | 30%+ | 30%+ | 30%+ | 30%+ | 30%+ |
| Hospital X rays & other radiology | 20%+ | $0+ | $0+ | $0+ | $0+ | $0+ | $0+ | $0+ | $0+ | $0+ | $0+ |
| Medical supplies | 20%+ | $0+ | $0+ | $0+ | $0+ | $0+ | $0+ | $0+ | $0+ | $0+ | $0+ |

## MEDICARE—MEDIGAP—HMO COVERAGE AND COST TABLE

| Hospital Outpatient Services* | Mdcr B You Pay | "A" You Pay | "B" You Pay | "C" You Pay | "D" You Pay | "E" You Pay | "F" You Pay | "G" You Pay | "H" You Pay | "I" You Pay | "J" You Pay |
|---|---|---|---|---|---|---|---|---|---|---|---|
| Professional only drugs | 20%+ | $0+ | $0+ | $0+ | $0+ | $0+ | $0+ | $0+ | $0+ | $0+ | $0+ |
| Professional only biologicals | 20%+ | $0+ | $0+ | $0+ | $0+ | $0+ | $0+ | $0+ | $0+ | $0+ | $0+ |
| Physical examinations: | | | | | | | | | | | |
| 1st $120/year | $120 | $120 | $120 | $120 | $120 | $0 | $120 | $120 | $120 | $120 | $0 |
| Over $120/year | 100% | 100% | 100% | 100% | 100% | 100% | 100% | 100% | 100% | 100% | 100% |
| Eye examinations for glasses | 100% | 100% | 100% | 100% | 100% | 100% | 100% | 100% | 100% | 100% | 100% |
| Ear examinations for hearing aid | 100% | 100% | 100% | 100% | 100% | 100% | 100% | 100% | 100% | 100% | 100% |
| Most prescription drugs: | | | | | | | | | | | |
| First $250 per year (deductible) | $250 | $250 | $250 | $250 | $250 | $250 | $250 | $250 | $250 | $250 | $250 |
| $1,250 maximum benefit for $2,500 in additional drugs | 100% | 100% | 100% | 100% | 100% | 100% | 100% | 100% | 50% | 50% | 50% |
| $3,000 maximum benefit for $6,000 in additional drugs | 100% | 100% | 100% | 100% | 100% | 100% | 100% | 100% | 100% | 100% | 50% |
| Beyond $6,250 per year | 100% | 100% | 100% | 100% | 100% | 100% | 100% | 100% | 100% | 100% | 100% |
| Most routine foot care | 100% | 100% | 100% | 100% | 100% | 100% | 100% | 100% | 100% | 100% | 100% |
| Outpatient blood transfusions | 100% | 100% | 100% | 100% | 100% | 100% | 100% | 100% | 100% | 100% | 100% |

*Prescription Drug Benefit of Medigap Plans H, I, J

You pay the first $250 of prescription drugs each year.
Medigap H & I pays 50% of the next $2,500 of prescription drugs you buy each year. ($1,250 is the maximum benefit.)
Medigap J pays 50% of the next $6,000 of prescription drugs you buy each year. ($3,000 is the maximum benefit.)

** Medigap pays 20% of the Medicare approved copayment and coinsurance charges.
Medicare pays for 80% of the Medicare approved copayment and coinsurance charges.

+ **You pay 20% (or 50% for "Outpatient mental health services") of the Billed Amount, which can be greater than 80% of Approved Amount**

Medicare Part B requires a 50% copayment for "Outpatient mental health services." Check with your Medigap insurer.

| Other Part B Provisions* | Mdcr B You Pay | "A" You Pay | "B" You Pay | "C" You Pay | "D" You Pay | "E" You Pay | "F" You Pay | "G" You Pay | "H" You Pay | "I" You Pay | "J" You Pay |
|---|---|---|---|---|---|---|---|---|---|---|---|
| Excess charges—up to 15% over Medicare allowable charges | 15% | 15% | 15% | 15% | 15% | 15% | $0 | 3% | 15% | $0 | $0 |
| Foreign travel emergency: | | | | | | | | | | | |
| 1st $250 in expenses | $250 | $250 | $250 | $250 | $250 | $250 | $250 | $250 | $250 | $250 | $250 |
| Charges over $250 | 100% | 100% | 100% | 20% | 20% | 20% | 20% | 20% | 20% | 20% | 20% |
| May have lifetime limit | | | | | | | | | | | |
| Durable medical equipment | 20% | $0 | $0 | $0 | $0 | $0 | $0 | $0 | $0 | $0 | $0 |
| Pap smear every 3 years | 20% | $0 | $0 | $0 | $0 | $0 | $0 | $0 | $0 | $0 | $0 |
| Mammogram every 2 years | 20% | $0 | $0 | $0 | $0 | $0 | $0 | $0 | $0 | $0 | $0 |
| Kidney dialysis ** | 20% | $0 | $0 | $0 | $0 | $0 | $0 | $0 | $0 | $0 | $0 |
| Kidney transplants ** | 20% | $0 | $0 | $0 | $0 | $0 | $0 | $0 | $0 | $0 | $0 |
| Heart transplants ** | 20% | $0 | $0 | $0 | $0 | $0 | $0 | $0 | $0 | $0 | $0 |
| Liver transplants ** | 20% | $0 | $0 | $0 | $0 | $0 | $0 | $0 | $0 | $0 | $0 |
| Ambulance between home & skilled nursing facility ** | 20% | $0 | $0 | $0 | $0 | $0 | $0 | $0 | $0 | $0 | $0 |
| hospital ** | 20% | $0 | $0 | $0 | $0 | $0 | $0 | $0 | $0 | $0 | $0 |
| Prosthetic devices ** | 20% | $0 | $0 | $0 | $0 | $0 | $0 | $0 | $0 | $0 | $0 |
| Therapeutic shoes for diabetics ** | 20% | $0 | $0 | $0 | $0 | $0 | $0 | $0 | $0 | $0 | $0 |
| Certain drugs & biologicals ** | 20% | $0 | $0 | $0 | $0 | $0 | $0 | $0 | $0 | $0 | $0 |

\* The 20% copay shown for some benefits indicates that Medicare pays 80% of the Medicare approved rate. The beneficiary is responsible for up to an additional 15%, if the services are rendered by a provider who does not accept assignment or is not a Medicare approved facility. The "$0" reference in the Medigap columns indicates that Medigap pays for the 20% copayment. See Medicare–Medigap–HMO Coverage and Cost Table for "Other Part B Provisions"

\* The "Other Part B Provisions", from "Kidney Dialysis" through "Certain drugs & biologicals", require specific definition of your benefits by your Social Security Administration office and Medigap coverage information from your local Medigap insurers. Application for more frequent pap smears and mammograms can also be made to your Social Security Administration office for special conditions or as a member of a risk group.

\*\* **Medicare "Helps Pay" for the following. Check with your Medicare and Medigap carriers re: your coverage.**

1. **What were my spouse's and my medical procedures (e.g., office visits, surgery, physical, mammogram, physical therapy) last year?** Use the "Medical Expenses" form to list them. (See "The Health Insurance Decision Process" in Chapter 4, "The Decision Making Process.")

**Status:** At this point in the process, you should know what your medical procedures were and whether Medicare, with or without Medigap or a Medicare HMO, would have provided coverage for your procedures. You should also know what your approximate costs would have been in the Medicare environment for last year's procedures, as listed on your "Medical Expenses" form.

2. **What coverages do I need that I don't have now?** Medicare and its supplements are designed to fill the needs of people 65 and over. By completing your "Medical Expenses" form; going through the Medicare, Medigap, and Medicare HMO offerings; and being aware of the Medicare gaps that are not filled, this question should be answered for you.

**Status:** You have been studying Medicare, and have seen many of its gaps. The coverage provided by Medicare Part A and Part B, combined with the filling of Medicare's gaps in the most cost effective way for you and your spouse, should be much of what you need.

You have been introduced to many combinations of coverage, which have evolved over the past 20 plus years, to help fill the Medicare gaps and extend coverage. Nevertheless, all the gaps will not be filled; we know there is a need for coverage of long-term skilled nursing home care and custodial care. We will discuss "Supplemental Insurance" in the next chapter. It might help.

If you have additional needs that you did not see specifically addressed, please talk to your Medicare carrier, the Medicare Hotline (1-800-638-6833) or your local Social Security Administration office about your needs. Medicare has some provisions for special situations and for members of high-risk groups. There may not be a ready answer or an inexpensive one for you, but I encourage you to check with Medicare.

3. **What's available?** You will see most of what's available in table format of the "Medicare—Medigap—HMO Coverage and Cost Worksheets." To get Medigap pricing, contact your Social Security Administration local office. Ask for the names of the Medicare-approved Medigap carriers and HMOs in your area. Call or write them to get their sales literature.

**Status:** At this point in the process, you should have reviewed the charts and received information from the Medicare HMOs and Medigap carriers in your area.

4. **Which plan meets my needs?** After gathering plan and pricing information from the Medicare-approved Medigap insurers and the Medicare HMOs, you will use evaluation techniques similar to those used in

evaluating employer and commercial health care plans and HMOs. The plan comparisons should be easier to make, because of the standardization of Medicare and Medigap. There are "Medicare–Medigap–HMO Coverage and Cost Worksheets" in the appendices to help you.

**Status:** By now you should know what is available from the local Medigap carriers and Medicare HMOs. You would have checked with the Better Business Bureau to see if there had been any complaints about the Medigap carriers and Medicare HMOs. You would have asked the Medicare HMOs and the Medigap carriers questions about coverage and quality of service. And you would have asked their clients and your doctor about them. From your doctor, the clients of the Medigap carriers, and the Medicare HMO members, you should have gained an insight into the kind of organization with which you would be working.

You should have narrowed your choices down to a few. Then you would have evaluated them against each other on the "Medicare–Medigap–HMO Coverage and Cost Worksheets." You would have consulted with your local Social Security office about your coverage needs and your selection of plans to meet those needs. You should be about ready to make a decision.

**5. Can I live with its rules?** Once again, asking the right questions will help. Use the "Medigap Carrier and Medicare HMO Questions," "Medigap Policyholder Questions," "Medicare HMO Member Questions," and "Questions to Ask Your Doctor." These questions are made up as forms for your use and can be found in the appendices.

**Status:** If you have asked the appropriate questions in the right way, you should have the information you need to make this decision. You should know what the local Medigap carriers' rules and the local Medicare HMOs' rules are. Hopefully, you can avoid one of the problems we learned about in the "Sample Example." You should have learned what coverages the locally available plans do and do not have, by reviewing their offerings in detail and asking them questions. You should know whether there are any Medigap carriers or Medicare HMOs with whom you would not want to work. You should have an insight into the level of their commitment to quality. Did what they said about themselves check out with what was said about them by their clients, members, and your doctor?

**6. Is it worth the price?** Only you can answer this question and the next one.

**Status:** By now I think you would know which option is "worth the price" to you. You might be wavering because of the attractiveness of some other plan's benefits, which are not worth the price. You will have to decide, if you haven't already.

**7. Can I afford it?**
**Status:** You decide.

**KEY POINTS**            **Making Your Medicare Decision**

1. "Medicare—Medigap—HMO Coverage and Cost Worksheets" can be found in the appendices.
2. Enter the coverages of each of the affordable, finalist Medigap and Medicare HMOs.
3. Compare the coverages and costs.
4. Decide.

### Glossary Update

**Attained-Age Rates**—Rates that provide for Medicare HMO pricing based on the age of the member at the time he or she joins a Medicare HMO which bases its pricing on this rating technique. Increases are planned to take effect as a member grows older. There is also an annual adjustment for inflation. These Medicare HMOs tend to be the lowest cost Medicare HMOs at age 65 and the highest cost Medicare HMOs in the member's advanced years.

**Block Grants**—The transfer of Federal Government budgeted funding to other governmental or quasi-governmental entities (e.g., state governments).

**Community Rates**—Rates that provide for Medicare HMO pricing based on the average age of the "community" of its members. All members pay the same membership fees. Prices cannot be raised except for inflation adjustments. Medicare HMOs using this rating technique tend to be the highest cost Medicare HMOs at age 65 and the lowest cost Medicare HMOs in a member's advanced years.

**Custodial Care**—The nature of care required by those who cannot perform the most basic of human functions on their own, but do not have major medical problems requiring physician or skilled nursing attention.

**Health Care Prepayment Plan**—One of five types of agreements that an insurance company or an HMO can have with Medicare. The Medicare HMOs who have this agreement with Medicare provide Medicare Part A coverage. They may provide Part B type of coverage, which would not be governed by Medicare rules.

**Home Health Care**—Medicare Part A benefits provided to patients who are confined to their homes under a physician's care and who need periodic skilled nursing care, physical therapy, or speech therapy. The services are provided without charge to the patient by a Medicare approved home health agency's skilled nurses or home health aides.

**Hospice Care**—The benefits provided by Medicare to those who are in terminal condition and within six months of death, in their physician's judgment.

**Issue-Age Rates**—Medicare HMO pricing based on the age of the member at the time he or she joined. Prices cannot be raised except to adjust for inflation. Medicare HMOs which use this rating technique tend to cost more at age 65 than Medicare HMOs using an "Attained-Age" rating technique. As a member advances in years, the cost goes up but only by the amount of inflation.

**Medicaid**—A joint federal and state program which provides health care to those members of our society who otherwise would not have access to any health care.

**Medicare**—A federally sponsored insurance program which provides health care insurance for Americans age 65 and older and the disabled of all ages who meet the requirements for coverage.

**Medicare Cost Plan**—One of five types of agreements that an insurance company or an HMO can have with Medicare. The Medicare HMOs who have this agreement with Medicare provide Medicare Part A and Part B coverage. Their members may pay copayments and receive all health care from providers affiliated with the Medicare HMO. If they go to other providers, Medicare will pay in accordance with its coverage provisions. The members would be responsible for deductibles and copayments to the non-affiliated providers.

**Medicare HMO**—A Health Maintenance Organization which has been approved to provide Medicare benefits in compliance with one of five types of agreements (e.g., "Medicare Cost Plan," "Health Care Prepayment Plan," "Medicare Risk Plan").

**Medicare HMO Agreements**—The contracts which insurance companies and HMOs sign with Medicare. These agreements (e.g., "Medicare Cost Plan," "Health Care Prepayment Plan," "Medicare Risk Plan") govern the insurer's and the HMO's relationship with Medicare and the way in which they can provide Medicare benefits.

**Medicare Part A**— Hospitalization insurance for Medicare beneficiaries.

**Medicare Part B**—Medical insurance for Medicare beneficiaries.

**Medicare Risk Plan**—One of five types of agreements that an insurance company or an HMO can have with Medicare. The Medicare HMOs who have this agreement with Medicare provide Medicare Part A and Part B coverage. Their members can be locked into receiving all health care from providers affiliated with the Medicare HMO.

**Medicare Select Plan**—One of five types of agreements that an insurance company or an HMO can have with Medicare. The "Select Plans" are managed care versions of the ten Medigap Plans. Twenty states are authorized to offer "Select Plans" as experimental extensions to Medigap.

**Medigap**—Ten standardized and approved insurance plans to fill some of the gaps in Medicare coverage. The plans pay some or all of a beneficiary's coinsurance responsibilities and also offer some extensions to Medicare coverage. Each of the ten plans has a different set of coverages to be offered by Medicare-approved insurance carriers at rates set by them. The carriers sign one of five "Medicare Agreements," known as the "Traditional Medicare Supplement Policy."

**Traditional Medicare Supplement Policy**—The agreement a Medigap carrier enters into with Medicare. It governs Medigap carriers and the policies they are allowed to offer to Medicare beneficiaries.

# Other Insurance

---

Let's spend a few pages talking about insurance we don't often think about until we need it. Then it falls into the category of:
"Should have bought it when I was young."
"Could have bought it when I was healthy."
"Would have bought it if I had known."

---

 **Supplemental Insurance Considerations**

During the last few years, I have become well acquainted with the value of four types of insurance to my family and me. I'd like to share what I know about them and how they have helped me. They range from inexpensive to expensive. Obviously, the policy cost is based on the odds that the insurance company will have to pay off and the cost to the insurer if it has to pay off.

My goal is to give you some food for thought, not to make you insurance poor. Keep in mind, the time to buy insurance is before you need it, while you are healthy and when you can afford it. Once you need it, you may not be able to get it, unless you are lucky enough to be offered an "open enrollment," as I was.

The first two policies are particularly good to have in our high-earning years when we are paying a mortgage, raising a family, saving for college tuitions, planning for retirement, and trying to have an enjoyable life all at the same time. It's not a time for an interruption in earnings. It's the time that we need disability income insurance. It's a time when even disability premium waiver insurance could help.

The other two policies are of more use to us when our parts start to wear out. We find that we could use more help in paying for the expenses associated with going into the hospital for repairs. And we don't have visions of sugar plums dancing in our head; instead we see friends our age who can no longer take care of themselves. We dread the thought that it could happen to us, and we would have to pay $3,000 to $5,000 a month for the same dreary existence. It would help to at least relieve some of the financial worry by having hospitalization supplemental insurance and long-term care insurance.

## What could you buy very inexpensively that could pay big dividends, but you would rather not collect on your investment?

### Disability Premium Waiver

You probably have this insurance, maybe without even knowing it. If you have life insurance policies, your insurance agent might have built in a rider to have your life insurance premium paid for you if you became disabled. It doesn't cost much. Not that many healthy people become disabled. If someone does, it does not cost the insurer very much to pay your premiums for you.

It's insurance on your insurance premiums. If you become disabled, the disability premium insurance pays the premiums on your behalf. If your policy has cash buildup provisions from investment of insurance dividends, for example, the buildup occurs just as though you are paying the premiums.

Disability premium waiver is inexpensive, and it's worth a call to your insurance agent to see if you have this coverage. I have several life insurance policies. A year after I became disabled I was reminded about disability premium waiver insurance and called my insurers. I found out I was covered on all the policies and had premium refunds coming. In my case it saved us thousands of dollars.

## Uncle Sam comes to the rescue—at least a little.

### Disability Insurance

The Social Security Administration provides disability insurance. The disabled person receives a monthly check resembling the amount he or she would receive in Social Security Retirement income. It is based on the individual's lifetime payroll contribution to Social Security.

A person who is disabled for 6 months can begin receiving monthly deposits in their bank account. If you are ever in this situation, apply at your local Social Security Administration office 60–90 days *before* the 6-month anniversary of your being disabled, so you can start receiving your monthly checks as soon as you are eligible. After being eligible to receive Social Security Disability Benefits for 24 months, you would automatically be enrolled in

Medicare Part A and invited to join Medicare Part B. You would receive your Medicare card approximately 90 days before your 2-year anniversary.

Disability insurance has been a real blessing for us. It is very expensive and difficult for an individual to get, because if you do need it, the cost to the insurer is high. The chances that you will ever need it are not very high. The cost of and ability to buy disability insurance is related to your occupation and your age. The premium is based on the monthly income you require in coverage, rather than your salary (e.g., $4,000 income per month).

Fortunately, my employer provides disability insurance which works in conjunction with Social Security disability insurance. If your employer does not provide this protection, you might want to ask about the availability of disability insurance through your employer's group insurer, at your expense. Ask if it can be done and how much it would cost you. You also might ask your insurance agent about disability insurance coverage.

There are a number of disability insurance plan types. Employer-provided disability insurance generally pays you a percentage of your salary. Coverage could be for a year or two or until you are 65. Some plans are tax free for 6 months to a year and then become taxable.

*"I was 55 a few months ago. Now I get supplemental insurance offers in the mail all the time. I just throw them away because I already have insurance coverage. Why would I need supplemental insurance?"*

Supplemental insurance has also been helpful to us. You will have to judge its value to you. My wife and I have two policies, "Hospitalization Supplemental Insurance" and "Long-Term Care Insurance." Let's start with "Hospitalization Supplemental Insurance."

### Hospitalization Supplemental Insurance

Hospitalization Supplemental Insurance pays you a flat amount in addition to any hospitalization insurance (including Medicare) for each day you spend in a hospital. It usually pays an amount for each inpatient day and twice that amount for each outpatient day. The purpose in having this rather inexpensive insurance is to help pay for additional costs you can incur while hospitalized. Our insurance pays $70 per inpatient hospital day and $140 per outpatient hospital day. It costs $18.90 per month for both of us.

I was in a hospital 70 miles from my home when I had my liver transplant and associated problems. I was an inpatient for 2½ months before moving to a skilled nursing facility close to home. During the time I was in the hospital my wife was by my side every day. She stayed in a room and ate out for this entire time except for occasional trips home. Hospitalization supplemental insurance would have offset at least some of the expenses she incurred. We did not have it at the time, but we do now and it has helped.

> The person who can no longer live alone or take care of himself or herself, but who does not need medical care,
> falls through the safety net of the Medicare program.

### Long-Term Care

Medicare has gaps in its coverage. The most notable of these gaps is thought to be "respite nursing home care." "Respite" means a time of rest and relaxation. "Respite nursing home care" refers to "rest home care," "custodial care," and "nursing home care." Medicare is a form of health insurance. "Respite nursing home care" is not primarily medical care and it was not a part of Medicare initially. Now with people living longer and with patients with Alzheimer's disease requiring the care of full-time attendants, we need some way of providing for it. With the pressure to cut the planned growth of Medicare spending, "respite nursing home care" is unlikely to become a Medicare benefit. It can be covered for a few years with "Long-Term Care Insurance," but it is an expensive solution.

Long-term care is another name for custodial care or nursing home care. Putting a member of our family in a nursing home is very difficult on all concerned. The person put in the home feels abandoned and no longer in control of his or her life, and the family feels guilty. When the decision is finally made by you or for you, the family then has the financial challenge of paying $3,000 to $5,000 per month out of their pocket or out of the patient's assets. Long-term care may be less in a rural area, but these are the going rates in urban America, and they're going up.

If you are a nursing home resident, you can apply to have your state's Medicaid program pay for your care when your assets have been depleted. Each state has it's own definition of inability to pay, with provisions to prevent spouses from becoming destitute.

There is supplemental long-term insurance available to pay a fixed amount per day for custodial care. My wife and I have long-term care insurance that we bought through my employer during an open enrollment period. It's not cheap, but will provide enough coverage for both of us to be in custodial care for 5 years, heaven help us. It costs us over $1,500 a year and pays up to $120 per day for 5 years for each of us.

If you want to look into long-term care, you might ask your insurance agent or your employer's Human Resources Department about it. Another source for long-term insurance is AARP. Call them at 1-800-424-3410 for information on a policy they make available.

Be very careful when buying long-term insurance. Have the policy you are considering evaluated by an independent party such as HICAP (Health Insurance Counseling and Advocacy Program) before you sign up. I will tell you about HICAP and how to contact them a little later. For now let me say that they evaluated my policy in a personal consultation that lasted over an hour. In the process, they told me about things to look for and concluded that I had a good policy. It was a free but valuable service. HICAP funding comes from public funds and donations. They're on our annual contribution list.

### How to Learn More About Nursing Homes

Consumers Union published a series of three articles about nursing homes in the August, September, and October 1995 issues of *Consumer Reports*. They are very well done and are available from Back Issues, Consumer Reports, P.O. Box 53016, Boulder, CO 80322-3016. The articles are titled

*"When a Parent Needs Care: Ratings of 43 Chains"*

*"Who Pays for Nursing Homes?"*

*"Can Your Loved Ones Avoid a Nursing Home?"*

 **KEY POINTS**             **Other Insurance**

1. Check your insurance policies to see if you have Disability Insurance Premium Waivers. If you do not, call your insurance agent to get a quote and consider it.

2. Disability Insurance is very expensive. Some employers provide it, and Social Security provides it on an individual earned credit basis.

3. Hospitalization Supplemental Insurance can be very helpful if you're seriously or chronically ill.

4. Long-Term Care Insurance is expensive but gives a lot of peace of mind.

 ## Glossary Update

**Custodial Care**—The nature of care required by those who cannot perform the most basic human functions on their own, but do not have major medical problems requiring physician or skilled nursing attention.

**Disability Insurance**—An insurance policy that provides you with a monthly income to help offset the loss of your regular income if you become disabled while the policy is in force.

**Disability Premium Waiver**—An insurance policy provision that is available at extra cost. It provides for the payment of your premium on the policy if you become disabled while the policy is in force.

**Hospitalization Supplemental Insurance**—An insurance policy that pays the policyholder(s) a preset amount for each day spent as a hospital inpatient or outpatient.

**Long-Term Care**—The non-medical assistance provided to a person who is unable to perform the most basic human functions on his or her own.

**Long-Term Insurance**—A form of insurance that helps pay for the daily cost of a stay in a nursing home for non-medical care.

**Nursing Home Care**—The non-medical assistance provided in a nursing home to a person who is unable to perform the most basic human functions on his or her own.

**Respite Care**—The non-medical assistance provided to a person who is unable to perform the most basic human functions on his or her own.

# PART IV

# Getting the Most Out of the Medical Systems

# U.S. Health Care Status and Directions, What You Can Do About It

---

From the family doctor who made house calls and
the loving care of not-for-profit hospitals,
to for-profit managed care corporations and hospitals.

---

 **The Information Age Changes All Our Lives**

### The Impact of Health Care Changes on Our Doctors

We have very well trained providers, high-technology equipment, and very good facilities. Our medical professionals can solve almost any medical problem if they catch it early enough. So far it sounds great, and it is. Then why are Americans so apprehensive about medical care? We have very high health care costs that are still rising. We cannot afford health care without insurance, and 40 million of us do not have insurance. Many cannot afford insurance unless it's part of an employer's benefit package.

    Our federal government is working to keep the cost of Medicare from growing as fast as it was planned to grow. With this pressure on the Medicare total budget, Medicare is driving down the reimbursement for each unit of medical care (CPT). Health Maintenance Organizations are working to control costs through managed care and preventive care. HMOs are able to offer lower cost health care plans and are gaining wider acceptance and growing. Fee-for-service insurers lower the cost of their health care plans with their Preferred Provider Organizations and have their own versions of managed care plans.

Medicare, HMOs, and Preferred Provider Organizations are each driving down the reimbursement for each unit of medical care (CPT code—explained in Chapter 13) in their own way. Combined they have tremendous buying power. Even the most highly specialized practices accept patients for discounted fees from PPOs and HMOs. As you might imagine, accepting sometimes deeply discounted fees can have a significant financial impact on providers and the viability of their practices and facilities. Not signing up to accept these patients can be even worse.

The American Medical Association (AMA) recently released a report on doctors' earnings, which went down in 1994 for the first time since the AMA has kept track. A friend of mine and his partners borrowed money to pay operating expenses when their insurance reimbursements stopped for 60 days. A friend of his lost 510 out of 512 patients from one employer who changed insurers, because he was not part of the new insurers Preferred Provider Organization. Another doctor I know went from 1,000 patients to 2 in one week, because of a contract change.

Doctors must be efficient. They must see more patients. They cannot afford to take more than the time scheduled for a patient unless the patient is in trouble. (I have more to tell you about this later.) If you are going to benefit from the knowledge and skills of our physicians, their highly trained medical associates, and the high-technology equipment at their disposal, you are going to have to be an effective patient. You are going to have to help your physician in every aspect of your health care. I'm going to show you how to do that in the next chapter.

The pressures of having to see more patients, the need to stay up-to-date with a heavy commitment to learning, and the realization that at any time their practice could lose all the employees from their community's biggest employers can combine to bring on anxiety for a physician. The effects of this pressure have been evidenced in newspaper and magazine articles and television reports in which some doctors say they wouldn't go into medicine again. The *New England Journal of Medicine* has served as a forum for physicians expressing their concerns for the future of their profession and their place in it.

Some doctors express a concern that they may have to choose between their medical ethics and the need to have a continuing stream of income. I've read about these concerns. Perhaps you have too. I am convinced that the person expressing this anxiety is sincere. I am even more convinced that not one of the many doctors who have treated me would be distracted by this kind of concern.

### HMOs and the Impact of Growth

*The HMO's problems are the best kind to have.*
*They are problems of growth.*

As more Americans sign up for HMO membership in which public funds are involved, HMOs, which are already regulated, get increased attention from media, consumer groups, and both federal and state governments. Hundreds of bills are reported to be in the process of becoming managed care laws or rules in the federal and state governments. In this environment, anecdotal evidence gets national attention. Newspapers and television feature news stories about managed care on a weekly, if not daily basis.

HMOs have their own set of problems with which to deal. They are growing fast with a missionary product—managed care. They are taking a new approach to old problems. They are sent patients from employers who stopped offering fee-for-service insurance with preferred provider options. These new members are not the most receptive audience for an HMO's message. An HMO has to sell the benefits of preventive and managed care, over and over, just like a missionary. They have to hold the line on the rules by which they exist, at the same time they are trying to build customer satisfaction.

### Hospitals Also Have Problems

*For our nation's hospitals it's anything but Sunday on the farm.*

We hear more and more about hospitals in our communities losing millions of dollars a year or even a month. There are many reasons given for their problems. Some cite over-building of hospitals and point to low occupancy rates on a national level. (In my region, occupancy is less than 50%.) Others blame the availability, cost, and need for the latest high-technology equipment so that a hospital can attract and keep the best physicians. Still others say the hospitals' financial problems are caused by insurance companies who require shorter inpatient stays with more procedures performed on an outpatient basis. Others point to Medicare and private health insurance reimbursement rates. Still others say it's mismanagement. It's probably some or all of the above.

Whatever the reasons for their problems, hospitals are not immune from bankruptcy. They have to find a way to become profitable, even if they are part of not-for-profit organizations. They need to cut costs and maximize the use of resources. Doing so can impact patients. As both an inpatient and an outpatient I have had to wait in my room or in a hallway on a gurney because the diagnostic equipment I needed was scheduled to its maximum capacity. Small non-profit hospital corporations are being acquired by large for-profit hospital corporations. When that happens, community education and therapy programs are assigned a much lower priority. In some cases they are abandoned.

### And Laboratories Too

Laboratories also feel the pressure for greater productivity. On a number of occasions I have found it not as easy to get a scheduled appointment at my convenience. I have also had to take a "fasting from midnight" radiological or other diagnostic test in the late morning or afternoon. Like hospitals, labs have to maximize the use of their facilities and their very expensive equipment.

*Like it or not, this is the health care world we live in today.*

*"Is there any good news, Bill?" Yes, there are three pieces of good news in this chapter alone. I told you about the first two. (1) The medical care available in the U.S.A is better than ever. (2) I am going to show you how to get the most out of it in the next chapter. The next piece of good news is coming up right now.*

### Some Good News

Before moving on, let's look at some things that have not changed. Routine office visits, examinations, laboratory work, and hospital stays may command less of our medical professionals' time. When you have a potentially serious problem, however, it's a different matter. You will undoubtedly find that your medical team is intense, focused, and oblivious of time.

To recall my personal experiences once again, I have had a number of occasions in which the help I received seemed boundless. To cite just one example, I was scheduled for a diagnostic procedure that was to take 45 minutes. We started with a physician, a surgical nurse, a technician, a lot of high-tech equipment, and me, of course, in a room. Instead of the scheduled 45 minutes, the procedure took 7 hours. At one point, there were over a dozen people in the room including doctors from two different specialty teams, along with nurses and support staff. The combined team transformed a radiological diagnostic procedure into an angioplastic stent insertion procedure, which remedied a problem I had for months. Incidentally, only one physician billed me and that was only for a small portion of the time that the procedure took.

This took place in 1995 and at the time it was an emotional high for everyone involved. My doctors were obviously proud of their success in having solved my problem, as they should have been. They were enthusiastic about the learning experience that they shared.

One of the specialists came to my room the next day. He brought a sequence of six X rays on one film, showing the collapsed veins, the balloon, and the three stents. He had also drawn a series of five diagrams showing my original liver with its plumbing (veins), how the liver was removed, how my new liver was installed, which veins had collapsed, and where the stents were inserted. He spent half an hour explaining it all to me. Nice touch!

> I have yet to find a medical professional
> who did not enjoy helping people.

*It's not like the old days no matter where you turn.*
*There's a lot that's better, but if you want the graciousness of the past,*
*Stay at an old five star hotel.*
*Or ride the Orient Express.*

 ## Nothing Is Like It Was in "The Good Old Days"

### The Impact of Health Care Change on You

The medical world is belatedly going through the kind of change we have seen in the rest or our lives. When I was young we traveled by pullman train. We had a private room with comfortable seats, and when we awoke, the shoes we left outside the night before were shined. We dressed and went to the dining car for a silver service breakfast. We didn't have a lot of money, but travel had a graciousness about it.

Today we stand by the door of the jetway. We have to get on early to have room for our carry-on luggage. As we are jammed into a crowded plane, we are handed a box lunch, if we're lucky. We cram our bodies into a tiny seat. We don't enjoy our journey but we get to our destination sooner. We don't like this treatment, but the air fares are held down, we think.

The rush, efficiency, and impersonalization has hit the medical world, and we don't like it. Neither does "the medical world," but that's the way it is. We can complain about it, but that only makes us feel worse. What we must do is take charge of our medical situation. Behave in a way that makes your office visit a bright spot in the day of your physician and the nurse. That doesn't mean that you have be Mr. or Ms. Sunshine, although a cheerful attitude and a smile would help. It means that they know that you will have done your homework. They won't have to draw everything out of you. They know that you will approach the encounter as their teammate in the "Your Health" project.

I have found that by doing the things that I'm going to show you how to do; my doctor, the nurse, and I have time left in my office visit to discuss things other than my enzymes and stamina, or lack thereof. The time for my giving information ends in the first few minutes of my visit—after that I get information and explanations. I actually look forward to my office visits with all my doctors.

Before we go deeper into the subject of how to work with your medical professionals, there is a very important piece of business that you and your spouse must put on your list of things to do.

---

Don't leave your fate in the hands of a stranger.

---

 **Vesting Others with Decision-Making Power**

One of the facts of modern medicine is that we can be kept "alive" by artificial means. We can predetermine, however, just how far we want our doctors to go to keep our heart beating. We can give the power to implement our decision to a family member or friend. It's something we should all do. The document used for this purpose is called a "Durable Power of Attorney for Health Care Decisions." Hospitals in my state pass out a standard form published by our state Medical Association. This document empowers your agent to make health care decisions on your behalf, if the situation warrants. Your state may have a similar form—one which is compatible with the laws of your state. Although it's a standard form, my wife and I consulted with our attorney before completing it and had him notarize it. I suggest you do the same in your state to make sure you are on solid legal ground.

---

We must learn how to participate in our own health care.
We must get the most out of our time with our doctors.
We must communicate well.

---

## Getting the Most Out of the Medical System

Our reaction to today's concern about productivity and costs may be one of confusion or anger. We could long for "the good old days" when doctors made house calls, when our family doctor took care of all our medical needs, and when life spans were shorter. But neither anger nor reminiscing will help us. We need to participate in our health care. Obviously, we need to follow instructions and use good judgment when we do not have specific instructions from our doctor(s). What may not be as obvious is the need for our participation as our health care providers' teammate through our fostering of effective communications.

You don't have to be a sophisticated medically trained person. Common sense, an interest in your own health care, telephone calls, and handwritten notes are all that's required. I will offer you some practical approaches by which you can help your doctor understand your health care needs and meet them under three sets of circumstances in which you could find yourself:

1. As a basically healthy person with occasional office visits.

2. As a patient with a chronic condition that requires monitoring and regularly scheduled doctor's care.

3. As a patient who has undetermined or serious health problems, and who is being tested and treated by multiple physicians.

 KEY POINTS U.S. Health Care Status and Directions

1. Doctors, hospitals, laboratories, and other health care providers are all feeling the pressure to do more for less.

2. Nothing is like "good old days," including medicine.

3. We cannot change the health care world we live in: We must learn to get the most out of it.

4. You have to take charge of your own health care. I developed "The McNally Method" for that purpose. Use it.

5. Make sure you have a "Durable Power of Attorney for Health Care Decisions" (a "Living Will").

# 12

# Enhancing Your Health Care

Good doctor/patient communications are the key
to your getting the best health care available to you.

 **Introduction**

Whether in a marriage, a corporate merger, peace talks, a doctor's appointment, or any other kind of meeting, effective two-way communications have always been the keystone of human interactions. Success is measured by the effectiveness of all parties involved in giving and getting information.

If you've been to see your physician recently, you have probably noticed that his or her schedule is tighter and better managed. You probably didn't have a lot of face to face time if you were there for a routine office visit. Doctors need to work harder and in a more structured fashion, with little or no unproductive time. And we need to be better patients.

*We all "go to see the doctor" at some time or other for a checkup or because we're sick. Let's start there.*

### The Office Visit

When you see your physician for an office visit, you should keep in mind that his or her preparation for your visit may have consisted of a quick look through your chart while walking down the hall. Don't assume that he or she is going to remember what you talked about last time. Don't rely on your physician to ask you all the right questions to elicit the most important issues that the two of you should be talking about.

Prepare for an office visit by writing down the things you think you should tell your doctor and the questions you want to ask. Between visits it's a good idea to jot down your questions, symptoms, and concerns whenever they pop into your mind. Your spouse and other family members will undoubtedly have things that they want to add to your list. Before you go for your appointment, be sure to consolidate your lists and make copies.

Let your doctor know about *all* your symptoms. Your doctor will sort out what's important from what isn't. Tell your doctor about your potentially bad health habits, such as the amount you smoke and drink, improper eating habits, drug usage, and anything else that's "bad for you."

The "Discussion Topics" example that follows has the sort of things you will want to write down in preparation for your office visit. If you have a potentially serious problem or have trouble talking about all your symptoms and bad habits, take your spouse, adult child, or close friend with you. From my experience, spouses are very open with doctors when talking about us.

The format of the notes that you take with you to your office visit is not important. What is important is that you communicate openly and completely with your physician. This means that you must ask all the questions that are on your mind. It also means that you must understand all the answers.

Medical professionals normally use biological and medical terminology. Your doctor may answer your questions and concerns with terms you do not understand. Tell him or her that you don't understand the answer and that you need it in lay person's terms. You must get answers that you understand. If the topic is important or involves detailed instructions, repeat your understanding of your doctor's explanation, to make sure that the two of you are communicating. It is extremely important that you understand what your doctor says to you. This is another reason to have your spouse, family member, or friend with you. Two can listen better than one and take more complete notes.

Whether you use the "Discussion Topics" format or not, write down the following as you prepare for your appointment:

- All your symptoms
- The special questions for which you want an answer
- Things that you may want your doctor to do for you
- Reminders to yourself of things you want to give to your doctor
- Other topics you want to discuss

Don't read the "Discussion Topics" to your physician. Hand a copy to him or her at the start of your office visit so that he or she can take a minute or two to read it. (Keep a copy for yourself.) You will have a much more productive visit with your doctor. You may find that your doctor will be a little surprised that you prepared for your visit and handed him or her the list. You may also find that your doctor will appreciate your having done so. With this preparation on your part, your physician will be able to get right to the point and not have to ask exploratory questions. Your doctor will be better able to ask pertinent questions and will know what your questions and concerns are. Your physician will be glad to address your questions and concerns.

> **DISCUSSION TOPICS**
> **DR. C. D. Beta**
> **AUGUST 22, 1996**
>
> 1. Symptom status:
>    Weight has stabilized at the 180 to 183 level ( up from 172 to 174 level as of 7/24/96).
>    Nothing has changed with skeletal problems and discomfort.
>    Am slightly less uptight.
>    Tremors have abated.
>    Continue to feel better.
>
> 2. Discuss bone density test results.
>    Bone density in "Wards Triangle" has improved by 50% in a year. (See test results.)
>    Dr. Alpha approved me for reconstructive pelvic/hip surgery. (See Dr. Alpha's notes.)
>
> 3. Discuss follow-up items from last two consultations and other items.
>    Will abdominal hernia operation be as an inpatient or as an outpatient?
>    Whom does Dr. Beta recommend for my orthopedic surgery?
>    When will Dr. Beta have Doppler Test results and recommendations?
>    How long will it take for coumadin to work its way out of my system after I stop taking it?
>    Are there any changes in my medications and/or dosages at this time (e.g., Prednisone)?
>
> 4. Give Dr. Beta the following:
>    Completed "Medforms" for the last four weeks;
>    "Medication Analysis" as of 8/17;
>    Bone Density Test results; and
>    Dr. Alpha's handwritten summary of our 5/23/96 consultation.
>
> ***Notes to me:***
>
> 1. Tell Dr. Beta that Dr. Alpha sent his regards.
>
> 2. Have nurse K. L. Omega give me my monthly injection.

*In this example I use "Notes to me:" on my copy as a reminder.

---

*There's an old adage which tells us
"It ain't what you do, it's the way how you do it."*

---

 ## Getting Answers from Your Doctor

If your doctor refuses to answer your questions or is vague, it is probably because you asked the right question in the wrong way. Let me explain. If you ask, "Will I recover?" you may be told, "We really cannot say for sure." On the other hand, if you had asked, "Do people having my illness recover?

If so, how often?" you might have been told something like, "On a national basis last year 80% of the patients treated for the disease you have, using the treatment plan that we propose for you, recovered. We had slightly better results, with 85% of our patients recovering."

Some doctors will take the question as originally stated, rephrase it into an answerable question, and then answer it. But don't count on it. It may take a little thought to phrase your questions in a manner that your doctor can answer, but it is worth the trouble. You won't walk out of your doctor's office saying, "My doctor never answers my questions." You will get the information you need, because you asked the question in a way your doctor could answer.

*Many people have chronic health problems that require disciplined behavior, sophisticated tests, and careful monitoring. When you find yourself suddenly having to live "under doctor's orders" for an extended period of time, it may be very difficult for you. By turning your regimen into a regular routine, you should more quickly get out of the "Woe is me!" phase of the illness.*

 **Chronic Illness**

### Tracking Your Progress

Some people have always had to live within a strict set of rules. HMO members are taught the importance of proper eating habits and exercise as part of the HMO's focus on preventive care and maintaining health. Others of us have been health care free spirits all our lives until a serious medical incident profoundly changed our lifestyle. All of a sudden we had new rules. We had to:

- Stop eating the things we like
- Measure what we eat
- Monitor our weight
- Take our vital signs
- Take medicine(s) every day
- Have an injection every day
- Some or all of the above plus more

When you find out that you have a serious medical problem, it's important that you get the initial shock of being ill out of your conscious thought as quickly as possible and turn your self-care into a positive process. There is something you can do that will help you in this situation. It will also satisfy your physician's need to know that you have followed instructions and to know the impact of your having done so on your vital signs and other important measurements. There is a "Medform" included in the Appendices for your use. I have included a sample "Medform" here in the text, as it might be tailored for a specific patient's use. Refer to the sample as I explain how you might use it.

## MEDFORM

| Time and Vital Sign | Medication | Dose | Sun | Mon | Tue | Wed | Thu | Fri | Sat |
|---|---|---|---|---|---|---|---|---|---|
| AM Temp | | | | | | | | | |
| AM B/P | | | / | / | / | / | / | / | / |
| AM Pulse | | | | | | | | | |
| AM Weight | | | | | | | | | |
| AM | Prograf (2) | 2mg | | | | | | | |
| Breakfast | Citracal (2) | 600mg | | | | | | | |
| Breakfast | Loperamide (3) | 6mg | | | | | | | |
| Breakfast | Multi-Vitamin (1) | | | | | | | | |
| Breakfast | Prednisone (1) | 5mg | | | | | | | |
| Breakfast | Prilosec (1) | 20mg | | | | | | | |
| Lunch | Citracal (3) | 900mg | | | | | | | |
| Afternoon | Prograf (1) | 1mg | | | | | | | |
| Dinner | Citracal (3) | 900mg | | | | | | | |
| Dinner | Loperamide (3) | 6mg | | | | | | | |
| Dinner | Prilosec (1) | 20mg | | | | | | | |
| Dinner | Rocaltrol (1) | .25mcg | | | | | | | |
| PM | Calcitonin Injection | 200 IU | | | | | | | |
| PM B/P | | | / | / | / | / | / | / | / |
| PM Pulse | | | | | | | | | |
| Medform Revised   /   / | | Patient Name: | | | | | | | |

Let's start with the column headings, reading from left to right.

- The leftmost column contains either the "Time" (e.g., "AM," "Breakfast," "Lunch"), or the "Vital Sign" to be monitored [e.g., "Temp" (temperature), "B/P" (blood pressure), "Pulse"] or both "Time" and "Vital Sign."
- The next column is for "Medication." The person using the example has entered the medications with number of pills or capsules in parenthesis.
- The dosages are in the next column.
- The next seven columns are for entry of the vital sign readings or a checkmark when the patient takes the medication.
- There is space to write in dates above the abbreviations "Sun"–"Sat."

The bottom of the form has spaces for date of the last revision of the "Medform." From my experience, medications are changed periodically. When they are changed, I modify my Medform to reflect the changes and make copies. At the bottom of the form on the right side there is room to print your name.

I suggest that you make copies of the blank "Medform" in the appendices for your use. Fill out a copy to reflect the daily doses of medications you take and vital sign monitoring. Make copies of your form and complete a column a day. By completing a form such as this on a daily basis, you'll be able to give your doctor a useful tool for analysis during your office visit. In preparing for your doctor's appointment, review your "Medforms." You may find a trend in one of your measurements. For example, suppose your blood sugar has not been out of normal range over a span of several weeks. By pointing out this fact to your physician, with verification on your completed Medform, you may be exempt from sticking your finger every day. This alone would make keeping track worthwhile. It worked for me.

## You and Your Doctor Are Partners

Whenever you have an observation or a suggestion to make to your physician, do so. *Don't feel intimidated because you are not a doctor!* Physicians are very well trained in their field, but they are not the god that we too often make them out to be. Regardless of their native skills, education, and training, they often need help from colleagues and patients. They want and need your help. After all, you are the patient and an intelligent and creative human being. It is your health, and perhaps your life, being threatened with illness, and you are the final responsible individual for the effort to grow well once again. So it is vital that you make an essential contribution to your own health care. Do so by letting your doctor know what you think. If your physician does not have a so-called "bedside manner," force him or her to listen to you!

I have never had a doctor who ignored what I had to say about my health unless it was not in his or her field. Let me explain. I have four physicians or teams of physicians working on my overall health from the perspective of their individual specialty. I also have worked with an orthopedic surgeon, who was very interested in the medical history I gave him before seeing him the first time. It was important background material. When I consulted with him about my hip, shoulder, and so forth, however, his interest was limited to those problems where he could have a positive impact on my care and related topics. He wanted to know about my bone density tests, X rays and any of my medications which could affect bones positively or negatively. As an orthopedic surgeon, he has a very specific area of interest. For example, I'd be wasting his time and mine if I discussed the fluid in my right pleural area.

A form such as a "Medform" will serve as a guide for you to take the proper medication and dosage. To help further reduce your daily regimen into a habit, use a dosage pillbox. A daily or weekly pillbox reduces the taking of medications to a simple task of taking what's in the next compartment. My daily pillbox cost $1.00 at our neighborhood drugstore. My wife has a weekly pillbox, which was free.

When you go in for office visits with your physician, your completed Medforms will be welcomed as an accurate and useful aid by your doctor and nurse. They will know that you are serious about helping yourself, which will encourage them to speak with you candidly and work with you closely. Once again you will have provided information your physician needed in caring for you.

***

*__Let's hope you and your family will not need prolonged treatment by multiple doctors in different specialty areas. If you do find yourself in that situation, however, there are some things you need to know and to do.__*

***

 ## Prolonged Serious Illness

### Some Personal Background

When my wife and I first went to visit the liver transplant team for a 2-day health status screening and indoctrination program, we were loaded down with reading material on my liver disease. The liver transplant team wanted us to know as much as possible about what to expect from the disease, how to live with it, and what to expect with a transplant operation.

If you suddenly find that you have a major medical problem, you will undoubtedly be given reading material as we were. With the booming "Information Age" you now can also have access to additional information through medical libraries, on-line medical libraries on the World Wide Web, and medical information service companies. You will find access information for these data sources included in the "Information Directory" section of the appendices under "Medical Databases."

If your medical condition requires the skills of multiple specialists, you may find that they do not communicate very well. The doctors involved might not know each other, see each other, or even talk to each other very often because of their different specialties. Communication among them can be even worse if they're in different locations. If you are an HMO member, a case manager should be assigned to your case. The interdiscipline communications problem may be alleviated or even prevented if the specialists are part of the organization. How ever it happens, the physicians must talk to each other in person or on the phone about the patient—not through a third party. You can help make that happen. I'll show you how.

Let me use my experience once again as an example. I work with five different individual physicians and teams of physicians. They practice out of three different hospitals in three different cities. Two of the cities are 60 miles apart, and the third is halfway between the other two. Each physician or a member of a team of physicians saw me regularly and examined, tested, performed procedures, or prescribed for me over a period of two years. Occasionally, another specialist who works out of one of their hospitals also becomes involved.

Perhaps the only thing that these physicians have in common, in addition to their profession, is that they are all responsible for treating me. Each of these doctors is, of course, doing what they do very well. Nevertheless, this situation can give rise to a conflict in approach—for example, in the choice of treatments that each selects for a particular condition. This is not to say that one opinion is right and the other is wrong; they just are different and both treatments may be effective in different ways. The most obvious conflict can occur in the prescribing of medicines. Sometimes the conflicts cannot be avoided.

Recently, when I went into liver rejection, the liver team increased my dosage of Prednisone (cortisone), which impacts the calcium retention of my bones. The physician treating me for osteoporosis needed to know about my new cortisone level. It is essential that all the teams of physicians know all the medicines I am taking. It's just too important to my well being for me to rely on extremely busy specialists to call each other every time they change my prescriptions.

In my case, whenever these apparent conflicts of approach have appeared, they have easily been resolved by the physician in charge of my overall care. Undoubtedly, this will happen for you as well, provided, of course, that each of your physicians knows what the others are doing for you. That's where you play a very important role. As I have done, take the initiative to make sure each member of the team knows what you know about your health care. You can fill this role relatively easily by using

- Providers list
- Copies of lab reports

- Medications history
- Procedures history
- Status reports

*A dictionary has all the words needed to create a great story, but does not do so. In much the same way, your doctors' files are full of facts about you. Facts, like words, are useful to know, but do not tell a story. They have to be synthesized and communicated. You can and must play a key role in this process.*

### List of Providers

The place to start is with a list of providers. The list should contain the names, addresses, telephone numbers, and specialties of your physicians and any laboratory you visit regularly for tests. (I left specialties off this example.) I carry copies of the list of my providers with me. To compile this list, be sure to pick up your providers' business cards when you visit each of their offices. Give a copy of the list you have created to each of your doctors and to their staffs. Members of your family and close friends should also have a copy, in the event that you become ill. My "Provider List" is similar to the example on the next page.

### Laboratory Reports

Make sure that all your doctors receive copies of your laboratory reports. Give a "List Of Providers" to the person who checks you in, for entry into their computer. Whether you are taking a regularly scheduled test or a test that only one of your doctors ordered, have them send copies of the reports for this test and subsequent tests to you and all your physicians. Do the same for hospital outpatient procedures (e.g., MRI, ultrasound). You should find that most reports will be fairly easy to understand at a summary level. File your copy. You may want to ask questions about it during your next office visit.

### Medication History

Whenever one of your doctors changes a prescription in any way—medication, dosage, frequency—you need to follow his or her instructions. If you are using a form such as the Medform, which we discussed earlier, you will have to record this change on it. By also recording the date of the change and the specifics of the change on a sheet of columnar paper, you will have created a useful analytical tool that you can then provide to your doctors. You will have a "Medication History" similar to the example which follows. There is a "Medication History" form included in the appendices.

## LIST OF PROVIDERS
## (PATIENT NAME)
## OCTOBER 12, 1996

A. B. Alpha, M.D., PhD  
100 Science Way  
Room A150  
Big City, U.S.A.

Telephone: 789-555-3665  
FAX: 789-555-3666

C. D. Beta, M.D.  
1932 Roosevelt Road  
Suite 841  
Next Town, U.S.A.

Telephone: 456-555-6519  
FAX: 456-555-6520  
Nurse: K. L. Omega, R.N.  
Telephone: 456-555-6521

E. F. Delta, M.D.  
1200 Washington Boulevard  
Suite 19  
Next Town, U.S.A.

Telephone: 456-555-1301  
FAX: 456-555-1310

G. H. Gamma, M.D.  
500 Caring Court  
Suite T  
Next Town, U.S.A.

Telephone: 456-555-4086  
FAX: 456-555-4097

I. J. Kappa, M.D.  
15 Adams Avenue  
Suite 2100  
Hometown, U.S.A.

Telephone: 123-555-8554  
FAX: 123-555-8570

**\* Laboratory tests are regularly preformed by:**

Patient's Lab  
1997 Medical Mall  
Suite 110  
Hometown, U.S.A.

Telephone: 123-555-1995  
FAX: 123-555-1996

\* Make sure you show the address and phone numbers of the site where you have your blood drawn. On a number of occasions, the doctor asked a nurse or administrator to "call the lab to get Mr. McNally's latest lab report faxed." The best way to get that done is to call the drawing site.

## MEDICATION HISTORY

| Patient name: | | | | | | | | | Year: 1996 | |
|---|---|---|---|---|---|---|---|---|---|---|
| Medication | 5/1 | 5/15 | 6/23 | 6/10 | 6/23 | 6/30 | 7/12 | 8/24 | 10/2 | |
| Calcitor in | .25 ml | .25 ml | .25 ml | .25 ml | .25 ml | .25 ml | .25 ml | .25 ml | .25 ml | |
| Prednisone | 7.5 mg | **5 mg** | **10 mg** | 10 mg | **7.5 mg** | 7.5 mg | 7.5 mg | 7.5 mg | **5 mg** | |
| Prilosec | 0 | **40 mg** | 40 mg | 40 mg | 40 mg | 40 mg | 40 mg | 40 mg | 40 mg | |
| Prograf | 4 mg | 4 mg | **5 mg** | **4 mg** | 4 mg | **3 mg** | 3 mg | 3 mg | 3 mg | |
| Citracal | 2400 mg | 2400 mg | 2400 mg | 2400 mg | 2400 mg | 2400 mg | 2400 mg | 2400 mg | 2400 mg | |
| Multi-Vitamin | 1 caplet | 1 caplet | 1 caplet | 1 caplet | 1 caplet | 1 caplet | 1 caplet | 1 caplet | 1 caplet | |
| Lasix | **160 mg** | **40 mg** | 0 | 0 | 0 | 0 | 0 | 0 | 0 | |
| Loperamide | 8 mg | 8 mg | 8 mg | 8 mg | 8 mg | 8 mg | **12 mg** | 12 mg | 12 mg | |
| Aldactone | 50 mg | **0 mg** | 0 | 0 | 0 | 0 | 0 | 0 | 0 | |
| Zantac | 300 mg | **0 mg** | 0 | 0 | 0 | 0 | 0 | 0 | 0 | |
| Rocaltrol | .25 mcg | .25 mcg | .25 mcg | .25 mcg | .25 mcg | .25 mcg | .25 mcg | .25 mcg | .25 mcg | |
| Coumadin | | **3 mg** | 3 mg | 3 mg | **3–4 mg** | 3–4 mg | 3–4 mg | **0 mg** | 0 mg | |
| | | | | | | | | | | |
| **Weight** | **197** | **163** | **170** | **175** | **177** | **175** | **175** | **184** | **193** | |

Looking at the "Medication History," you will notice that there is a place to enter your name. Be sure to write your name on this form, and on all other forms you give to your doctor, to help make sure that it gets filed in your medical records. Write in the year on the right side of the top line so you can merely write in the month and date over the columns. If you don't often have changes in your medications, simply write the year as part of the date over the columns.

Notice on the "Medication History" that the names of the medicines are written down the left side. When a doctor prescribes a new medicine add it to your list. Enter the date of the prescription change, new medication, or dosage at the top of the next available column. Highlight prescription changes to make them more noticeable. I highlight the change by using bold typeface (against a tinted background). You may want to circle new dosages or use a highlighting pen. Unchanged prescription dosages are simply copied in the new column from the prior column in regular typeface.

This form gives your doctors an historical view of your prescriptions. You'll notice that the bottom line of the "Medication History" shows "Weight" for the day of the change. This is an example of how another relevant fact might be related to a change in your prescriptions.

### Procedures List

With a prolonged and complicated illness, tests and diagnostic procedures will be a way of life. It is very useful to keep track of them on a list such as

178 ■ THE MCNALLY METHOD FOR MANAGING YOUR HEALTH CARE

the "Procedures List" which follows. I started keeping track of my procedures when I found myself working with several doctors and having a lot of "procedures." My definition of a "procedure" is a diagnostic test or operation. This does not include blood draws, but it includes everything from an X ray session to a liver transplant.

## PROCEDURE LIST

**Patient:**

| Date | Procedure | Site* | Status | Reason | Ordering Doctor |
|---|---|---|---|---|---|
| 5/1/96 | Bone Density Test | LCMC | O/P | Evaluate Bone Health for Operation | Alpha |
| 5/3/96 | Thoracentesis | Y/C | O/P | Fluid Removal | Kappa |
| 5/3/96 | Chest X ray | Y/C | O/P | Check for Potential Lung Collapse | Kappa |
| 5/5/96 | MRI | AUMC | O/P | Evaluate Liver (Blood Vessels) | Beta |
| 5/8/96 | Doppler-Hepatic Veins | AUMC | O/P | Look for Partial Blockage of Outflow | Beta |
| 5/10/96 | Thoracentesis | Y/C | O/P | Remove Fluid in Right Pleural Area | Kappa |
| 5/10/96 | Chest X ray | Y/C | O/P | Check for Collapse of Lung | Kappa |
| 5/11/96 | Chest X ray | K/O | O/P | Check Partially Collapsed Right Lung | Kappa |
| 5/12/96 | Ultrasound | AUMC | I/P | Evaluate Inferior Venacavea (IVC) | Delta |
| 5/12/96 | Venogram | AUMC | I/P | Insert Stents in IVC & Anastomosis | Delta |
| 5/15/96 | Ultrasound/Doppler | AUMC | I/P | Baseline for Future Stent U/S & D/T | Delta |
| 5/30/96 | Chest X ray | K/O | O/P | Check Right Lung and Pleural Fluid | Kappa |
| 6/10/96 | Chest X ray | K/O | O/P | Check Right Lung and Pleural Fluid | Kappa |
| 8/24/96 | Ultrasound/Doppler | AUMC | O/P | Assess Vein Wall Integration of Stents | Beta |
| 9/28/96 | Pelvis/Left Hip X ray | LCMC | O/P | Evaluate Pelvis & Left Hip Healing | Alpha |
| 10/9/96 | Chest X rays | K/O | O/P | Check Right Pleural Area for Fluid | Kappa |
| 10/12/96 | Repair Abdom. Hernias | AUMC | O/P | Repaired Incisional Hernias | Gamma |

**\* SITE LEGEND:**
LCMC    Large City Medical Center
Y/C    Your Community Hospital
AUMC    A University Medical Center
K/O    Dr. Kappa's Office

To keep track of your tests and procedures, add them to a list as they occur. Indicate the date, procedure/test name, site, status, reason, and ordering physician. Note that "status" signifies either O/P for outpatient or I/P for inpatient. By simply keeping track of your procedures and tests in this fashion, you will be able to provide your physicians with a valuable clinical tool. You will also be able to quickly communicate your medical history to newly assigned specialists, in a very efficient and effective way.

If you become disabled and have disability insurance or insurance policies with insurance premium waivers, you will periodically be asked to have your doctor complete a questionnaire. They will also have you fill out a form and ask for a list of your hospital stays or the treatments. If you have this list, you can simply attach a copy to your form.

### Status Reports

It's a good idea to send periodic updates to your physicians, especially those whom you see less frequently. The report will remind them of your situation and update them on your status. It's also a good way to say thank you to your caretaking doctor for a job well done. You might use this means to express concern about a problem of unknown origin that has been bothering you. Be certain you inform the doctor how long the problem has existed.

I sent a "Status Report" to my physicians which focused on a particular problem I was having at the time. The issue was unresolved. In my view the situation needed special attention. Three of my doctors contacted me and communicated with one another in response to the report. They worked together, consulted with others, and devised a diagnostic plan of attack. The coordinating doctor had me go through a series of tests. They diagnosed my problem, brought in a specialty team, and saw to it that the problem was resolved. The issue was not life-threatening, but it was discomforting and medically complex. My "Status Report" helped bring my problem to the top of their priority list.

An example of a "Status Report" follows. There is no form in the appendices because it is free form. The example on the next page is in the format I use.

### The Benefits of Patient/Doctor Communications

*So what's the point of preparing and sharing all this information? From my experience, there are a number of points.*

With some effort on my part, I

- am involved as a responsible patient, instead of being a passive victim.
- help my doctors to help me.
- get maximum productivity out of my doctors and their staffs.
- have effective two-way communications with my physicians.
- answer their questions and they answer mine.

> **"Patient Name"**
> **Status Report #5**
> **September 8, 1996**
>
> *Shattered Bones:*
> I met with Dr. Alpha on 5/23/96 to review the results of my bone density test of 5/1/96. My left hip bone density has improved by 50% in the last year. It is now in the normal range and ready to be operated upon.
>
> *Shoulder:*
> There has been no measurable change in my right shoulder. In certain positions of its range of motion it is weak. It also is still sore all the time and painful when stressed.
>
> *Breathing:*
> I have not had any fluid buildup and consequent breathing difficulties since insertion of stents during the venogram procedure of 5/12/96. My breathing is greatly improved. I will no longer report on this problem.
>
> *Esophagus/Stomach:*
> I do not often have discomfort after eating. When I do it is not as severe as it was. Dr. Beta will be ordering an endoscopy to determine whether the ulcerated spots in my stomach have healed. Until then I am to stay on Prilosec.
>
> *Abdominal Hernia:*
> On 8/24/96 Dr. Beta discontinued my taking of coumadin. Surgery to repair my abdominal hernias will be performed sometime after my corrective pelvic/hip surgery.
>
> *Medication:*
> I have enclosed a copy of a "Medication History." It shows the medications I have been taking from 5/1/96 to date.
>
> *Liver Condition:*
> My liver measurements are within range and stable. Prograf and prednisone are subject to dosage tuning. My kidney measurements have also improved.

- am able to demonstrate issues and communicate my concerns.
- enhance communications among my doctors.
- am a teammate with my physicians and their staffs.
- feel more in control of my day-to-day life.
- understand my condition and my doctor's treatment plan.
- find it's much easier to check in with a hospital, clinic, laboratory, or new doctor.
- am doing what must be done to be an effective patient.
- get excellent health care.

*AND YOU CAN HAVE THE SAME RELATIONSHIP WITH YOUR HEALTH CARE PROVIDERS, STARTING NOW! BEFORE MOVING ON TO THE NEXT CHAPTER, WRITE DOWN YOUR SYMPTOMS AND QUESTIONS FOR YOUR NEXT OFFICE VISIT.*

## ▼ KEY POINTS  Enhancing Your Health Care

1. Doctor/Patient communications are the key to getting the best health care available to you.

2. We all "go to see the doctor." Give your doctor a list of symptoms, questions, and discussion topics at the start of each "Office Visit."

3. Ask questions in a way that your doctor can answer.

4. Our attitude toward health problems and diminished physical abilities is critical.

    If we harbor a "Woe is me, victim attitude," we will feel worse and get worse.

    The sooner we reduce our daily medication and diet to a regimen we don't have to think about, the better.

5. We need to take charge of our health care by using "The McNally Method" tools and techniques:

    Pillbox

    Medform

    List of Providers

    Copies of Lab Reports to all providers

    Medications History

    Procedures History

    Status Reports

    Some of the above, or all of the above

6. The solution should not be more complex than the problem we are trying to solve.

7. Most of us are healthy and only need to prepare for office visits and possibly use a pillbox for now.

8. The chronically and seriously ill and their family support teams need to use *The McNally Method for Managing Your Health Care* as a key reference book.

*Let's update our Glossary with terms from this chapter and the next one.*

 **Glossary Update**

**Advocacy Program**—The function within an HMO that supports the HMO's members when they have a grievance.

**Advocate**—A person who speaks on behalf of another. In the context of this text, an advocate is someone who represents a patient's position against the members of the medical profession or insurance industry.

**Chronic Illness**—An ongoing and recurring health problem requiring periodic treatment.

**CPT Code**—The "Physicians' Current Procedural Terminology," which is a systematic listing of codes used for the procedures and services performed for patients by medical providers. Members of the medical profession and the health care insurance industry use the term CPT Codes to refer to these five-digit codes.

**Disallowed Charges**—The charges that an insurer refuses to reimburse. Disallowed charges can occur when a patient's insurance policy does not provide coverage for the procedure, or when the provider and the insurance company have an agreement that certain CPT codes will not be reimbursable under specific circumstances or when the procedure performed is not a normal test or treatment for the patient's disease.

**Enzyme**—A complex protein produced in living cells. It is able to cause changes in other cells without being changed itself. It is a catalyst. As used in this text, it is a condition in the cells of the body detected by certain tests as part of a diagnostic regimen. The tests indicate whether the enzymes are at an abnormal level in given cells, too low, or too high.

**Explanation of Benefits (EOB)**—A report sent to the provider and the patient, if the provider submitted the claim or just to the patient if the patient submitted a claim for insurance reimbursement. It shows the amount charged for each procedure, the amount reimbursed, and the detailed explanation of the reasons for the payment or non-payment of parts or all of the claim. It accompanies any payment that is made.

**Federal ID**—A number assigned to an individual or a corporate entity and used by the person or corporate entity for identification and to relate his, her, or its role in a particular situation.

**ICD-9**—The commonly used term for *The International Classification of Diseases, 9th Revision*, which is a listing of diseases associated with a five-digit code, three to the left of the decimal and two to the right. There are instances of codes using alphabetic characters and other instances with one or no entries to the right of the decimal point. It depends upon the number of digits that are needed to the right of the decimal point to define the disease. These codes are used to specify the disease for which the patient is being treated.

**Medform**—A form developed by the author for keeping track of vital signs and medications prescribed and taken.

**Office Visit**—The encounter a patient has when he or she "goes to the doctor."

**Pending Charges**—The charges for procedure codes which an insurer will not reimburse without further explanation.

**Status Post (S/P)**—A modifier used to describe that the procedure has been performed or a condition has been remedied, as in "Liver Transplant S/P."

**Third Party Administrator (TPA)**—The role filled by an insurance company when, for a fee, it performs all the insurance processes for a policy funded by an employer or other group.

**Vital Sign**—The critical conditions and processes of the human body (e.g., pulse, blood pressure).

# Managing Medical Bills and Insurance Reimbursement

---

The following discussion assumes that you have health insurance,
Fee-For-Service with/without a Preferred Provider Option or
Medicare with/without Medigap;
or
that you are a member of an HMO or a Medicare HMO.

---

 ## The Business Relationship with Health Care Providers and Insurers

When bills and insurance claim reports begin to arrive, it's too late to thoroughly investigate your health insurance alternatives. Hopefully, the insurance you have will meet your needs. If you do not have sufficient insurance, you will be obligated to pay your medical bills, no matter how long it takes: even if it means spending your life savings to do so. This is the problem some refer to as applying to *only* 20% of Americans. (Imagine referring to 50+ million Americans as *"only."*) In fact, this is a growing problem. A recent estimate quoted the number of uninsured at 63 million.

If you have no medical insurance and you are not wealthy enough to pay major medical expenses out of pocket, your hospital and doctor's insurance coordinators may be able to help. They will insist on knowing how you are going to pay for the services you have received and any additional services you may need. Once they know your situation, however, they may come up with some creative alternatives using endowments or research funds in the case of major surgery or illness. Don't count on it. It's much more likely that you would be put on a time payment plan, if anything.

Before going any further, let me remind you of three important points. First, my experience with billing and insurance is as a fee-for-service patient with a preferred provider option ultimately responsible for my medical bills. Second, as a member of an HMO, I would have been responsible for my HMO dues and copays. The HMO is responsible to deliver care, as stipulated in their membership agreements. Third, both fee-for-service insurance and HMO membership impose rules on the insured or member as the basis upon which their rates are built. To avoid unexpected billing, all who are insured must know and follow the rules of their policy or membership.

*With fee-for-service insurance, you are responsible for paying provider bills. As an HMO member, your HMO is responsible for paying providers.*

### HMO Billing

As an HMO member, you should not receive any provider bills unless the procedure wasn't covered (e.g., cosmetic surgery, substance abuse rehabilitation). When you become an HMO member, you agree to pay fees and coinsurance, as specified by the agreement you sign. You also agree to use only HMO providers, and only with a referral or authorization from your Primary Care Physician

The HMO agrees to provide for your health care needs according to the terms of your agreement. The HMO is responsible to pay providers who treat you, as long as you follow the HMO's rules. The HMO is not responsible to pay bills that you incur on your own. When you go to a provider other than your Primary Care Physician without a referral or a pre-authorization, you establish a fee-for-service relationship with that provider. You are responsible to pay any charges which result from your encounter.

### HMO Advocacy Program for Problem Resolution

As an HMO member, you should not receive a bill from a provider. Whether you are a member as an individual, through your employer, or through Medicare, you will have a procedure to follow should you erroneously receive a bill. Follow the procedure given to you by your HMO for correcting the situation. Start executing the procedure as soon as you receive the bill to prevent collection activity.

In lieu of a procedure or to augment the HMO's procedure, you might want to consider taking the following steps as soon as you receive the bill.

1. If you are a member of an HMO with "Point of Service" provisions, call your HMO's, "Member Services" to find out how to proceed.
   If you do not have "Point of Service" provisions, go to Step #2.

2. Ask yourself whether you had a procedure that is not covered.
   Look it up on your "Coverage Spreadsheet" if you are not sure.
   If it is not covered, you must pay the bill.

3. If it is a covered procedure, ask yourself whether you followed the HMO's procedure for referral or pre-authorization.

4. If you did follow the proper procedure, call the provider's office (Step #9).

5. If you went to a physician without a referral from your Primary Care Provider, you must pay the bill.

6. If you did not follow the HMO's procedure for pre-authorization because of the emergency nature of the situation, did you follow the post-authorization procedure, (e.g., call within 48 hours)?

7. If you did not get post-authorization, call your HMO's "Member Services." State your case for the granting of an exception. Send them copies of your documentation and notes, as appropriate. Follow their direction.

8. If you did get a post-authorization, call the provider's office (Step #9).

9. Call the provider's billing office at the number shown on the bill or statement. Take names and notes. Tell them why you should not have been billed.

10. If they agree, make sure they tell you what they are going to do to correct the billing. Consider confirming the conversation in writing.

11. If they do not agree, ask why you were billed.

12. If you are satisfied with explanation and agree that you should pay the bill, pay it.

13. If you are not satisfied with the explanation, you have two choices:

    (a) Call your HMO's Member Services group. Go through your situation with them. Send them a copy of your documentation and notes. Follow their direction.

    (b) Escalate your request to have the provider cancel the charges they entered into your account and confirm that they have done so. Make sure that you state your case fully and positively. Include names, dates, and notes on the conversations you have had on the subject. Direct your letter to the provider's administrator. If the practice consists of a single doctor, you can subsequently appeal to him or her if necessary. If it is a large practice, escalate to the president, medical director, or board of directors of the practice.

If the provider billing persists or you have some other complaint, your HMO has an advocate for you to call and a "Grievance Procedure" to follow. HMOs are required to have a member advocacy program by federal law, known as the Knox-Keene Legislation. HMO management must closely scrutinize their complaint resolution systems to protect their federal franchise to operate, especially as it applies to their approval as a Medicare provider.

Follow the advocate's direction. If you are not ready to accept the answer and explanation you are given, you might wish to escalate the complaint in writing with supporting documentation to executive levels within the HMO. Before you do, keep in mind that if you clearly abridged the rules of the HMO which you agreed to abide by, you are responsible for the bill.

If there are extenuating circumstances, you may want to escalate to executive management. For example, suppose you were unconscious and hemorrhaging and taken to the nearest hospital by ambulance, and you are being billed because you did not get pre-authorization. If you were also physically unable to follow the HMO procedure for post-authorization approval, it might be worthwhile to bring to the attention of the HMO's executive management or Medical Director for review.

If you do not accept the answer you are given at that level and want a review by someone outside the HMO, call the appropriate executive or the Medical Director. Leave a message that you intend to seek the help of an outside advocate. Reference your appeal and the date on which you intend to contact an advocate. If you are not contacted by the executive or a representative, consider that as your final answer.

If you feel you need an advocate, call your state "Department of Consumer Affairs" or its equivalent in your state. Their number should be listed in the State Government section of the white pages in your local telephone directory. When you call, be ready to briefly describe the nature of your problem. Tell them you need a consumer advocate in the department or agency with regulatory authority over Health Maintenance Organizations, your provider, or health insurance company, or all of them. They should be able to point you in the right direction.

### The Fee-For-Service Billing and Reimbursement System

As long as you stay within the limits of your insurance coverage and follow the rules, you should have no concerns about insurance coverage and billing. Unfortunately, problems can still occur because of the complexity of the health care network, systemic inadequacies in the billing and reimbursement processes, and human error. If you understand how the medical billing and insurance reimbursement process works, you will be better able to deal with it. On that premise, I will describe the billing process for charges you incur as a person having fee-for-service insurance with a preferred provider option.

There are four key pieces of data that your provider uses: what was done for you (CPT Code), why it was done (ICD-9 Code), who you are (Patient and Insurance Identification Numbers), and who the provider is (Federal Identification Number). They will also use policy and group numbers. A brief explanation of the four key codes follows:

**CPT Code** is a standard five-digit number used to describe a procedure performed and its complexity. CPT stands for "Physicians' Current Procedural Terminology," a listing which precisely defines all procedures, using a five-digit code structure. For example: a "Detailed Moderate Complexity Office Visit" for an established patient is 99214. If the same patient has a "Complicated High Complexity Office Visit," it is coded as 99215. Each procedure (e.g., X ray, blood draw, blood test, liver transplant operation) is assigned a unique CPT code.

**ICD-9** is the current listing of the *International Classification of Diseases, ninth revision*. The ICD-9 codes are controlled by the World Health Organization. An ICD-9 code reflects the physician's diagnosis of the patient's condition. For example a person who has ICD-9 codes of 996.82, 733.0, 811 and 808.8 is someone who has had a liver transplant and who has osteoporosis, a fractured right shoulder and a fractured pelvis. (The correct description for code 996.82 is "liver transplant status post" or "liver transplant S/P.")

**Patient ID** is the number that your insurance company uses to refer to you. Often it's your Social Security Number, but it can also be your Medicare Number, your insurance company assigned number, or your employee number in the case of employer-provided insurance.

**Federal ID** is a number which the Federal Government, upon written application, assigns to a person or a corporate entity. It looks like a Social Security Number. In the case of a health insurer, it is used by an insurance company to identify the provider who performed a procedure and his or her relationship with the insurer. Each provider can have multiple Federal ID Numbers. A physician may have one number to be used when treating Medicare patients and filing a claim for reimbursement, another number for each insurance company with which he or she has a PPO contract, a non-PPO number for the insurance companies with whom he or she has a fee-for-service relationship, and so on.

---

*"How does the system work?*
*Or does it?"*
*The system does work, most of the time.*
*Let's look at an example.*

---

Assume the person having the ICD-9 codes spelled out under "ICD-9" above goes to a lab to have blood drawn and tested. At check-in, the lab would enter insurance and patient identification numbers. They would also enter the "liver transplant status post" ICD-9 code (996.82), the CPT codes for a blood draw (36415), and codes for each of the tests to be performed on the drawn blood. These identification numbers and codes would indicate that the patient is a preferred provider policyholder, using a preferred provider to have blood drawn and tested for the status of his or her liver enzymes. After the procedures were performed, a claim would be sent to the insurance company, usually electronically.

If everything checked out, the insurance company would send the laboratory a check with an Explanation of Benefits (EOB). They would also send a copy of the EOB to the patient. If the patient owed money because of an annual deductible, or out-of-pocket obligation, or owed a copayment, this information would be noted on the EOB. The lab's billing department would bill the patient for the amount he or she owes, and if the patient pays promptly, that is the end of the process. If the patient does not pay promptly, collection efforts will begin. And that's the way it should go. What could go wrong? Here are a few examples of the kind of errors that can occur.

> The lab could have entered the patient's osteoporosis ICD-9 code (733.0) instead of 996.82, the code for "liver transplant S/P." In this case the Explanation of Benefits sent to the lab would have indicated that the procedures (blood tests) were not allowed for that diagnosis code and that the patient owed the entire amount to the lab.
>
> The lab could have put in the wrong Federal ID, in which case the lab might be paid as a fee-for-service provider. The Explanation of Benefits would have told the lab to get the rest of their money from the patient.
>
> The patient could have employer provided insurance with Medicare as a secondary insurer. The lab might have sent the claim to Medicare first instead of the primary insurance carrier, or maybe they sent it to the primary insurance carrier and failed to send it to Medicare as a secondary insurer.

Errors such as I described above can more easily occur when the provider is a lab because of volume, multiple orders for one patient, and the fact that communications with the lab are usually passed through the patient. Problems can also occur in large medical facilities with hundreds of doctors, thousands of patients, and remote billing centers. It should not occur often in a small practice.

The first case I cited above, in which the wrong ICD-9 code was entered into the system (osteoporosis instead of liver transplant S/P), can easily occur. The doctor treating the patient for a secondary problem, osteoporosis in this case, writes an order for the patient to be tested for calcium levels with the osteoporosis diagnostic code written on the order. When the patient next goes in for regular blood tests, the osteoporosis tests are added to the regularly scheduled liver enzyme tests. If the administrative person at the check-in desk enters the osteoporosis diagnostic code instead the liver transplant S/P code, the liver enzyme tests would not be allowed. The Explanation of Benefits would show the charges for the liver enzyme tests as collectable from the patient.

*When you receive your first Explanation of Benefits, don't be intimidated. They can be read. Let me show you how.*

## Explanation of Benefits (EOB)

An Explanation of Benefits can be confusing when you first see it. One feature that seems to confuse people is the Explanation of Benefit's format. It has clusters of information. They're logical, once you get used to the form.

Another cause of confusion is the way an Explanation of Benefits uses numerical codes or letter codes for explanations. The number codes, or as in the case of Medicare, letter codes, are printed next to an entry on the Explanation of Benefits. The codes indicate that there is a message concerning the entry. The codes are printed elsewhere on the form with the printed message. After you become accustomed to the format of the Explanation of Benefits, when you see a code you will automatically switch your focus to the code explanation and back to the entry.

Until you get used to reading them, Explanations of Benefits can be confusing and frustrating. I will explain how to read an EOB, using an example that ties back to the "Sample Example." I'm going to start using "EOB" to refer to Explanations of Benefits. As is the case with HMO, CPT, and ICD-9, EOB is the term used by medical and insurance personnel.

### An EOB Example

What follows is an EOB for the blood draw and tests which Mrs. Sally Sample had in connection with her physical examination. After showing you this example of an EOB, I will explain its entries. The EOB is based on the PPO coverage provisions for the Sample family on the "Insurance Option Summary." Later we will use this EOB to explain how to use a "Tracking Form."

## EXPLANATION OF BENEFITS
### Your Health Insurance, Inc.
### 1234 Health Insurance Road
### Big City, U.S.A.

I.M. Sample  
987 Happy Way  
Hometown, U.S.A.

EOB Date: 10/11/96  
Provider: Mu Nu, M.D.

**1996 YTD PPO Insurance Plan Status**
**For Patient: Mrs. Sally Sample**

|  | Plan | YTD | Left |
|---|---|---|---|
| Your ded | 200.00 | 200.00 | 0.00 |
| Fam ded | 600.00 | 400.00 | 200.00 |
| Your OOP | 1,000.00 | 15.00 | 985.00 |
| Fam OOP | 3,000.00 | 525.00 | 3,472.00 |

**Claim Information**

| | |
|---|---|
| Claim # | 123AB45 |
| Date Rcd | 26-Sep-96 |
| Policy # | 1481 |
| Group # | 201 |
| Benefit Yr | 1996 |

**Claim Summary**

| | |
|---|---|
| Charges | 261.00 |
| Disallow. | 50.00 |
| Pending | 46.25 |
| Deduct. | 5.00 |
| OOP | 15.00 |
| Copay | 0.00 |
| Ins Paid | 85.00 |
| Pat. pays | 20.00 |

| Svc. Date | Billed Amt | PPO Amt | Amt Not Allowed | Rsn Cde | Amt Pending | Rsn Cde | Cvge % | Ins. Paid | Ded. Amt. | OOP Amt. | Copay Amt | Patient Pays |
|---|---|---|---|---|---|---|---|---|---|---|---|---|
| 20-Sep-96 | 27.50 | 0.00 | | | 27.50 | a | | 0.00 | 0.00 | 0.00 | 0.00 | 0.00 |
| 20-Sep-96 | 50.00 | 0.00 | 50.00 | b | | | | 0.00 | 0.00 | 0.00 | 0.00 | 0.00 |
| 20-Sep-96 | 22.50 | 20.00 | | | | | 85% | 12.75 | 5.00 | 2.25 | 0.00 | 7.25 |
| 20-Sep-96 | 40.00 | 23.00 | | | | | 85% | 19.55 | 0.00 | 3.45 | 0.00 | 3.45 |
| 20-Sep-96 | 65.00 | 33.30 | | | | | 85% | 28.30 | 0.00 | 5.00 | 0.00 | 5.00 |
| 20-Sep-96 | 20.00 | 15.50 | | | | | 85% | 13.18 | 0.00 | 2.32 | 0.00 | 2.32 |
| 20-Sep-96 | 17.25 | 13.20 | | | | | 85% | 11.22 | 0.00 | 1.98 | 0.00 | 1.98 |
| 20-Sep-96 | 18.75 | 0.00 | | | 18.75 | a | | 0.00 | 0.00 | 0.00 | 0.00 | 0.00 |
| Totals | 261.00 | 105.00 | 50.00 | | 46.25 | | | 85.00 | 5.00 | 15.00 | 0.00 | 20.00 |

**Notes:**
a. Charge is pending further information requested from provider.
b. Charge is not allowed per the terms of the PPO contract.

## EOB Explanation

Let's go through the EOB for Mrs. Sample's blood draw charges from top to bottom and left to right. Remember she has a fee-for-service policy with a preferred provider option.

1. "Explanation of Benefits" in the top center clearly identifies the form.
2. The EOB is from "Your Health Insurance, Inc."
3. In the upper left, the EOB is addressed to the policyholder.
4. In the upper right is the "EOB Date: 10/11/96."
5. In the upper right is the "Provider: Dr. Mu Nu."
6. Below the "mail to" address is "1996 YTD Insurance Plan Status." It shows us that:
   - The patient is Mrs. Sally Sample
   - Her $200 annual deductible is paid up (as of this EOB)
   - The family has paid $400 of their $600 family annual deductible
   - Mrs. Sample has only paid $15 of her $1,000 annual Out-of-Pocket coinsurance (as of this FOB)
   - The family has paid $525 of their $3,000 annual Out-of-Pocket coinsurance
7. In the center of the EOB is the "Claim Information" section. It gives us:
   - The claim number—123AB45
   - The date on which the claims office received the claim—9/26/96
   - The policy number—1481
   - The group number—201
   - The benefit year—1996
8. On the right side of the form is the claim summary, which shows us:

   | | |
   |---|---|
   | Charges totaled | $261.00 |
   | Disallowed charges of | $ 50.00 |
   | Pending charges of | $ 46.25 |
   | Deductible of | $  5.00 |
   | Out-Of-Pocket of | $ 15.00 |
   | Copayment of | $  0.00 |
   | Insurance payment of | $ 85.00 |

   - Total patient payment due of $ 20.00 ($5.00 deductible and $15.00 Out-of-Pocket).
9. The details on the charges and payments are in the columns across the bottom half of the page as follows:
   - Service date for all eight charges is 9/20/96.
   - Billed amount column shows eight charges totaling $261. The entries are as follows:

- The first is for $27.50. It shows up in the "Amount Pending" column.

  In the Reason Code column next to it is a code "a."

  Looking under "Notes:" at the bottom of the page, the note "a" indicates that the insurance company is holding it, pending the receipt of further information. This means that the insurance company is awaiting an explanation as to why this particular test was ordered. They might need a secondary diagnosis code (ICD-9).

- The second charge of $50.00 is not allowed. The reason code of "b" in the next column, and at the bottom of the page indicates that this charge is not allowed under the terms of the contract.

- The third item is a $22.50 charge which is discounted to a $20.00 charge. Mrs. Sample pays $5.00, paying off her $200 annual deductible. (See "Ded. Amt." column). Insurance pays 85% of the $15.00 balance ($12.75 in the "Ins. Paid column). Mrs. Sample pays 15% of the $15.00 balance ($2.25 in the "OOP" column).

- The next four charges have the insurance company (85%) and Mrs. Sample (15% for her annual out-of-pocket coinsurance obligation) sharing the PPO discounted amount of the charges.

- The last charge has the same explanation as the first charge. It is a pending charge awaiting further information before it can be paid. (See note "a.")

*If your Fee-For-Service, Preferred Provider Insurer does not have a good, or any, Patient Advocate Function, and anyone in billing, reimbursement, or account posting makes a mistake, it will be up to you to spot it, prove it, and get it corrected.*

 **Working with the Billing/Reimbursement System(s)**

There are steps you can take to stay on top of your insurance coverage and reimbursement, so that managing the financial aspect of your health problems does not distract you from the important task of getting well.

*If you want to get the most out of your insurance, you better know its rules and follow them.*

### Know the Rules of Your Policy

As we discussed in the "Insurance Plan Options" section, make sure that your insurance company or your employer gives you a "Coverage Summary" similar to the "Insurance Options Summary." You should not have to create your own. You don't have to memorize all the rules regarding coverage. Get a good understanding of what your insurance covers and what it does not cover. Keep your "Coverage Summary" handy for its detailed coverage and coinsurance information.

*Knowing where your reimbursement money comes from, should help you work with the insurance claims office representatives, who control its distribution.*

### Understand the Environment of Insurance Claims Office Personnel

Some large employers fund their own health care insurance benefits. They contract with an insurance company to act on their behalf as a Third Party Administrator (TPA), who administers an employer's health care insurance benefit programs for a fee. The Third Party Administrator reimburses the medical providers from your employer's funds according to the provisions of employer's policy. They are, in effect, an extension of your employer's Human Resource organization and are likely to treat you accordingly.

Most companies who provide group health insurance to their employees buy the coverage from an indemnity insurer. The insurance company provides coverage to the employees by paying the health care providers out of their funds. In this arrangement, the insurance company can make money in two ways. First, they can hold administrative costs below the level they built into the premium they charge your employer. Second, they can try to stay under budget for reimbursed health care benefits. You are likely to find more of a "prove it to me" atmosphere in dealing with the insurer.

Don't be offended: just be prepared. The claims office representatives are not questioning your integrity when they ask you questions. They need to make sure of what you are saying. It's their job. They might not always have the best "bedside manner," but you need to be courteous and friendly. Remember, you want and need their help.

*"What should I do when an EOB arrives in the mail?"*
*Let me tell you what I do.*

## What To Do When an EOB Arrives

Here are the steps I go through when I receive an EOB.

1. Check to see whether the patient owes money.
2. Check to see who is shown as the patient on the EOB.
3. Make sure that the charge is valid. Did the patient receive these services from the provider on the service date shown. If not tell the Claims Office.
4. Make sure the EOB is correct for the provider, fee-for-service vs. preferred provider. If not, tell the Claims Office.
5. Make sure that this EOB is not a duplicate payment by checking the service date on the "Tracking Form" and in the EOB binder. If it is, tell the Claims Office.
6. If the patient does not owe money and the EOB is not a duplicate payment to the provider, post the EOB to a "Tracking Form" and file it alphabetically in a binder on top of the most recent EOB from the same provider.
7. If the patient is shown as owing money, check to see if the EOB shows a deductible, copayment, or coinsurance (out-of-pocket) amount due from the patient.
8. If the EOB amount due from the patient is correct, post the EOB information to the "Tracking Form" for the patient and this provider. Wait for the provider's bill.
9. If the EOB amount is not correct, tell the Claims Office.
10. When the provider's bill arrives, check the amount against the amount shown on the "Tracking Sheet" or EOB.
11. If it's correct, pay the bill.
12. If it's not correct, call the provider's billing service to have them send you a corrected bill before you pay. Depending on prior experience with the provider, consider sending in the correct amount with a letter and a copy of the EOB.

## Know How Billing and Insurance Reimbursement Work

If you do not use a preferred provider, you will probably have to pay for the services rendered. You will then have to send your insurance company a copy of the provider's detailed bill (receipt) with a claim form. The insurance company will reimburse you, based on the provisions of your policy, for a portion of the cost you incurred. Whatever is not reimbursed is your expense.

If you go to a preferred provider for your health care needs, the provider will send a claim to your insurance company for reimbursement. Your insurance company will reimburse the provider for the provider's portion of the charges. They will also instruct the provider on the EOB to write off charges that are not billable under the Preferred Provider Agreement. The EOB will also let the provider know how much you owe.

Problems can develop if your insurance company incorrectly reimburses a preferred provider, as though the provider were not a member of their PPO (Preferred Provider Organization). If this happens, your provider's billing group will send you a statement showing that you owe the difference. Once this charge is entered into the billing organization's computer, getting your account record corrected can be very difficult and frustrating. With the number of mergers, consolidations, restructurings and spin-offs in the medical industry, this type of error is far too common. This is a problem you should be able to spot and have rectified before it gets into the provider's billing system. Make sure that you examine the insurance company's EOBs for errors as soon as you receive them.

For preferred providers, the insurance EOBs should show an amount that was billed and amount that was "allowed," an amount that was paid, and any amount that the patient owes (for the deductible, out-of-pocket expense, copayment, etc.) It might also have notes explaining that your provider has agreed to accept the amount "allowed."

If the EOB does not show "Contract Amounts," "Allowed Amounts," "PPO Amounts," "PPO Notes," or the correct coinsurance amounts (e.g., 70% vs. 85% as on the "Insurance Options Summary"), the provider has been reimbursed as a fee-for-service provider instead of a preferred provider. If that is not correct, call the insurance company immediately and go through the EOB with them. They should be able to quickly issue a corrected EOB, thereby preventing a billing error from being posted to your account. Once you have a commitment from the insurer to send the provider a corrected EOB, call the provider's billing department. Let them know that your insurer is going to issue a corrected EOB. Your goal is to prevent the erroneous EOB, which shows that you owe money or more money than you owe, from being entered into their billing and accounts receivable systems.

If you miss the error on an EOB, you will receive a statement from the provider showing that you owe money. If this happens, call the insurance company and review the EOB with them. Once you have their commitment to reissue the EOB, call the billing organization's number as shown on the statement. Have the statement and the EOB handy. Go through the situation with them and tell them that the insurance company is going to issue a revised EOB. You might prevent dunning notices.

## Keep Track of Your Payments for the Year

*Don't let the solution become more complex than the problem you are trying to solve.*

If you and your family only go to the doctor for minor problems and checkups, there is no great need to keep track of your payments. Keep copies of the bills and insurance EOBs for each member of your family in a file folder by date. If later in the year someone in your family has more serious medical problems, you can refer to his or her folder to make sure that you are not overpaying deductibles, out-of-pocket (OOP) expenses, and copayments.

On the other hand, if you have a chronic illness or other serious medical problems with which you must deal, you should file EOBs and statements by patient, by provider, and by date. I use a three-ring binder for this purpose with alphabetized dividers. When I receive an EOB, I file it alphabetically in a binder on top of the last EOB received for the same provider. If I talk to the provider's billing staff or my insurer, I put the dated notes of those conversations in the binder and stapled to the EOB. I file provider billing statements, reissued EOBs, letters, and anything pertaining to the EOB's service date in the binder, attached to the original EOB for the same service date.

Keep track of your bills and reimbursements as your family's medical expenses start to grow. You need to avoid overpayment of deductibles, out-of-pocket expenses, and copayments. If you are overcharged in these categories, you will need all your documentation to prove it to your insurance company. It can happen.

Since there is potential for an income tax deduction, keep track of other medical expenses as well. Prescriptions, dental care, eyeglasses, mileage, and living expenses might qualify. Form 1040 lists examples of medical deductions that can qualify for entry on Form 1040 Schedule A. Check with the Internal Revenue Service or a competent tax advisor to get detailed guidance. The telephone numbers for the Internal Revenue Service (IRS) can be found under "United States Government" in the white pages of your local telephone directory.

If your family starts to have more complex medical assistance requirements, the paperwork will rapidly become unmanageable. As mistakes are made in your medical bill reimbursements, you will not be able to simply sort through a few sheets of paper to refresh your memory and find the right bill or EOB. There is an alternative to digging through a pile of bills, EOBs, and checkbook stubs every time a billing or reimbursement problem comes up. Keep an up-to-date summary of every EOB.

The format for keeping track of medical expenses and reimbursements should not be more complex than the problem you are trying to solve or avoid. If you have a single insurance company, you may want to use a "Tracking Form" with one sheet for each provider. We will post Mrs. Sample's blood draw and tests EOB to a "Tracking Form" upon completion of this topic to show you how to use a "Tracking Form."

If you have a complex insurance tracking problem, you will still be able to manage it with multiple "Tracking Forms," but it will be difficult to see the big picture. Multiple insurance policies (e.g., employer provided insurance, Medicare, and Medigap), large volumes of bills, and EOBs for many providers could benefit from a more complex solution. In my case, my stack of EOBs, bills, and notes for one year was over six inches tall. I built a database on my personal computer to help keep track of where I stood. If I had tracked it all manually with "Tracking Forms," I would have used separate sheets for each provider. I would have had a chronological file for each provider within an alphabetized notebook of the sheets for all the providers, but the database made it easier.

## Posting Mrs. Sample's EOB to a Tracking Form

Let's go through the posting of Mrs. Sally Sample's EOB to her Tracking Form (see next two pages) for this provider, Dr. Mu Nu. After going through the Tracking Form for Mrs. Sample, I will make some general comments about posting to Tracking Forms and using them. Notice that I only entered a one line summary for the eight lines on the EOB, the total line on the EOB. All of your references to these charges will be related to the EOB date and, secondarily, the Service Date. The Tracking Form is an up-to-date status summary for each of a patient's EOBs. Post to it in pencil.

Going across the top of the form, I entered the patient name found in the "1996 YTD PPO Insurance Plan Status" box on the upper left side of the form. The provider's name is in the upper right corner of the EOB. This form would be used for all of Mrs. Sample's EOBs for Dr. Mu Nu. After filling out the top of the form, I posted to the body of the form as follows:

1. "Svc Date" from the date in the "Svc Date" column on the EOB.
2. "Billed Amt" from the total for "Billed Amt" column on the EOB.
3. "PPO Amt" from the total for "PPO Amt" column on the EOB.
4. "Ins EOB Date" from the upper right corner of the EOB.
5. "Ins Amt Paid" from the total for "Ins Paid" column on the EOB.
6. "Ded Amt" from the total for "Ded Amt" column on the EOB.
7. "OOP Amt" from the total for "OOP Amt" column on the EOB.
8. "Copay Amt" from the total for "Copay Amt" column on the EOB.
9. "Pers Due" from the total for "Patient Pays" column on the EOB.
10. "Pers Paid" is "0.00" since the patient has not paid anything yet.

**EXPLANATION OF BENEFITS**
Your Health Insurance, Inc.
1234 Health Insurance Road
Big City, U.S.A.

I.M. Sample
987 Happy Way
Hometown, U.S.A.

EOB Date: 10/11/96
Provider: Mu Nu, M.D.

**1996 YTD PPO Insurance Plan Status**
**For Patient: Mrs. Sally Sample**

|  | Plan | YTD | Left |
|---|---|---|---|
| Your ded | 200.00 | 200.00 | 0.00 |
| Fam ded | 600.00 | 400.00 | 200.00 |
| Your OOP | 1,000.00 | 15.00 | 985.00 |
| Fam OOP | 3,000.00 | 525.00 | 3,472.00 |

**Claim Information**

| | |
|---|---|
| Claim # | 123AB45 |
| Date Rcd | 9/26/96 |
| Policy # | 1481 |
| Group # | 201 |
| Benefit Yr | 1996 |

**Claim Summary**

| | |
|---|---|
| Charges | 261.00 |
| Disallow. | 50.00 |
| Pending | 46.25 |
| Deduct. | 5.00 |
| OOP | 15.00 |
| Copay | 0.00 |
| Ins Paid | 85.00 |
| Pat. pays | 20.00 |

| Svc. Date | Billed Amt | PPO Amt | Amt Not Allowed | Rsn Cde | Amt Pending | Rsn Cde | Cvge % | Ins. Paid | Ded. Amt. | OOP Amt. | Copay Amt | Patient Pays |
|---|---|---|---|---|---|---|---|---|---|---|---|---|
| 9/20/96 | 27.50 | 0.00 | | | 27.50 | a | | 0.00 | 0.00 | 0.00 | 0.00 | 0.00 |
| 9/20/96 | 50.00 | 0.00 | 50.00 | b | | | | 0.00 | 0.00 | 0.00 | 0.00 | 0.00 |
| 9/20/96 | 22.50 | 20.00 | | | | | 85% | 12.75 | 5.00 | 2.25 | 0.00 | 7.25 |
| 9/20/96 | 40.00 | 23.00 | | | | | 85% | 19.55 | 0.00 | 3.45 | 0.00 | 3.45 |
| 9/20/96 | 65.00 | 33.30 | | | | | 85% | 28.30 | 0.00 | 5.00 | 0.00 | 5.00 |
| 9/20/96 | 20.00 | 15.50 | | | | | 85% | 13.18 | 0.00 | 2.32 | 0.00 | 2.32 |
| 9/20/96 | 17.25 | 13.20 | | | | | 85% | 11.22 | 0.00 | 1.98 | 0.00 | 1.98 |
| 9/20/96 | 18.75 | 0.00 | | | 18.75 | a | | 0.00 | 0.00 | 0.00 | 0.00 | 0.00 |
| Totals | 261.00 | 105.00 | 50.00 | | 46.25 | | | 85.00 | 5.00 | 15.00 | 0.00 | 20.00 |

**Notes:**
a. Charge is pending further information requested from provider.
b. Charge is not allowed per the terms of the PPO contract.

## TRACKING FORM

**PATIENT:** Sally Sample  **PROVIDER:** Dr. Mu Nu  **YEAR:** 1996

| SVC DATE | BILLED AMT | PPO AMT | INS EOB DATE | INS AMT PAID | DED AMT | OOP AMT | COPAY AMT | PERS DUE | PERS PAID | PERS DTE PD | TOTAL PAID | BALANCE DUE | COMMENTS |
|---|---|---|---|---|---|---|---|---|---|---|---|---|---|
| 9/20 | 261.00 | 105.00 | 10/11 | 85.00 | 5.00 | 15.00 | 0.00 | 20.00 | 0.00 | | 85.00 | 20.00 | Waiting for pvdr. bill |
| | | | | | | | | | | | | | |
| | | | | | | | | | | | | | |
| | | | | | | | | | | | | | |
| | | | | | | | | | | | | | |
| | | | | | | | | | | | | | |

11. "Pers Dte Pd" is blank since the patient has not paid anything yet.
12. "Total Paid" is the sum of the "Ins Amt Paid" and "Pers Paid" on this line of the Tracking Form.
13. "Blnce Due" is "Pers Due" minus "Pers Paid."
14. "Comments" section is intended for the summary of the status of this EOB. In this case the patient is waiting for the provider's bill.

Never pay a provider before receiving a bill or statement. If you do, there's a very good chance that the payment will not be posted to your account. You need to include the bill or a portion of it with your payment so the person who posts receipts knows which account gets credit for the payment.

When you receive a bill from the provider and pay it, post to "Pers Due," "Pers Paid," "Pers Dte Pd," "Total Paid," and "Blnce Due." Then change the "Comments." I usually write: "Paid in full on (date)."

There is no need to track charges which are not allowed and those which are pending. The payment or non-payment of these charges is between the provider and your insurer. If the provider satisfied your insurer's request for more information on the two pending charges, your insurer would reimburse the preferred provider and issue an EOB, with a copy sent to you. You would be able to easily relate the follow-on EOB(s) to the original one, post to Tracking Form line for the 9/20/96 Service Date, and file the follow-on EOB in the binder with the original EOB.

If you have a personal computer, it's an easy matter to update the original EOB data from a new EOB for the same Service Date. If you do not have a personal computer, you can update the line on the Tracking Form. Make all your entries with a #2 pencil and use a good eraser. If you received an EOB showing that the two charges that were pending are now processed and paid, you would erase the original entries and post the updated amount.

In this example, you would add the "PPO Amt" from the new EOB to the "PPO Amt" of $105.00 on the Tracking Form and post the new total to the Tracking Form "PPO Amt." The "Billed Amt" would not be changed. The pending charges were included in the "Billed Amt" column of the original EOB. You would post to the summary line, adding the totals from the new EOB "Ins Paid" to "Ins Amt Paid" and "Total Paid"; "Ded Amt" to "Ded Amt"; "OOP Amt" to "OOP Amt"; "Copay Amt" to "Copay Amt"; and "Patient Pays" to the "Pers Due" and "Blnce Due." Mrs. Sample paid the last $5.00 of her $200 annual deductible; therefore, the "Ded Amt" would not change. There also would not be any changes in the "Copay Amt" column, since there were no copay charges for the procedures performed.

There are times when a single EOB has several pages. When that happens, I consider each page as a separate EOB and post one line for each page. There are other times when two service dates are on one page of an EOB. I post one line per service date per EOB. As long as I have the EOB date in the entry, I can find the original EOB, which I file as one EOB. I vary from "One EOB = One Tracking Form," but keep the EOBs together in the binder. I do this to make it easier to keep track of where I am and to be able to find the original EOB and subsequent documentation when disputes arise.

When disputes arise and last for months, you need to be very clear in your understanding of the situation. You need to know where you stand and why. You won't want to reconstruct everything that has happened on the charges in question every time you receive an EOB or a billing statement. That's when you will really be glad that you kept your Tracking Forms and your filing current. You will also be thankful that you kept good notes and have them filed with the EOBs. That leads us into our next topic.

*Write down the topics to be discussed and the questions you want to ask before you place a call. Write the date, time, and name of the person with whom you speak on the same sheet of paper. Then use the paper for notes during the phone conversation.*

### Take Notes When You Call

Whenever you speak to anyone at the insurance company or the medical provider's office about your account, a specific bill, or an Explanation of Benefits, take names and notes. Write the date and time of the conversation, the name of the person with whom you spoke, and the commitments he or she made on a sheet of paper. Include your notes with the EOB or provider statement in your binder or file folder. If you have to follow up at a later time, your notes will lend authenticity to your recounting of the conversation and commitments that were made.

As you prepare to make a call, it's a good idea to list the points that you want to make on a sheet of paper. During the conversation, use the same sheet of paper to write down the name of the person with whom you spoke, the date, time, and notes of the conversation. The EOB referencing a patient, provider, and service date is the centerpiece of the medical billing and insurance reimbursement process. All documentation should be kept with that document for ease of reference.

If you have to follow up with the insurance or billing organization on unfulfilled commitments, call them again, reminding them of what they had promised to do. This time confirm the conversation with a letter.

*"What if I get dunning notices for a charge that I do not owe?"*
*Don't be bullied. You can do something about it.*

## Dealing with Dunning Notices

If after all your efforts to straighten out your account you receive demands for payment of money you do not owe, don't despair. You could be dealing with a billing service under contract to your provider. Perhaps your provider is part of a large organization, in which case you're dealing with a corporate billing department. The people in billing may be dealing with thousands of small transactions every day and are likely under pressure to do more. You may find that the people you talk to on the phone are pleasant and helpful, but not in control of the system that is causing you a headache. I found myself in this situation many times.

From my experience there are steps you can take if the people you call or write do not correct the error in your account. First, call their manager. I was never able to reach a billing department or insurance manager by phone. In one case, I tried three times to reach a particular manager without success. My persistence, however, paid off. A member of the manager's staff was authorized to work on and solve my problem after I left my third voice mail message. The problem was quickly resolved.

Second, write to their manager. I did this a number of times. I never received a reply, but my problems were sometimes solved at this level. Third, write the physician in charge of the practice. Give the doctor a brief outline of the problem and what you have done to try to resolve it. Enclose copies of letters and any pertinent documentation you have sent to the billing department. Ask the doctor to give the letter and documentation to his or her office manager with instructions to resolve the problem. One letter to the doctor in charge of the practice finally resolved twenty billing problems I had been calling and writing to the billing department about for six months. Obviously, this is not something that you should have to do on a regular basis.

If, after writing to the billing manager, your doctor, the doctor in charge of the practice, or to the CEO, dunning notices continue, call the office of the person you wrote and leave a message. Let the appropriate executive or doctor know that you are going to an outside advocate. Briefly describe your reason for doing so and the date on which you intend to contact an advocate. If corrective action is not taken and you are not contacted by the executive or his or her representative, consider that as your final answer.

I never had to go to an outside advocate, but I was ready to do so on one occasion. I said that I would do so if the problem was not resolved in 48 hours. A series of problems going back nine months were resolved within 24 hours.

If you feel you need an advocate, call your state "Department of Consumer Affairs" or its equivalent in your state. Their number should be listed in the State Government section of the white pages of your local telephone directory. When you call, be ready to briefly describe the nature of your problem. Tell them you need a consumer advocate in the department or agency with regulatory authority over your provider or health insurance company or both. They should be able to point you in the right direction.

## ▼ KEY POINTS     Managing Medical Bills and Insurance Reimbursement

1. HMO members should not receive bills from providers if they use HMO resources.

2. HMOs are required by law to have a patient advocacy function.

3. Fee-For-Service and Preferred Provider Options billing and reimbursement systems are error prone, especially with high volume, specialized health care providers.

4. Learn how to read your Explanation of Benefits (EOBs) and Explanation of Medicare Benefits (EOMBs). Compare them to the EOB example and explanation in this chapter.

5. Know the rules of your policy.

6. React immediately when you receive an incorrect bill, EOB, or EOMB.

7. Take notes, dates, times, and names during telephone conversations.

8. Keep track of insurance and your payments for the year.

9. Don't be intimidated by dunning notices: use the techniques found in this chapter to deal with them.

# Summary

---

Once in a while, read this summary,
the Key Points highlighted throughout the book,
the glossary to sharpen up your vocabulary,
and the section on preparing for an office visit.

---

- Sooner or later you or a member of your family will have to deal with a serious medical problem emotionally, medically, and financially. Don't worry about it, but be prepared to deal with it.
- If you're going to get the care you need and not be in the dark, you need to participate in the management of your health care.
- The more freedom of choice, the more it costs. The more managed your care, the less it costs.
- Remember a lesson we learned from the "Sample Example." "You do not know what your insurance covers until you know what it does not cover."
- By studying your options, you can have quality health care as a Medicare beneficiary at relatively low cost.
- The person who can no longer live alone, but who does not need medical care, falls through the safety net of the Medicare Program.
- "When does Medicaid take over?" Hopefully for your sake, never.
- Don't leave your fate in the hands of a stranger. Execute a Durable Power of Attorney for health care decisions.
- If you're going to deal effectively with billing companies or departments, you need to know your financial responsibilities and stay on top of your insurance plan, commercial or Medicare.
- Good doctor/patient communications are the key to your getting the best health care available to you.

- When asking your doctor about your prognosis, the old adage is true. "It ain't what you say: it's the way how you say it."
- When talking to the insurer's claims office or the provider's billing department, take names, dates, times and make notes.
- I have yet to meet a medical professional who did not enjoy helping people.

# PART V

# Appendices

# Glossary

**Advocacy Program**—The function within an HMO that supports the HMO's members when they have a grievance.

**Advocate**—A person who speaks on behalf of another. In the context of this text, an advocate is someone who represents a patient's position against the members of the medical profession or insurance industry.

**Attained-Age Rates**—Rates that provide for Medicare HMO pricing based on the age of the member at the time he or she joins a Medicare HMO which bases its pricing on this rating technique. Increases are planned to take effect as a member grows older. There is also an annual adjustment for inflation. These Medicare HMOs tend to be the lowest cost Medicare HMOs at age 65 and the highest cost Medicare HMOs in the member's advanced years.

**Block Grants**—The transfer of Federal Government budgeted funding to other governmental or quasi-governmental entities (e.g., state governments).

**CAP**—The limit on the amount of coverage that the insurance company will provide (e.g., $250,000 lifetime limit per patient).

**Capitation**—One of the techniques used by HMOs to pay providers for specific services performed for members of the HMO. The HMO pays a set amount per member per month or quarter multiplied by the number of members in the HMO (e.g., $1/month × 50,000 members = $50,000).

**Carve-Outs**—An HMO practice of contracting with a highly specialized practice (e.g., cancer treatment center, liver transplant team) to treat members needing their services. The HMO is said to "carve-out" in this example, cancer treatment and liver transplants.

**Case Management**—An HMO function which monitors and coordinates the treatment of patients who are seriously or chronically ill, have long term hospital stays, or have other problems requiring multi-specialty long-term care. This function is over and above the health care management role of the "Primary Care Physician" ("PCP").

**Chronic Illness**—An ongoing and recurring health problem requiring periodic treatment.

**Claims Office**—The insurance claims processing and reimbursement function of an insurance company.

**COBRA**—The law (Consolidated Omnibus Budget Reconciliation Act) that allows employees having employer health insurance to convert it, at the time of their resignation or involuntary termination from employment, into personal and family health insurance for 18 months (36 months with certain health problems).

**Community Rates**—Rates that provide for Medicare HMO pricing based on the average age of the "community" of its members. All members pay the same membership fees. Prices cannot be raised except for inflation adjustments. Medicare HMOs using this rating technique tend to be the highest cost Medicare HMOs at age 65 and the lowest cost Medicare HMOs in a member's advanced years.

**Copayments**—A stipulated amount that the patient must pay each time he or she receives a specified service (e.g., $15/office visit).

**CPT Code**—The "Physicians' Current Procedural Terminology," which is a systematic listing of codes used for the procedures and services performed for patients by medical providers. Members of the medical profession and the health care insurance industry use the term "CPT Codes" to refer to these five-digit codes.

**Credentialing**—An on-going assessment of a physician's qualifications to practice medicine and in the doctor's chosen specialty, if he or she is considered a specialist.

**Custodial Care**—The nature of care required by those who cannot perform the most basic of human functions on their own, but do not have major medical problems requiring physician or skilled nursing attention.

**Deductible**—The amount a patient must pay for health care within a year (e.g., $200) before receiving insurance benefits (e.g., reimbursement).

**Direct Contract Model HMO**—An HMO that contracts with individual physicians to provide health care services to its patients under protocols defined by the HMO.

**Disability Insurance**—An insurance policy that provides a disabled person with a monthly income to help offset the loss of his or her regular income if he or she became disabled while the policy was in force.

**Disability Premium Waiver**—An insurance policy provision that is available at extra cost. It provides for the payment of your premium on the policy if you become disabled while the policy is in force.

**Disallowed Charges**—The charges that an insurer refuses to reimburse. Disallowed charges can occur when the procedure is not appropriate for the disease as defined by the ICD-9 code, a patient's insurance policy does not provide coverage for the procedure, or when the provider and the insurance company have an agreement that certain CPT codes will not be reimbursable under specific circumstances.

**Encounter**—A term used by physicians, medical staffs, and claims office personnel to refer to interactions with patients without disclosing the nature of the patient's visit (e.g., office visit, consultation, examination).

**Enzyme**—A complex protein produced in living cells. It is able to cause changes in other cells without being changed itself. It is a catalyst. As used in this text, it is a condition in the cells of the body detected by certain tests as part of a diagnostic regimen. The tests indicate whether the enzymes are at an abnormal level in given cells, too low, or too high.

**Exclusive Provider Option**—A health care insurance plan in which the providers are members of a local physician network which has been recruited by an employer to provide discounted managed care to the employer's employees.

**Explanation Of Benefits (EOB)**—A report sent to the provider and the patient if the provider submitted the claim or just to the patient if the patient submitted a claim for insurance reimbursement. It shows the amount charged for each procedure, the amount reimbursed, and the detailed explanation of the reasons for the payment or non-payment of parts or all of the claim. It accompanies any payment that is made.

**Facilities**—Facility health care providers including **laboratories** (e.g., chemical, radiology), **emergency care centers**, **hospitals**, **clinics**, and **other facilities**.

**Facility Sources**—Ways in which HMOs provide their members with access to health care facilities such as hospitals, laboratories, and other facilities.

**Federal ID**—A number assigned to an individual or a corporate entity and used by the person or corporate entity for identification and to relate his, her, or its role in a particular situation.

**Fee-For-Service**—The practice of going to a medical provider (e.g., doctor, laboratory) of our choice and paying for the service performed, personally or through insurance. It offers maximum flexibility and choice for the patient, at maximum cost.

**Formulary**—The list of low cost drugs your HMO physician may use to prescribe to you, if you have prescription coverage with the HMO.

**Gatekeeper**—A colloquial name given to the "Primary Care Physician" who, in a managed care or an HMO environment, controls access to other providers.

**Group Contracted**—Facilities under contract to "Medical Groups."

**Group Model HMO**—An HMO whose members receive medical care, under protocols defined by the HMO, from doctors belonging to a "Medical Group," also known as "Group Practice."

**Group Practice**—A number of physicians who are organized as a partnership, professional corporation, or in some other type association. The Group's administrative function compensates its physicians and enters into contractual relationships with other organizations (e.g., hospitals, HMOs) on their behalf.

**Health Care Prepayment Plan**—One of five types of agreements that an insurance company or an HMO can have with Medicare. The Medicare HMOs who have this agreement with Medicare provide Medicare Part A coverage. They may provide Part B type of coverage, which would not be governed by Medicare rules.

**The Health Insurance Portability and Accountability Act**—The law that assures employees having employer group health care insurance that they and their covered dependents will be insurable under a new employer's health insurance plan within one year of employment and that they can buy the coverage they had until their new employer insurance becomes effective.

**Health Maintenance Organization (HMO)**—A form of health insurance based on preventive medicine and maintaining of the wellness of its enrollees. Individuals join as members and receive their care through the personnel and facilities that are part of the organization or are under contract to provide health care to the organization's members.

**Health Plan Employer Data and Information Set (HEDIS)**—A computer-resident database containing individual HMO's data on 60 "quality of care measurements" (e.g., credentialing, average duration of appointments, specialist appointments average wait times).

**HMO Contracted**—Facilities under contract to an HMO.

**HMO Owned**—The HMO's own facilities.

**Home Health Care**—Medicare Part A benefits provided to patients who are confined to their homes under a physician's care and who need periodic skilled nursing care, physical therapy, or speech therapy. The services are provided without charge to the patient by a Medicare approved home health agency's skilled nurses or home health aides.

**Hospice Care**—The benefits provided by Medicare to those who are in terminal condition and within six months of death, in their physician's judgment.

**Hospitalization Supplemental Insurance**—An insurance policy that pays the policyholder(s) a preset amount for each day spent as a hospital inpatient or outpatient.

**ICD-9**—The commonly used term for *The International Classification of Diseases, 9th Revision,* which is a listing of diseases associated with a five-digit code, three to the left of the decimal and two to the right. These codes are used to specify the disease for which the patient is being treated.

**Indemnity Insurance Company**—An organization that will indemnify (pay for) pre-identified types of losses, which you may incur, in return for your payment of premiums, based on the indemnity insurance company's actuarial risk of incurring losses.

**Independent Physician Association (IPA)**—An organization formed by entrepreneurial doctors to perform services for its member physicians with the bargaining power of an association and at a reduced cost to the individual physicians.

**IPA Model HMO**—An HMO whose members receive medical care, under protocols defined by the HMO, from doctors who are part of an "Independent Physician Association."

**Issue-Age Rates**—Medicare HMO pricing based on the age of the member at the time he or she joined. Prices cannot be raised except to adjust for inflation. Medicare HMOs which use this rating technique tend to cost more at age 65 than Medicare HMOs using an "Attained-Age" rating technique. As a member advances in years, the costs goes up but only by the amount of inflation.

**Long-Term Care**—The non-medical assistance provided to a person who is unable to perform the most basic human functions on his or her own.

**Long-Term Care Insurance**—A form of insurance that helps pay for the daily cost of a stay in a nursing home for non-medical care.

**Managed Care Plan**—A Fee-For-Service type plan in which the policyholder sees an assigned doctor who manages his or her care and who, as needed, refers the patient to providers who participate in the plan.

**Medform**—A form developed by the author for keeping track of vital signs and medications prescribed and taken.

**Medicaid**—A joint federal and state program which provides health care to those members of our society who otherwise would not have access to any health care.

**Medicare**—A federally sponsored insurance program which provides health care insurance for Americans age 65 and older and the disabled of all ages who meet the requirements for coverage.

**Medicare Cost Plan**—One of five types of agreements that an insurance company or an HMO can have with Medicare. The Medicare HMOs who have this agreement with Medicare provide Medicare Part A and Part B coverage. Their members may pay copayments and receive all health care from providers affiliated with the Medicare HMO. If they go to other providers, Medicare will pay in accordance with its coverage provisions. The members would be responsible for deductibles and co-payments to the non-affiliated providers.

**Medicare HMO**—A Health Maintenance Organization which has been approved to provide Medicare benefits in compliance with one of five types of agreements (e.g., "Medicare Cost Plan," "Health Care Prepayment Plan," "Medicare Risk Plan").

**Medicare HMO Agreements**—The contracts which insurance companies and HMOs sign with Medicare. These agreements (e.g., "Medicare Cost Plan," "Health Care Prepayment Plan," "Medicare Risk Plan") govern the insurer's and the HMO's relationship with Medicare and the way in which they can provide Medicare benefits.

**Medicare Part A**—Hospitalization insurance for Medicare beneficiaries.

**Medicare Part B**—Doctor and other medical insurance for Medicare beneficiaries.

**Medicare Risk Plan**—One of five types of agreements that an insurance company or an HMO can have with Medicare. The Medicare HMOs who have this agreement with Medicare provide Medicare Part A and Part B coverage. Their members can be locked into receiving all health care from providers affiliated with the Medicare HMO.

**Medicare Select Plan**—One of five types of agreements that an insurance company or an HMO can have with Medicare. The "Select Plans" are managed care versions of the ten Medigap Plans. Twenty states are authorized to offer "Select Plans" as experimental extensions to Medigap.

**Medigap**—Ten standardized and approved insurance plans to fill some of the gaps in Medicare coverage. The plans pay some or all of a beneficiary's coinsurance responsibilities and also offer some extensions to Medicare coverage. Each of the ten plans has a different set of coverages to be offered by Medicare-approved insurance carriers at rates set by them. The carriers sign one of five "Medicare Agreements," known as the "Traditional Medicare Supplement Policy."

**Membership Agreement**—The HMO document that spells out the details of your coverage and restrictions.

**National Committee for Quality Assurance (NCQA)**—An organization made up of representatives from HMOs and large corporations. It has its roots in the 1980s, when a number of employers wanted a way to evaluate the HMO plans that they had begun offering as part of their employee benefit plans. This group developed HEDIS for this purpose and have continued to refine it and expand its usage.

**Network Model HMO**—An HMO that contracts with two or more group practices to provide health care services to the HMO's patients, under protocols defined by the HMO.

**Nursing Home Care**—The non-medical assistance provided in a nursing home to a person who is unable to perform the most basic human functions on his or her own.

**Office Visit**—The encounter a patient has when he or she "goes to the doctor."

**Other Model HMOs**—HMO variations that use non-HMO medical personnel and facilities. The HMO may have some employee staff members and own some facilities, but if it also contracts with others for physicians, medical staff, and facilities, it is not a "Staff Model HMO."

**Out-of-Pocket Expense (OOP)**—The amount of money a patient must pay annually as a percentage of the cost of his or her health care, after having paid an annual deductible amount, if that provision is also part of the patient's insurance policy. OOP is also referred to as "coinsurance."

**Pending Charges**—The charges for procedure codes which an insurer will not reimburse without further explanation.

**Per Diem**—The arrangement HMOs sometimes make with hospitals to pay a fixed rate per day of hospital occupancy, per member, per type of care provided by the hospital (e.g., surgery, critical care, maternity).

**Point of Service HMO Plan**—An HMO plan that offers members the freedom to go to preferred providers at an additional cost and to go to any licensed provider at still greater cost.

**Pre-Authorization**—The requirement for an HMO member to obtain permission before visiting an emergency room or other facility for medical care.

**Preferred Provider**—A professional or facility that provides health care and has signed a contract with an insurance company to do so at a discount for its policyholders.

**Preferred Provider Option (PPO Plan)**—An option provided as an adjunct to a Fee-For-Service Plan. The insured can use any of the Preferred Providers who have signed a contract with the insurance company to accept discounted fees for their services and file for reimbursement directly with the insurance company's claims office.

**Preferrer Provider Organization (PPO)**—The insurance company's view of the "Preferred Providers." The insurance company signs providers to a contract as "Preferred Providers" and is then able to sell a "Preferred Provider Plan."

**Preferred Provider Organization Contract**—A document signed by health providers agreeing to file claims directly with a claims office and to accept discounted reimbursement for their services.

**Primary Care Physician (PCP)**—The physician assigned as a health care manager to each patient having Managed Care Insurance and to each member of an HMO. He or she also functions as a "Gatekeeper," controlling all access to other providers.

**Protocols**—The set of written procedures that are to be followed under given medical situations.

**Provider**—A professional or facility that provides health care.

**Quality Compass**—A report on the quality of care provided in 200 HMOs, as measured using HEDIS.

**Respite Care**—The non-medical assistance provided to a person who is unable to perform the most basic human functions on his or her own.

**Self-refer**—The right of a patient to determine when and to whom to go for health care.

**Staff Model HMO**—An HMO with physicians and medical personnel on its payroll and its own hospitals, laboratories, clinics, and other facilities to minister to the preventive and other health care needs of its members.

**Status Post (S/P)**—A modifier used to describe that the procedure has been performed or a condition has been remedied, as in "Liver Transplant Status Post" or "Liver Transplant S/P."

**Stop-Loss**—An insurance policy that indemnifies the policy buyer from costs above a pre-set limit (e.g., $250,000), at which level the indemnifying organization starts to pay.

**Third Party Administrator (TPA)**—The role filled by an insurance company when, for a fee, it performs all the insurance processes for a policy funded by an employer or other group.

**Traditional Medicare Supplement Policy**—The agreement a Medigap carrier enters into with Medicare. It governs Medigap carriers and the policies they are allowed to offer to Medicare beneficiaries.

**Usual and Customary**—The phrase that describes allowable insurance claim charge amounts for the procedures performed in the provider's community.

**Utilization Management**—A process used by insurance companies and HMOs to evaluate the diagnostic, treatment and billing practices that a doctor has used over a period of time.

**Utilization Review**—An insurance company's or HMO's evaluation of a procedure proposed by a physician. The evaluation is based on the patient's problem, the need to perform the procedure, and a judgment of the effectiveness of the proposed procedure in the given situation. The physician may be required to personally justify the procedure proposed for the patient. If he or she cannot justify it, it will not be allowed.

**Vital Sign**—The critical conditions and processes of the human body (e.g., pulse, blood pressure).

# Information Directory

 ### Doctor Information

*The American Medical Directory*, American Medical Association (AMA)
Available in Public Libraries

**Biographical Information on Specific Doctors (Fee Service)**

American Medical Association (AMA)
Department of Physician Data Services
Dept. P
515 North State Street
Chicago, IL 60610

**Board Certification Information**

The American Board of Medical Specialties (1-800-776-2378)

**Disciplined Physicians List for Each State (Fee Service)**

Public Citizen Health Research Group
Dept. P
1600 20th Street, N.W.
Washington, D.C. 20009

**Discipline and Formal Charge Information**

Your State Medical Board

## Health Maintenance Organizations (HMO)

National Committee for Quality Assurance (NCQA)
1-202-955-3515
http://www.ncqa.org

 ## Long-Term Care Insurance

National Association of Insurance Commissioners
120 West 12th Street
Kansas City, MO 64105

United Seniors Health Cooperative
(1-202-393-6222)

 ## Medicaid

Your county's Social Services Agency
(Look under County Government Offices in the Government Pages of your local telephone directory)

Local office of the Social Security Administration
(Local office of the Social Security Administration is listed in the business section or in the United States Government pages of your local telephone directory white pages, or call the Social Security Hotline, 1-800-638-6833, for the number.)

 ## Medical Database Access and Report Services

CANHELP
Port Ludlow, WA
Voice: 1-206-437-2291

Georgia Consumer Center
Atlanta, GA
Voice: 1-404-256-2528

HealthGate™ Data Corp.
380 Pleasant Street
Suite 230
Malden, MA 02148
Voice: 1-800-434-4283
FAX: 1-617-321-2262
http://www.healthgate.com
info@healthgate.com (Mail)
(Layman language database queries)

Health Responsibility Systems, Inc.
585 Grove Street
Suite 320
Herndon, VA 22070
Voice: 1-703-904-6900
FAX: 1-703-904-6908
(Access to database of medical articles through America On-line, Inc.)

H.E.R.M.E.S.
Consumer Medical Search
Marina, CA
Voice: 1-800-484-9863 Ext. 5773

MEDcetera, Inc.
4515 Merrie Lane
Bellaire, TX 77401
Voice: 1-800-748-6866
 1-713-664-3222
FAX: 1-713-664-6891
(Standard and customized reports with treatment options, including alternative medicine)

MEDSCAN
Johnson City, NY
1-800-MED-8145

PaperChase®
350 Longwood Avenue
Boston, MA 02115
Voice: 1-800-722-2075
 1-617-278-3900
FAX: 1-617-278-9792
http://www.paperchase.com
(Database searches through a variety of access methods including CompuServe)

The Health Resource, Inc.
564 Locust Street
Conway, AR 72032
Voice: 1-800-949-0090
 1-501-329-5272
FAX: 1-501-329-9489
(Standard and customized reports with treatment options, including alternative medicine)

Planetree
San Francisco, CA
1-415-923-3681

Schine On-Line
   Providence, RI
   1-800-FIND-CURE

World Research Foundation
   Sherman Oaks, CA
   1-818-907-5483

## ▶ Medicare

Local Social Security Administration office
   (Local office is listed in business section or the "United States Government" pages of your local telephone directory white pages or call the Social Security Administration Hotline 1-800-638-6833)

## ▶ Medigap

Local Social Security Administration office
   (Local office is listed in the business section or in the "United States Government" pages of your local telephone directory white pages or call the Social Security Administration Hotline 1-800-638-6833)

*Consumer Reports* (Articles 8/94 & 9/94)
   Consumers Union
   Bulk Reprints
   101 Truman Avenue
   Yonkers, NY 10703-1057

## ▶ Nursing Homes

*Consumer Reports* (Articles 8/95, 9/95, 10/95)
   Consumers Union
   Bulk Reprints
   101 Truman Avenue
   Yonkers, NY 10703-1057

The National Association for Home Care
   (1-202-547-7424)

The National Council on Aging
   (1-202-479-1200)

**Senior Organizations**

Information on State and Local Agencies
  The Eldercare Locator (1-800-677-1116)

American Association of Retired Persons
  (1-800-424-3410)

Council On Aging
  (Look under Council on Aging in business section of local white pages or call your county's information number to be found under County Government Offices in the Government Pages of your local white pages)

Health Insurance Counseling and Advocacy Program (HICAP)
  (Look under HICAP or Council on Aging in business section of local white pages or call your county's information number to be found under County Government Offices in the Government Pages of your local white pages)

Health Insurance Information and Counseling
  (Office for your region or state is listed in Your Medicare Handbook or call the Social Security Administration Hotline 1-800-638-6833)

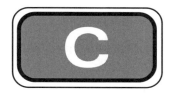

# Reading List

Health care is in the news on a daily basis, and all of us need to keep up with developments. We can no longer rely on employers to hire us and provide us with rich insurance and retirement benefits. We each need to be informed about federal and state legislation and its impact on our health care coverage, costs, and security. We need to know what insurance we have now—what our current options are and what to expect as we plan for our retirement years.

Based on this need for information, I put together a reading list. Television news and documentaries are good sources of information but cannot supplant the print media, which can afford to go into more depth on the subject.

 **Current Information News Sources:**

1. Your local newspaper

2. A major city newspaper

3. Weekly news magazines

4. "The Jim Lehrer News Hour" (Public Broadcasting System, Monday–Friday)

### Current Insurance Status and Options:

1. Your current health care insurance policy or its coverage summary
2. Coverage and cost summary of other options offered to you by your employer
3. Information available from local insurers and HMOs
   (Write or call in response to radio, TV, and newspaper ads)

### Retirement Planning and Senior Insurance Information:

**Medicare Publications:**
**(Publication Number Appears in Parentheses)**

*Medicare* (ICN 460000)

*Your Medicare Handbook* (SSA ICN 61250)

*Guide to Health Insurance for People with Medicare* (518B)*

*Medicare: Coverage for Second Surgical Opinion* (521B)*

*Medicare: Hospice Benefits* (591B)*

*Medicare and Managed Care Plans* (592B)*

*Medicare and Other Health Benefits* (593B)*

*Medicare Coverage of Kidney Dialysis and Kidney Transplant Services* (594B)*

*Medicare: Savings for Qualified Beneficiaries* (596B)*

*Medicare and Your Physician's Bill* (520B)*

*Medicare and Advance Directives* (519B)*

*Continuous Improvement* (637A)*

*Manual De Medicare* (595B)*

(*Available free of charge from: Consumer Information Center, Department 33, Pueblo, CO 81009)

**AARP Publications:**

*Medicare—What It Covers—What It Doesn't*

*Knowing Your Rights* (Medicare's Prospective Payment System)

*Medigap–Medicare Supplemental Insurance* (A Consumer's Guide)

*Tomorrow's Choices* (Preparing Now for Future Legal, Financial, and Health Care Decisions)

*A Matter of Choice* (Planning Ahead for Health Care Decisions)

*Making Wise Decisions for Long-term Care Before You Buy* (A Guide to Long-Term Care Insurance)

**Council on Aging Agency Publications:**

Health Insurance Counseling and Advocacy Program (HICAP) Bulletins and Newsletters

Information Referral Services

*Directory of Senior Services and Agencies* (aka, Senior Handbook)

**Consumer Reports:**

*Filling the Gaps in Medicare (Part 1: Medigap Insurance Policies)* – 8/94

*Medicare Under Siege (Part 2: Medigap Insurance)* – 9/94

*Nursing Homes (Part 1: When a Parent Needs Care—Ratings)* – 8/95

*Nursing Homes (Part 2: Who Pays for Nursing Homes?)* – 9/95

*Nursing Homes (Part 3: Alternatives—Assisted Living & Home Care)* – 10/95

# Forms

 **Forms for Manual Usage**

Medical Expenses
Health Care Plan Evaluation
HMO and Insurance Company Questions
Health Plan Enrollee Questions
Questions of Your Doctor About Commercial HMOs
Medigap Carrier and Medicare HMO Questions
Medigap Policyholder Questions
Medicare HMO Member Questions
Questions to Ask Your Doctor
Blank Question Form
Medicare–Medigap–HMO Coverage and Cost Worksheets
Medform
Medication History
Procedure Chronology
Tracking Form

**NOTE:** The reader of this book has the publisher's permission to reproduce the forms in this appendix. If you are borrowing this book from a library, please be considerate of the next reader by not marking on the forms.

## MEDICAL EXPENSES

| Expense Item | Monthly or Quarterly Expense | X 12 or X 4 Expenses | Annual Expense |
|---|---|---|---|
| Premium Expense | | | |
| Chiropractor | | | |
| Dentist | | | |
| Doctor | | | |
| Durable Equipment | | | |
| Hospital | | | |
| Laboratory | | | |
| Medicine | | | |
| Total Insurable Expenses | | | |
| Food | | | |
| Housing | | | |
| Mileage | | | |
| Total Other Expense | | | |
| Total Medical Expenses | | | |

## HEALTH CARE PLAN EVALUATION

| Date of Service | Family Member | Encounter | Billed Amount | Family Paid | Insurance Paid | Comments |
|---|---|---|---|---|---|---|
| | | | | | | |
| | | | | | | |
| | | | | | | |
| | | | | | | |
| | | | | | | |
| | | | | | | |
| | | | | | | |
| | | | | | | |
| | | | | | | |
| | | | | | | |
| | | | | | | |
| | | | | | | |
| | | | | | | |
| | | | | | | |
| | | | | | | |
| | | | | | | |
| | | | | | | |

## HMO AND INSURANCE COMPANY QUESTIONS

Plans: All          Importance: _____          Score: _____          Weighted Score: _____

Is there a maximum lifetime benefit?

If yes, how much is it?

Is it for each patient or for my whole family?

---

Plans: All          Importance: _____          Score: _____          Weighted Score: _____

Do you have disease or procedural limits?

If yes, what are they?

How much are they by disease or procedure?

---

Plans: All          Importance: _____          Score: _____          Weighted Score: _____

What procedures are considered "experimental"?

---

Plans: All          Importance: _____          Score: _____          Weighted Score: _____

Do you have carve-outs for certain diseases?

If yes, what are they?

Where do you send the patients for each disease?

---

Plans: All          Importance: _____          Score: _____          Weighted Score: _____

Is this a national policy or HMO?

If not, am I insured outside of your region?

How does that coverage work?

## HMO AND INSURANCE COMPANY QUESTIONS

| Plans: All | Importance: _____ | Score: _____ | Weighted Score: _____ |

Will I have worldwide health care coverage?

If yes, how does it work?

If no, what happens to my family or me if we need care while abroad?

---

| Plans: All | Importance: _____ | Score: _____ | Weighted Score: _____ |

May I have a list of your providers?

If not, why not?

---

| Plans: All | Importance: _____ | Score: _____ | Weighted Score: _____ |

What percentage of your providers out of residency for 5 years are board certified?

What percentage passed their Boards on the first try?

What percentage failed and are not Board Certified?

---

| Plans: HMO & M/C | Importance: _____ | Score: _____ | Weighted Score: _____ |

May I select my own Primary Care Physician?

If yes, will the PCP I want be available? (Ask before you sign up.)

---

| Plans: HMO & M/C | Importance: _____ | Score: _____ | Weighted Score: _____ |

From what fields do you draw your Primary Care Providers?

Can women have a gynecologist as their PCP?

Do you have pediatricians as PCPs?

## HMO AND INSURANCE COMPANY QUESTIONS

| Plans: HMO & M/C | Importance: _____ | Score: _____ | Weighted Score: _____ |

Are patients with chronic problems allowed to have a specialist as their PCP?

| Plans: HMO & M/C | Importance: _____ | Score: _____ | Weighted Score: _____ |

If being treated by a specialist for a problem that requires follow-up or continuing care, can my specialist become my PCP either temporarily or permanently?

| Plans: HMO & M/C | Importance: _____ | Score: _____ | Weighted Score: _____ |

If being treated by a specialist for a problem that requires follow-up or continuing care, do I have to have a PCP referral for each follow-up visit?

| Plans: HMO & M/C | Importance: _____ | Score: _____ | Weighted Score: _____ |

Are annual gynecological examinations and mammograms allowed without referral?

If not, why not?

| Plans: HMO & M/C | Importance: _____ | Score: _____ | Weighted Score: _____ |

Can infants and children be taken to pediatrician without a referral?

If not, why not?

| Plans: HMO & M/C | Importance: _____ | Score: _____ | Weighted Score: _____ |

What is the average wait (days) for a PCP appointment?

| Plans: HMO & M/C | Importance: _____ | Score: _____ | Weighted Score: _____ |

What is the average length (minutes) of PCP office visits?

## HMO AND INSURANCE COMPANY QUESTIONS

| | | | |
|---|---|---|---|
| Plans: HMO & M/C | Importance: _____ | Score: _____ | Weighted Score: _____ |

When a referral to a specialist occurs, what is the average length of wait (days) between being seen by the PCP and a specialist?

| | | | |
|---|---|---|---|
| Plans: HMO & M/C | Importance: _____ | Score: _____ | Weighted Score: _____ |

What is the average length (minutes) of specialist office visits?

| | | | |
|---|---|---|---|
| Plans: All | Importance: _____ | Score: _____ | Weighted Score: _____ |

What specialties participate in your plan?

What specialties do not participate in your plan?

| | | | |
|---|---|---|---|
| Plans: All | Importance: _____ | Score: _____ | Weighted Score: _____ |

What percentage of your specialists are Board Certified in their specialty?

What percentage passed on their first try?

What percentage failed and never have been Board Certified?

| | | | |
|---|---|---|---|
| Plans: HMO & M/C | Importance: _____ | Score: _____ | Weighted Score: _____ |

Where will I be referred if I need highly specialized medical care (e.g., rare disease treatment, transplant)?

| | | | |
|---|---|---|---|
| Plans: All | Importance: _____ | Score: _____ | Weighted Score: _____ |

May I request and receive a second opinion?

If yes, how would I go about getting the second opinion?

## HMO AND INSURANCE COMPANY QUESTIONS

| Plans: All | Importance: _____ | Score: _____ | Weighted Score: _____ |

What hospitals do you use?

| Plans: All | Importance: _____ | Score: _____ | Weighted Score: _____ |

What are the rules regarding Emergency Room care?

| Plans: All | Importance: _____ | Score: _____ | Weighted Score: _____ |

What is the procedure for pre-authorizations?

Emergency Room?

Outpatient?

Inpatient?

| Plans: All | Importance: _____ | Score: _____ | Weighted Score: _____ |

What are the coverage provisions if I have a life-threatening emergency (e.g., heart attack, hemorrhage, serious accident) and do not get a pre-authorization? If I'm unconscious? If my family is too distraught?

| Plans: All | Importance: _____ | Score: _____ | Weighted Score: _____ |

What is the procedure for pre-authorization exceptions?

| Plans: All | Importance: _____ | Score: _____ | Weighted Score: _____ |

What is the prescription drug benefit?

## HMO AND INSURANCE COMPANY QUESTIONS

| Plans: All | Importance: _____ | Score: _____ | Weighted Score: _____ |

I have a list of my current prescriptions and need to know which of my medications are not in your formulary?

| Plans: All | Importance: _____ | Score: _____ | Weighted Score: _____ |

Do you have other brands of the same drug?

If so what are they?

| Plans: All | Importance: _____ | Score: _____ | Weighted Score: _____ |

Do you have substitute drugs?

If so, what are they?

| Plans: All | Importance: _____ | Score: _____ | Weighted Score: _____ |

What are the caps on your prescription benefits?

| Plans: All | Importance: _____ | Score: _____ | Weighted Score: _____ |

Does your prescription benefit have copayment or coinsurance provisions?

If yes, what are they?

Is that all I have to pay?

| Plans: All | Importance: _____ | Score: _____ | Weighted Score: _____ |

Do you have a formal complaint program?

If yes, please describe it.

## HMO AND INSURANCE COMPANY QUESTIONS

| | | | |
|---|---|---|---|
| Plans: All | Importance: _____ | Score: _____ | Weighted Score: _____ |

Do your patients have an Advocate to whom they can appeal?

If yes, please describe how that function works.

| | | | |
|---|---|---|---|
| Plans: All | Importance: _____ | Score: _____ | Weighted Score: _____ |

If after going through your advocacy or grievance program I am not satisfied with the answer, to whom do I go in your management?

To whom do I go for outside advocacy or arbitration?

| | | | |
|---|---|---|---|
| Plans: All | Importance: _____ | Score: _____ | Weighted Score: _____ |

What measurement criteria are used in the evaluation of your doctors?

What is the weighting for each of the measurement criteria?

| | | | |
|---|---|---|---|
| Plans: HMO | Importance: _____ | Score: _____ | Weighted Score: _____ |

What was the NCQA rating by your HMO membership for each of the last 3 years?

| | | | |
|---|---|---|---|
| Plans: HMO | Importance: _____ | Score: _____ | Weighted Score: _____ |

What was your overall NCQA rating for each of the last 3 years?

| | | | |
|---|---|---|---|
| Plans: | Importance: _____ | Score: _____ | Weighted Score: _____ |

## HMO AND INSURANCE COMPANY QUESTIONS

Plans:  Importance: _____  Score: _____  Weighted Score: _____

Plans:  Importance: _____  Score: _____  Weighted Score: _____

Plans:  Importance: _____  Score: _____  Weighted Score: _____

Plans:  Importance: _____  Score: _____  Weighted Score: _____

Plans:  Importance: _____  Score: _____  Weighted Score: _____

Plans:  Importance: _____  Score: _____  Weighted Score: _____

Plans:  Importance: _____  Score: _____  Weighted Score: _____

## HEALTH CARE PLAN ENROLLEE QUESTIONS

| | | | |
|---|---|---|---|
| Plans: All | Importance: _____ | Score: _____ | Weighted Score: _____ |

How do you like the plan?

| | | | |
|---|---|---|---|
| Plans: All | Importance: _____ | Score: _____ | Weighted Score: _____ |

How long have you been receiving care under this plan?

| | | | |
|---|---|---|---|
| Plans: All | Importance: _____ | Score: _____ | Weighted Score: _____ |

What plan did you have before this one?

| | | | |
|---|---|---|---|
| Plans: All | Importance: _____ | Score: _____ | Weighted Score: _____ |

Why did you change over to this plan?

| | | | |
|---|---|---|---|
| Plans: HMO & M/C | Importance: _____ | Score: _____ | Weighted Score: _____ |

How do you like your Primary Care Physician?

| | | | |
|---|---|---|---|
| Plans: HMO & M/C | Importance: _____ | Score: _____ | Weighted Score: _____ |

How long do you have to wait to get an appointment with your Primary Care Physician?

| | | | |
|---|---|---|---|
| Plans: HMO & M/C | Importance: _____ | Score: _____ | Weighted Score: _____ |

How are you treated on the phone when you call for an appointment?

| | | | |
|---|---|---|---|
| Plans: HMO & M/C | Importance: _____ | Score: _____ | Weighted Score: _____ |

Have you ever had any problems that required help from a specialist?

If yes, how long did it take to get to see the specialist?

## HEALTH CARE PLAN ENROLLEE QUESTIONS

| Plans: HMO & M/C | Importance: _____ | Score: _____ | Weighted Score: _____ |

Does your Primary Care Physician listen to you?

| Plans: HMO | Importance: _____ | Score: _____ | Weighted Score: _____ |

Have you ever been sent a bill that you should not have received?

If yes, how did your HMO deal with it?

Was it a problem? Or did one phone call take care of it?

| Plans: PPO & M/C | Importance: _____ | Score: _____ | Weighted Score: _____ |

When the Claims Office sends out an erroneous Explanation of Benefits (EOB):

Do they admit the error and take charge of correcting it?

Does it take more than one call from you?

Do you have to manage communications between the Claims Office and the Provider?

| Plans: All | Importance: _____ | Score: _____ | Weighted Score: _____ |

Have you ever received an incorrect statement from your insurer?

If yes, how did your insurer deal with it?

What caused the problem?

Did one phone call take care of it?

Who corrected it?

How long did it take to straighten it out?

## HEALTH CARE PLAN ENROLLEE QUESTIONS

| Plans: All | Importance: _____ | Score: _____ | Weighted Score: _____ |

What do you like most about the plan?

| Plans: All | Importance: _____ | Score: _____ | Weighted Score: _____ |

What do you like least about the plan?

| Plans: All | Importance: _____ | Score: _____ | Weighted Score: _____ |

I'm thinking of signing up for this plan; do you recommend it?

If yes (for HMO and M/C), who is your PCP?

| Plans: | Importance: _____ | Score: _____ | Weighted Score: _____ |

| Plans: | Importance: _____ | Score: _____ | Weighted Score: _____ |

| Plans: | Importance: _____ | Score: _____ | Weighted Score: _____ |

| Plans: | Importance: _____ | Score: _____ | Weighted Score: _____ |

| Plans: | Importance: _____ | Score: _____ | Weighted Score: _____ |

## QUESTIONS OF YOUR DOCTOR ABOUT COMMERCIAL HMOS

| Plans: HMO | Importance: _____ | Score: _____ | Weighted Score: _____ |

Do you have HMO patients?

If yes, from which HMOs?

| Plans: HMO | Importance: _____ | Score: _____ | Weighted Score: _____ |

Are you a Primary Care Provider for any HMOs?

If yes, which ones?

| Plans: HMO | Importance: _____ | Score: _____ | Weighted Score: _____ |

In your opinion, which HMOs do the best job on utilization reviews?

| Plans: HMO | Importance: _____ | Score: _____ | Weighted Score: _____ |

Do you feel that any of the HMOs intrude on your professional judgment?

| Plans: HMO | Importance: _____ | Score: _____ | Weighted Score: _____ |

With which HMOs are you able to refer patients to specialists by name?

Do you or your staff arrange for the appointment?

If not, does the HMO let you know when they have set it up?

| Plans: HMO | Importance: _____ | Score: _____ | Weighted Score: _____ |

If you were running an HMO and had a choice of how to pay physicians (e.g., capitation, hold backs, fees, salary), how would you do it?

Why?

## QUESTIONS OF YOUR DOCTOR ABOUT COMMERCIAL HMOS

Plans: HMO        Importance: _____        Score: _____        Weighted Score: _____

How are you compensated by the HMOs with whom you work?

Plans: HMO        Importance: _____        Score: _____        Weighted Score: _____

With which of the HMOs do you have the best working relationship?

Plans: HMO        Importance: _____        Score: _____        Weighted Score: _____

With which of the HMOs do you not have a good working relationship, if any?

Plans: HMO        Importance: _____        Score: _____        Weighted Score: _____

If you were going to recommend an HMO to a family member who had a choice of several HMOs offered through an employer benefits program, which one would you recommend?

Plans:        Importance: _____        Score: _____        Weighted Score: _____



Plans:        Importance: _____        Score: _____        Weighted Score: _____



Plans:        Importance: _____        Score: _____        Weighted Score: _____



Plans:        Importance: _____        Score: _____        Weighted Score: _____

## MEDIGAP CARRIER AND MEDICARE HMO QUESTIONS

Plans: Medigap  Importance: _____  Score: _____  Weighted Score: _____

How quickly do you turn around claims?

How do you measure claim turnaround?

What are your statistics on claim turnaround?

---

Plans: Medigap  Importance: _____  Score: _____  Weighted Score: _____

If you make an error on a claim, how do you handle making the correction?

Who is responsible for making the correction?

---

Plans: Medigap  Importance: _____  Score: _____  Weighted Score: _____

What is your claim error rate?

---

Plans: Medigap  Importance: _____  Score: _____  Weighted Score: _____

How do you measure and manage the quality of your claim processing?

What are your statistics on errors in claim processing?

---

Plans: Medigap  Importance: _____  Score: _____  Weighted Score: _____

If a client tells you that he or she is being billed by a provider, who sent in a claim months ago and was never reimbursed, what action do you take?

---

Plans: Medigap  Importance: _____  Score: _____  Weighted Score: _____

What will the providers tell me when I ask them about your claim processing?

## MEDIGAP CARRIER AND MEDICARE HMO QUESTIONS

| Plans: Medigap | Importance: _____ | Score: _____ | Weighted Score: _____ |

What will the providers tell me when I ask them whether they enjoy working with you?

| Plans: Medigap | Importance: _____ | Score: _____ | Weighted Score: _____ |

Do you have an advocacy system for clients?

How does it work?

Where does the advocate report in your organization?

What is the level of the reporting executive?

| Plans: Medigap | Importance: _____ | Score: _____ | Weighted Score: _____ |

How do you like working here?

| Plans: Both | Importance: _____ | Score: _____ | Weighted Score: _____ |

Is there a maximum lifetime benefit?

If yes, how much is it?

| Plans: Both | Importance: _____ | Score: _____ | Weighted Score: _____ |

Do you have disease or procedural limits?

If yes, what are they?

How much are they by disease or procedure?

| Plans: Both | Importance: _____ | Score: _____ | Weighted Score: _____ |

What procedures are considered "experimental"?

## MEDIGAP CARRIER AND MEDICARE HMO QUESTIONS

| Plans: HMO | Importance: _____ | Score: _____ | Weighted Score: _____ |

Do you have carve-outs for certain diseases?

If yes, what are they?

Where do you send the patients for treatment of each disease?

| Plans: Both | Importance: _____ | Score: _____ | Weighted Score: _____ |

Is this a national HMO or Medigap plan?

If not, do I have coverage outside of your region?

How does that coverage work?

| Plans: Both | Importance: _____ | Score: _____ | Weighted Score: _____ |

Will I have worldwide health care coverage?

If yes, how does it work?

Does it have deductibles, copays, and limits?

If I am not covered, what happens to my family or me if we need care while abroad?

| Plans: HMO | Importance: _____ | Score: _____ | Weighted Score: _____ |

May I have a list of your providers?

If not, why not?

## MEDIGAP CARRIER AND MEDICARE HMO QUESTIONS

| Plans: HMO | Importance: _____ | Score: _____ | Weighted Score: _____ |

What percentage of your providers out of residency for 5 years are Board Certified?

What percentage passed their Boards on the first try?

What percentage failed and are not Board Certified?

| Plans: HMO | Importance: _____ | Score: _____ | Weighted Score: _____ |

May I select my own Primary Care Physician?

Is the one I want available? (A follow-up question before you sign up)

| Plans: HMO | Importance: _____ | Score: _____ | Weighted Score: _____ |

From what fields do you draw your Primary Care Providers?

| Plans: All | Importance: _____ | Score: _____ | Weighted Score: _____ |

Can women have a gynecologist as their PCP?

| Plans: HMO | Importance: _____ | Score: _____ | Weighted Score: _____ |

Are patients with chronic problems allowed to have a specialist as their PCP?

| Plans: HMO | Importance: _____ | Score: _____ | Weighted Score: _____ |

If being treated by a specialist for a problem that requires follow-up or continuing care, can my specialist become my PCP, either temporarily or permanently?

| Plans: HMO | Importance: _____ | Score: _____ | Weighted Score: _____ |

If being treated by a specialist for a problem that requires follow-up or continuing care, do I have to have a PCP referral for each follow-up visit?

## MEDIGAP CARRIER AND MEDICARE HMO QUESTIONS

| Plans: All | Importance: _____ | Score: _____ | Weighted Score: _____ |

Are women allowed to have annual mammograms in this plan?

| Plans: All | Importance: _____ | Score: _____ | Weighted Score: _____ |

Are women allowed to have annual Pap smears in this plan?

| Plans: All | Importance: _____ | Score: _____ | Weighted Score: _____ |

Are men allowed to have an annual sigmoidoscopy in this plan?

| Plans: HMO | Importance: _____ | Score: _____ | Weighted Score: _____ |

Are annual gynecological examinations and mammograms allowed without referral?

If not, why not?

| Plans: HMO | Importance: _____ | Score: _____ | Weighted Score: _____ |

What is the average wait (days) for a PCP appointment?

| Plans: HMO | Importance: _____ | Score: _____ | Weighted Score: _____ |

What is the average length (minutes) of PCP office visits?

| Plans: HMO | Importance: _____ | Score: _____ | Weighted Score: _____ |

When a referral to a specialist occurs, what is the average length of wait (days) between being seen by the PCP and a specialist?

## MEDIGAP CARRIER AND MEDICARE HMO QUESTIONS

Plans: HMO    Importance: _____    Score: _____    Weighted Score: _____

What is the average length (minutes) of specialist office visits?

Plans: All    Importance: _____    Score: _____    Weighted Score: _____

Does this plan provide allergy treatment?

If yes, how does it work.

If no, how would I go about getting allergy treatment?

Plans: HMO    Importance: _____    Score: _____    Weighted Score: _____

What specialties participate in your plan?

What specialties do not participate in your plan?

Plans: HMO    Importance: _____    Score: _____    Weighted Score: _____

What percentage of your specialists are Board Certified in their specialty?

What percentage passed on their first try?

What percentage failed and never have been Board Certified?

Plans: HMO    Importance: _____    Score: _____    Weighted Score: _____

Where will I be referred if I need highly specialized medical care (e.g., rare disease treatment, transplant)?

## MEDIGAP CARRIER AND MEDICARE HMO QUESTIONS

| Plans: HMO | Importance: _____ | Score: _____ | Weighted Score: _____ |

May I request and receive a second opinion?

If yes, how would I go about getting the second opinion?

| Plans: All | Importance: _____ | Score: _____ | Weighted Score: _____ |

What is the prescription drug benefit?

| Plans: All | Importance: _____ | Score: _____ | Weighted Score: _____ |

I have a list of my current prescriptions and need to know which of my medications are not in your formulary?

| Plans: All | Importance: _____ | Score: _____ | Weighted Score: _____ |

Do you have other brands of the same drug?

If so what are they?

| Plans: All | Importance: _____ | Score: _____ | Weighted Score: _____ |

Do you have substitute drugs?

If so, what are they?

| Plans: All | Importance: _____ | Score: _____ | Weighted Score: _____ |

What are the caps on your prescription benefits?

## MEDIGAP CARRIER AND MEDICARE HMO QUESTIONS

Plans: All      Importance: _____      Score: _____      Weighted Score: _____

Does your prescription benefit have a copayment or coinsurance provision?

If yes, what are they?

Is that all I have to pay?

---

Plans: All      Importance: _____      Score: _____      Weighted Score: _____

Do you have a formal complaint program?

If yes, please describe it.

---

Plans: All      Importance: _____      Score: _____      Weighted Score: _____

Do your patients have an Advocate to whom they can appeal?

If yes, please describe how that function works.

---

Plans: All      Importance: _____      Score: _____      Weighted Score: _____

If after going through your advocacy or grievance program I am not satisfied with the answer, to whom do I go in your management?

To whom do I go for outside advocacy or arbitration?

---

Plans: All      Importance: _____      Score: _____      Weighted Score: _____

What measurement criteria are used in the evaluation of your doctors?

What is the weighting for each of the measurement criteria?

## MEDIGAP CARRIER AND MEDICARE HMO QUESTIONS

| Plans: HMO | Importance: _____ | Score: _____ | Weighted Score: _____ |
|---|---|---|---|

What was the NCQA rating by your HMO membership for each of the last 3 years?

| Plans: HMO | Importance: _____ | Score: _____ | Weighted Score: _____ |
|---|---|---|---|

What was your overall NCQA rating for each of the last 3 years?

| Plans: | Importance: _____ | Score: _____ | Weighted Score: _____ |
|---|---|---|---|

| Plans: | Importance: _____ | Score: _____ | Weighted Score: _____ |
|---|---|---|---|

| Plans: | Importance: _____ | Score: _____ | Weighted Score: _____ |
|---|---|---|---|

| Plans: | Importance: _____ | Score: _____ | Weighted Score: _____ |
|---|---|---|---|

| Plans: | Importance: _____ | Score: _____ | Weighted Score: _____ |
|---|---|---|---|

| Plans: | Importance: _____ | Score: _____ | Weighted Score: _____ |
|---|---|---|---|

## MEDIGAP POLICYHOLDER QUESTIONS

Plans: Medigap        Importance: _____        Score: _____        Weighted Score: _____

Who is your Medigap carrier?

---

Plans: Medigap        Importance: _____        Score: _____        Weighted Score: _____

How long have you been with this carrier?

---

Plans: Medigap        Importance: _____        Score: _____        Weighted Score: _____

Which Medigap Plan do you have (A–J)?

Do you like it?

---

Plans: Medigap        Importance: _____        Score: _____        Weighted Score: _____

Have you had any Medigap claims?

(If yes, go to the next questions.)

---

Plans: Medigap        Importance: _____        Score: _____        Weighted Score: _____

How long does it take to get claims processed?

---

Plans: Medigap        Importance: _____        Score: _____        Weighted Score: _____

Have you had to deal with many claims errors?

---

Plans: Medigap        Importance: _____        Score: _____        Weighted Score: _____

Have you been able to make one phone call to your Medigap carrier to get errors resolved?

If not, what usually happens?

## MEDIGAP POLICYHOLDER QUESTIONS

| Plans: Medigap | Importance: _____ | Score: _____ | Weighted Score: _____ |

Have you ever had to manage communications between the Claims Office and the Provider?

| Plans: Medigap | Importance: _____ | Score: _____ | Weighted Score: _____ |

Do you find it pleasant to work with your Medigap carrier?

Do they take responsibility for their errors and fix them?

Are they polite?

| Plans: Medigap | Importance: _____ | Score: _____ | Weighted Score: _____ |

I'm considering Medigap, would you recommend your carrier?

Why or why not?

| Plans: | Importance: _____ | Score: _____ | Weighted Score: _____ |

| Plans: | Importance: _____ | Score: _____ | Weighted Score: _____ |

| Plans: | Importance: _____ | Score: _____ | Weighted Score: _____ |

| Plans: | Importance: _____ | Score: _____ | Weighted Score: _____ |

## MEDICARE HMO MEMBER QUESTIONS

| Plans: HMO | Importance: _____ | Score: _____ | Weighted Score: _____ |
|---|---|---|---|

How do you like your Medicare HMO plan?

| Plans: HMO | Importance: _____ | Score: _____ | Weighted Score: _____ |
|---|---|---|---|

How long have you been receiving care under this Medicare HMO plan?

| Plans: HMO | Importance: _____ | Score: _____ | Weighted Score: _____ |
|---|---|---|---|

What plan did you have before this one?

Was it another Medicare HMO?

Another plan with the same Medicare HMO?

| Plans: HMO | Importance: _____ | Score: _____ | Weighted Score: _____ |
|---|---|---|---|

Have you had a Medigap plan?

If yes, which plan (A–J)?

Who was the carrier?

Why did you leave that plan?

| Plans: HMO | Importance: _____ | Score: _____ | Weighted Score: _____ |
|---|---|---|---|

Why did you change over to this plan?

| Plans: HMO | Importance: _____ | Score: _____ | Weighted Score: _____ |
|---|---|---|---|

How do you like your Primary Care Physician?

| Plans: HMO | Importance: _____ | Score: _____ | Weighted Score: _____ |
|---|---|---|---|

How long do you have to wait to get an appointment with your Primary Care Physician?

## MEDICARE HMO MEMBER QUESTIONS

| Plans: HMO | Importance: _____ | Score: _____ | Weighted Score: _____ |

How are you treated on the phone when you call in to get an appointment?

| Plans: HMO | Importance: _____ | Score: _____ | Weighted Score: _____ |

Have you ever had any problems which required help from a specialist?

If yes, how long did it take to get to see the specialist?

| Plans: HMO | Importance: _____ | Score: _____ | Weighted Score: _____ |

Does your doctor listen to you?

| Plans: HMO | Importance: _____ | Score: _____ | Weighted Score: _____ |

Have you ever been sent a bill that you should not have received?

If yes, how did your Medicare HMO deal with it?

Was it a problem? Or did one phone call take care of it?

| Plans: HMO | Importance: _____ | Score: _____ | Weighted Score: _____ |

What do you like most about the plan?

| Plans: HMO | Importance: _____ | Score: _____ | Weighted Score: _____ |

What do you like least about the plan?

| Plans: HMO | Importance: _____ | Score: _____ | Weighted Score: _____ |

I'm thinking of signing up for this plan; do you recommend it?

If yes, who is your PCP?

## QUESTIONS TO ASK YOUR DOCTOR

| Plans: HMO | Importance: _____ | Score: _____ | Weighted Score: _____ |

Do you have Medicare HMO patients?

If yes, from which Medicare HMOs?

---

| Plans: HMO | Importance: _____ | Score: _____ | Weighted Score: _____ |

Are you a Primary Care Physician for any Medicare HMOs?

If yes, which ones?

---

| Plans: HMO | Importance: _____ | Score: _____ | Weighted Score: _____ |

In your opinion, which Medicare HMOs do the best job on utilization reviews?

---

| Plans: HMO | Importance: _____ | Score: _____ | Weighted Score: _____ |

Do you feel that any of the Medicare HMOs intrude on your professional judgment?

---

| Plans: HMO | Importance: _____ | Score: _____ | Weighted Score: _____ |

With which Medicare HMOs are you able to refer patients to specialists by name?

Do you or your staff arrange for the appointment?

If not, does the Medicare HMO let you know when they have set it up?

---

| Plans: HMO | Importance: _____ | Score: _____ | Weighted Score: _____ |

If you were running a Medicare HMO and had a choice of how to pay physicians (e.g., capitation, hold backs, fees, salary), how would you do it?

Why?

## QUESTIONS TO ASK YOUR DOCTOR

| Plans: HMO | Importance: _____ | Score: _____ | Weighted Score: _____ |

How are you compensated by the Medicare HMOs with whom you work?

| Plans: HMO | Importance: _____ | Score: _____ | Weighted Score: _____ |

With which of the Medicare HMOs do you have the best working relationship?

| Plans: HMO | Importance: _____ | Score: _____ | Weighted Score: _____ |

With which of the Medicare HMOs do you not have a good working relationship?

| Plans: HMO | Importance: _____ | Score: _____ | Weighted Score: _____ |

If you were going to recommend a Medicare HMO to a family member, which one would you recommend?

| Plans: | Importance: _____ | Score: _____ | Weighted Score: _____ |

| Plans: | Importance: _____ | Score: _____ | Weighted Score: _____ |

| Plans: | Importance: _____ | Score: _____ | Weighted Score: _____ |

| Plans: | Importance: _____ | Score: _____ | Weighted Score: _____ |

## BLANK QUESTION FORM

Plans:          Importance: _____     Score: _____     Weighted Score: _____

Plans:          Importance: _____     Score: _____     Weighted Score: _____

Plans:          Importance: _____     Score: _____     Weighted Score: _____

Plans:          Importance: _____     Score: _____     Weighted Score: _____

Plans:          Importance: _____     Score: _____     Weighted Score: _____

Plans:          Importance: _____     Score: _____     Weighted Score: _____

Plans:          Importance: _____     Score: _____     Weighted Score: _____

## MEDICARE—MEDIGAP—HMO COVERAGE AND COST WORKSHEET

| Hospital Inpatient | Mdcr A You Pay | "A" You Pay | "B" You Pay | "C" You Pay | "D" You Pay | "E" You Pay | "F" You Pay | "G" You Pay | "H" You Pay | "I" You Pay | "J" You Pay |
|---|---|---|---|---|---|---|---|---|---|---|---|
| Part A annual deductible | $760 | $760 | $0 | $0 | $0 | $0 | $0 | $0 | $0 | $0 | $0 |
| Semiprivate room days 1–60 | $0 | $0 | $0 | $0 | $0 | $0 | $0 | $0 | $0 | $0 | $0 |
| Semiprivate room days 61–90 | $190/day | $0 | $0 | $0 | $0 | $0 | $0 | $0 | $0 | $0 | $0 |
| Reserve days (60) 91–150* | $380/day | $0 | $0 | $0 | $0 | $0 | $0 | $0 | $0 | $0 | $0 |
| Extra 365 days | 100% | $0 | $0 | $0 | $0 | $0 | $0 | $0 | $0 | $0 | $0 |
| All meals | $0 | $0 | $0 | $0 | $0 | $0 | $0 | $0 | $0 | $0 | $0 |
| Special diets | $0 | $0 | $0 | $0 | $0 | $0 | $0 | $0 | $0 | $0 | $0 |
| Regular nursing services | $0 | $0 | $0 | $0 | $0 | $0 | $0 | $0 | $0 | $0 | $0 |
| Special care units | $0 | $0 | $0 | $0 | $0 | $0 | $0 | $0 | $0 | $0 | $0 |
| Drugs | $0 | $0 | $0 | $0 | $0 | $0 | $0 | $0 | $0 | $0 | $0 |
| Blood—first 3 pints | 100% | $0 | $0 | $0 | $0 | $0 | $0 | $0 | $0 | $0 | $0 |
| Blood—after first 3 pints | $0 | $0 | $0 | $0 | $0 | $0 | $0 | $0 | $0 | $0 | $0 |
| Lab tests | $0 | $0 | $0 | $0 | $0 | $0 | $0 | $0 | $0 | $0 | $0 |
| X rays other radiology | $0 | $0 | $0 | $0 | $0 | $0 | $0 | $0 | $0 | $0 | $0 |
| Radiation therapy | $0 | $0 | $0 | $0 | $0 | $0 | $0 | $0 | $0 | $0 | $0 |
| Medical supplies | $0 | $0 | $0 | $0 | $0 | $0 | $0 | $0 | $0 | $0 | $0 |
| Wheelchairs & appliances | $0 | $0 | $0 | $0 | $0 | $0 | $0 | $0 | $0 | $0 | $0 |
| Operating room | $0 | $0 | $0 | $0 | $0 | $0 | $0 | $0 | $0 | $0 | $0 |
| Recovery room | $0 | $0 | $0 | $0 | $0 | $0 | $0 | $0 | $0 | $0 | $0 |
| Rehabilitation services | $0 | $0 | $0 | $0 | $0 | $0 | $0 | $0 | $0 | $0 | $0 |
| Private room required | $0 | $0 | $0 | $0 | $0 | $0 | $0 | $0 | $0 | $0 | $0 |
| Private room not required | 100% | 100% | 100% | 100% | 100% | 100% | 100% | 100% | 100% | 100% | 100% |
| Private duty nurses | 100% | 100% | 100% | 100% | 100% | 100% | 100% | 100% | 100% | 100% | 100% |
| Personal items | 100% | 100% | 100% | 100% | 100% | 100% | 100% | 100% | 100% | 100% | 100% |

\* **One-time 60 reserve days are used in this example to extend coverage from 90 days to 150 days.**

## MEDICARE—MEDIGAP—HMO COVERAGE AND COST WORKSHEET

| Skilled Nursing Facility Inpatient | Mdcr A You Pay | "A" You Pay | "B" You Pay | "C" You Pay | "D" You Pay | "E" You Pay | "F" You Pay | "G" You Pay | "H" You Pay | "I" You Pay | "J" You Pay |
|---|---|---|---|---|---|---|---|---|---|---|---|
| Semiprivate room days 1–20 | $0 | $0 | $0 | $0 | $0 | $0 | $0 | $0 | $0 | $0 | $0 |
| Semiprivate room days 21–100 | $95/day | $95/day | $95/day | $0 | $0 | $0 | $0 | $0 | $0 | $0 | $0 |
| All meals | $0 | $0 | $0 | $0 | $0 | $0 | $0 | $0 | $0 | $0 | $0 |
| Special diets | $0 | $0 | $0 | $0 | $0 | $0 | $0 | $0 | $0 | $0 | $0 |
| Regular nursing services | $0 | $0 | $0 | $0 | $0 | $0 | $0 | $0 | $0 | $0 | $0 |
| Therapy | $0 | $0 | $0 | $0 | $0 | $0 | $0 | $0 | $0 | $0 | $0 |
| Drugs | $0 | $0 | $0 | $0 | $0 | $0 | $0 | $0 | $0 | $0 | $0 |
| Blood transfusions | $0 | $0 | $0 | $0 | $0 | $0 | $0 | $0 | $0 | $0 | $0 |
| Medical supplies | $0 | $0 | $0 | $0 | $0 | $0 | $0 | $0 | $0 | $0 | $0 |
| Wheelchair & other appliances | $0 | $0 | $0 | $0 | $0 | $0 | $0 | $0 | $0 | $0 | $0 |
| Private room medically required | $0 | $0 | $0 | $0 | $0 | $0 | $0 | $0 | $0 | $0 | $0 |
| Private room (not required) | 100% | 100% | 100% | 100% | 100% | 100% | 100% | 100% | 100% | 100% | 100% |
| Private duty nurses | 100% | 100% | 100% | 100% | 100% | 100% | 100% | 100% | 100% | 100% | 100% |
| Personal items (e.g., phone, TV) | 100% | 100% | 100% | 100% | 100% | 100% | 100% | 100% | 100% | 100% | 100% |
| Any other billed services | 100% | 100% | 100% | 100% | 100% | 100% | 100% | 100% | 100% | 100% | 100% |

## MEDICARE—MEDIGAP—HMO COVERAGE AND COST WORKSHEET

| Home Health Services | Mdcr A You Pay | "A" You Pay | "B" You Pay | "C" You Pay | "D" You Pay | "E" You Pay | "F" You Pay | "G" You Pay | "H" You Pay | "I" You Pay | "J" You Pay |
|---|---|---|---|---|---|---|---|---|---|---|---|
| Part-time & Intermittent nursing | $0 | $0 | $0 | $0 | $0 | $0 | $0 | $0 | $0 | $0 | $0 |
| Home health aide services | $0 | $0 | $0 | $0 | $0 | $0 | $0 | $0 | $0 | $0 | $0 |
| Home health care extensions 8 wks.; at $40/visit; $1,600 maximum | 100% | 100% | 100% | 100% | $0 | 100% | 100% | $0 | 100% | $0 | $0 |
| Physical therapy | $0 | $0 | $0 | $0 | $0 | $0 | $0 | $0 | $0 | $0 | $0 |
| Speech therapy | $0 | $0 | $0 | $0 | $0 | $0 | $0 | $0 | $0 | $0 | $0 |
| Occupational therapy | $0 | $0 | $0 | $0 | $0 | $0 | $0 | $0 | $0 | $0 | $0 |
| Medical social services | $0 | $0 | $0 | $0 | $0 | $0 | $0 | $0 | $0 | $0 | $0 |
| Medical supplies | $0 | $0 | $0 | $0 | $0 | $0 | $0 | $0 | $0 | $0 | $0 |
| Durable medical equipment | 20% | 20% | 20% | 20% | 20% | 20% | 20% | 20% | 20% | 20% | 20% |
| 24-hour nursing | 100% | 100% | 100% | 100% | 100% | 100% | 100% | 100% | 100% | 100% | 100% |
| Drugs & biologicals | 100% | 100% | 100% | 100% | 100% | 100% | 100% | 100% | 100% | 100% | 100% |
| Meals delivered to home | 100% | 100% | 100% | 100% | 100% | 100% | 100% | 100% | 100% | 100% | 100% |
| Homemaker services | 100% | 100% | 100% | 100% | 100% | 100% | 100% | 100% | 100% | 100% | 100% |
| Blood transfusions | 100% | 100% | 100% | 100% | 100% | 100% | 100% | 100% | 100% | 100% | 100% |

## MEDICARE—MEDIGAP—HMO COVERAGE AND COST WORKSHEET

| Hospice Services (At Home) | Mdcr A You Pay | "A" You Pay | "B" You Pay | "C" You Pay | "D" You Pay | "E" You Pay | "F" You Pay | "G" You Pay | "H" You Pay | "I" You Pay | "J" You Pay |
|---|---|---|---|---|---|---|---|---|---|---|---|
| Nursing services | $0 | $0 | $0 | $0 | $0 | $0 | $0 | $0 | $0 | $0 | $0 |
| Doctor services | $0 | $0 | $0 | $0 | $0 | $0 | $0 | $0 | $0 | $0 | $0 |
| Inpatient drugs | $0 | $0 | $0 | $0 | $0 | $0 | $0 | $0 | $0 | $0 | $0 |
| Outpatient pain & symptom drugs up to $5 each | ≥$5 | ≥$5 | ≥$5 | ≥$5 | ≥$5 | ≥$5 | ≥$5 | ≥$5 | ≥$5 | ≥$5 | ≥$5 |
| Physical therapy | $0 | $0 | $0 | $0 | $0 | $0 | $0 | $0 | $0 | $0 | $0 |
| Occupational therapy | $0 | $0 | $0 | $0 | $0 | $0 | $0 | $0 | $0 | $0 | $0 |
| Speech-language therapy | $0 | $0 | $0 | $0 | $0 | $0 | $0 | $0 | $0 | $0 | $0 |
| Medical social services | $0 | $0 | $0 | $0 | $0 | $0 | $0 | $0 | $0 | $0 | $0 |
| Medical supplies | $0 | $0 | $0 | $0 | $0 | $0 | $0 | $0 | $0 | $0 | $0 |
| Medical appliances | $0 | $0 | $0 | $0 | $0 | $0 | $0 | $0 | $0 | $0 | $0 |
| Inpatient respite care—up to 5 days Mdcre allowed rate (approx. $5/day) | ~$5 | ~$5 | ~$5 | ~$5 | ~$5 | ~$5 | ~$5 | ~$5 | ~$5 | ~$5 | ~$5 |
| Counseling | $0 | $0 | $0 | $0 | $0 | $0 | $0 | $0 | $0 | $0 | $0 |
| Non-terminal pain treatment | $0 | $0 | $0 | $0 | $0 | $0 | $0 | $0 | $0 | $0 | $0 |
| Non-terminal symptom treatment | 100% | 100% | 100% | 100% | 100% | 100% | 100% | 100% | 100% | 100% | 100% |

## MEDICARE—MEDIGAP—HMO COVERAGE AND COST WORKSHEET

| Doctor Services* | Mdcr B You Pay | "A" You Pay | "B" You Pay | "C" You Pay | "D" You Pay | "E" You Pay | "F" You Pay | "G" You Pay | "H" You Pay | "I" You Pay | "J" You Pay |
|---|---|---|---|---|---|---|---|---|---|---|---|
| Part B deductible | $100 | $100 | $100 | $0 | $100 | $100 | $0 | $100 | $100 | $100 | $0 |
| Medical & surgical services | 20% | $0 | $0 | $0 | $0 | $0 | $0 | $0 | $0 | $0 | $0 |
| Anesthesia | 20% | $0 | $0 | $0 | $0 | $0 | $0 | $0 | $0 | $0 | $0 |
| Diagnostic tests & procedures | 20% | $0 | $0 | $0 | $0 | $0 | $0 | $0 | $0 | $0 | $0 |
| Inpatient radiologist services | 20% | $0 | $0 | $0 | $0 | $0 | $0 | $0 | $0 | $0 | $0 |
| Outpatient radiologist services | 20% | $0 | $0 | $0 | $0 | $0 | $0 | $0 | $0 | $0 | $0 |
| Inpatient pathologist services | 20% | $0 | $0 | $0 | $0 | $0 | $0 | $0 | $0 | $0 | $0 |
| Outpatient pathologist services | 20% | $0 | $0 | $0 | $0 | $0 | $0 | $0 | $0 | $0 | $0 |
| Inpatient mental illness treatment | 20% | $0 | $0 | $0 | $0 | $0 | $0 | $0 | $0 | $0 | $0 |
| X rays including at home | 20% | $0 | $0 | $0 | $0 | $0 | $0 | $0 | $0 | $0 | $0 |
| Doctor's office nurse services | 20% | $0 | $0 | $0 | $0 | $0 | $0 | $0 | $0 | $0 | $0 |
| Professional only drugs | 20% | $0 | $0 | $0 | $0 | $0 | $0 | $0 | $0 | $0 | $0 |
| Professional only biologicals | 20% | $0 | $0 | $0 | $0 | $0 | $0 | $0 | $0 | $0 | $0 |
| Blood—1st 3 pints | 100% | $0 | $0 | $0 | $0 | $0 | $0 | $0 | $0 | $0 | $0 |
| Blood—after 1st 3 pints | $0 | $0 | $0 | $0 | $0 | $0 | $0 | $0 | $0 | $0 | $0 |
| Medical supplies | 20% | $0 | $0 | $0 | $0 | $0 | $0 | $0 | $0 | $0 | $0 |
| Physical therapy | 20% | $0 | $0 | $0 | $0 | $0 | $0 | $0 | $0 | $0 | $0 |
| Occupational therapy | 20% | $0 | $0 | $0 | $0 | $0 | $0 | $0 | $0 | $0 | $0 |
| Speech pathology services | 20% | $0 | $0 | $0 | $0 | $0 | $0 | $0 | $0 | $0 | $0 |
| Physical examinations: 1st $120/year | $120 | $120 | $120 | $120 | $120 | $120 | $120 | $120 | $120 | $120 | $0 |
| Over $120/year | 100% | 100% | 100% | 100% | 100% | 100% | 100% | 100% | 100% | 100% | 100% |
| Routine foot care | 100% | 100% | 100% | 100% | 100% | 100% | 100% | 100% | 100% | 100% | 100% |
| Routine dental care | 100% | 100% | 100% | 100% | 100% | 100% | 100% | 100% | 100% | 100% | 100% |
| Eye examinations for glasses | 100% | 100% | 100% | 100% | 100% | 100% | 100% | 100% | 100% | 100% | 100% |

# MEDICARE—MEDIGAP—HMO COVERAGE AND COST WORKSHEET

| Doctor Services* (cont.) | Mdcr B You Pay | "A" You Pay | "B" You Pay | "C" You Pay | "D" You Pay | "E" You Pay | "F" You Pay | "G" You Pay | "H" You Pay | "I" You Pay | "J" You Pay |
|---|---|---|---|---|---|---|---|---|---|---|---|
| Hearing aid examinations | 100% | 100% | 100% | 100% | 100% | 100% | 100% | 100% | 100% | 100% | 100% |
| Hearing aids | 100% | 100% | 100% | 100% | 100% | 100% | 100% | 100% | 100% | 100% | 100% |
| Most immunizations | 100% | 100% | 100% | 100% | 100% | 100% | 100% | 100% | 100% | 100% | 100% |
| Most prescription drugs: | | | | | | | | | | | |
| First $250 per year | $250 | $250 | $250 | $250 | $250 | $250 | $250 | $250 | $250 | $250 | $250 |
| $2,500 in additional drugs | 100% | 100% | 100% | 100% | 100% | 100% | 100% | 100% | 50% | 50% | 50% |
| $6,000 in additional drugs | 100% | 100% | 100% | 100% | 100% | 100% | 100% | 100% | 100% | 100% | 50% |
| Beyond $6,250 per year | 100% | 100% | 100% | 100% | 100% | 100% | 100% | 100% | 100% | 100% | 100% |
| Elective cosmetic surgery | 100% | 100% | 100% | 100% | 100% | 100% | 100% | 100% | 100% | 100% | 100% |

\* The 20% copay shown for some benefits indicates that Medicare pays 80% of the Medicare approved rate. The beneficiary is responsible for up to an additional 15%, if the services are rendered by a provider who does not accept assignment or is not a Medicare approved facility. The "$0" reference in the Medigap columns indicates that Medigap pays for the 20% copayment. See Medicare–Medigap–HMO Coverage and Cost Table for "Other Part B Provisions"

Prescription Drug Benefit of Medigap Plans H, I, J
You pay the first $250 of prescription drugs each year.
Medigap H & I pays 50% of the next $2,500 of prescription drugs you buy each year. ($1,250 is the maximum benefit.)
Medigap J pays 50% of the next $6,000 of prescription drugs you buy each year. ($3,000 is the maximum benefit.)

# MEDICARE—MEDIGAP—HMO COVERAGE AND COST WORKSHEET

| Hospital Outpatient Services* | Mdcr B You Pay | "A" You Pay | "B" You Pay | "C" You Pay | "D" You Pay | "E" You Pay | "F" You Pay | "G" You Pay | "H" You Pay | "I" You Pay | "J" You Pay |
|---|---|---|---|---|---|---|---|---|---|---|---|
| Emergency room services | 20%+ | $0+ | $0+ | $0+ | $0+ | $0+ | $0+ | $0+ | $0+ | $0+ | $0+ |
| Clinic services | 20%+ | $0+ | $0+ | $0+ | $0+ | $0+ | $0+ | $0+ | $0+ | $0+ | $0+ |
| Same day surgery (ER & clinic) | 20%+ | $0+ | $0+ | $0+ | $0+ | $0+ | $0+ | $0+ | $0+ | $0+ | $0+ |
| Laboratory tests | $0+ | $0+ | $0+ | $0+ | $0+ | $0+ | $0+ | $0+ | $0+ | $0+ | $0+ |
| Mental health services** | 50%+ | 30%+ | 30%+ | 30%+ | 30%+ | 30%+ | 30%+ | 30%+ | 30%+ | 30%+ | 30%+ |
| X rays & other radiology | 20%+ | $0+ | $0+ | $0+ | $0+ | $0+ | $0+ | $0+ | $0+ | $0+ | $0+ |
| Medical supplies | 20%+ | $0+ | $0+ | $0+ | $0+ | $0+ | $0+ | $0+ | $0+ | $0+ | $0+ |
| Professional only drugs | 20%+ | $0+ | $0+ | $0+ | $0+ | $0+ | $0+ | $0+ | $0+ | $0+ | $0+ |
| Professional only biologicals | 20%+ | $0+ | $0+ | $0+ | $0+ | $0+ | $0+ | $0+ | $0+ | $0+ | $0+ |
| Physical examinations: | | | | | | | | | | | |
| 1st $120/year | $120 | $120 | $120 | $120 | $120 | $0 | $120 | $120 | $120 | $120 | $0 |
| Over $120/year | 100% | 100% | 100% | 100% | 100% | 100% | 100% | 100% | 100% | 100% | 100% |
| Eye examinations for glasses | 100% | 100% | 100% | 100% | 100% | 100% | 100% | 100% | 100% | 100% | 100% |
| Ear examinations for hearing aid | 100% | 100% | 100% | 100% | 100% | 100% | 100% | 100% | 100% | 100% | 100% |
| Most prescription drugs: | | | | | | | | | | | |
| First $250 per year (deductible) | $250 | $250 | $250 | $250 | $250 | $250 | $250 | $250 | $250 | $250 | $250 |
| $2,500 in additional drugs | 100% | 100% | 100% | 100% | 100% | 100% | 100% | 100% | 50% | 50% | 50% |
| $6,000 in additional drugs | 100% | 100% | 100% | 100% | 100% | 100% | 100% | 100% | 100% | 100% | 50% |
| Beyond $6,250 per year | 100% | 100% | 100% | 100% | 100% | 100% | 100% | 100% | 100% | 100% | 100% |
| Most routine foot care | 100% | 100% | 100% | 100% | 100% | 100% | 100% | 100% | 100% | 100% | 100% |
| Outpatient blood transfusions | 100% | 100% | 100% | 100% | 100% | 100% | 100% | 100% | 100% | 100% | 100% |

*Prescription Drug Benefit of Medigap Plans H, I, J

You pay the first $250 of prescription drugs each year; Medigap H & I pays 50% of the next $2,500 of prescription drugs you buy each year. ($1,250 is the maximum benefit.); Medigap J pays 50% of the next $6,000 of prescription drugs you buy each year. ($3,000 is the maximum benefit.)

** Medigap pays 20% of the Medicare approved copayment and coinsurance charges; Medicare pays for 80% of the Medicare approved copayment and coinsurance charges.

**+ You pay 20% (or 50% for "Outpatient mental health services") of the Billed Amount, which can be greater than 80% of Approved Amount** for "Outpatient mental health services." Check with your Medigap insurer.

Medicare Part B requires a 50% copayment for "Outpatient mental health services."

# MEDICARE—MEDIGAP—HMO COVERAGE AND COST WORKSHEET

| Other Part B Provisions* | Mdcr B You Pay | "A" You Pay | "B" You Pay | "C" You Pay | "D" You Pay | "E" You Pay | "F" You Pay | "G" You Pay | "H" You Pay | "I" You Pay | "J" You Pay |
|---|---|---|---|---|---|---|---|---|---|---|---|
| Excess charges—up to 15% over Medicare allowable charges | 15% | 15% | 15% | 15% | 15% | 15% | $0 | 3% | 15% | $0 | $0 |
| Foreign travel emergency: | | | | | | | | | | | |
| 1st $250 in expenses | $250 | $250 | $250 | $250 | $250 | $250 | $250 | $250 | $250 | $250 | $250 |
| Charges over $250 | 100% | 100% | 100% | 20% | 20% | 20% | 20% | 20% | 20% | 20% | 20% |
| May have lifetime limit | | | | | | | | | | | |
| Durable medical equipment | 20% | | | $0 | $0 | $0 | $0 | $0 | $0 | $0 | $0 |
| Pap smear every 3 years | 20% | | | $0 | $0 | $0 | $0 | $0 | $0 | $0 | $0 |
| Mammogram every 2 years | 20% | | | $0 | $0 | $0 | $0 | $0 | $0 | $0 | $0 |
| Kidney dialysis ** | 20% | | | $0 | $0 | $0 | $0 | $0 | $0 | $0 | $0 |
| Kidney transplants ** | 20% | | | $0 | $0 | $0 | $0 | $0 | $0 | $0 | $0 |
| Heart transplants ** | 20% | | | $0 | $0 | $0 | $0 | $0 | $0 | $0 | $0 |
| Liver transplants ** | 20% | | | $0 | $0 | $0 | $0 | $0 | $0 | $0 | $0 |
| Ambulance between home & skilled nursing facility ** hospital ** | 20% | | | $0 | $0 | $0 | $0 | $0 | $0 | $0 | $0 |
| Prosthetic devices ** | 20% | | | $0 | $0 | $0 | $0 | $0 | $0 | $0 | $0 |
| Therapeutic shoes for diabetics ** | 20% | | | $0 | $0 | $0 | $0 | $0 | $0 | $0 | $0 |
| Certain drugs & biologicals ** | 20% | | | $0 | $0 | $0 | $0 | $0 | $0 | $0 | $0 |

* The 20% copay shown for some benefits indicates that Medicare pays 80% of the Medicare approved rate. The beneficiary is responsible for up to an additional 15%, if the services are rendered by a provider who does not accept assignment or is not a Medicare approved facility. The "$0" reference in the Medigap columns indicates that Medigap pays for the 20% copayment. See Medicare—Medigap—HMO Coverage and Cost Table for "Other Part B Provisions"

* The "Other Part B Provisions", from "Kidney Dialysis" through "Certain drugs & biologicals," require specific definition of your benefits by your Social Security Administration office and Medigap coverage information from your local Medigap insurers. Application for more frequent pap smears and mammograms can also be made to your Social Security Administration office for special conditions or as a member of a risk group.

** **Medicare "Helps Pay" for these charges. Check with your Medicare and Medigap carriers re: your coverage.**

270

## MEDFORM

| Time and Vital Sign | Medication | Dose | Sun | Mon | Tue | Wed | Thu | Fri | Sat |
|---|---|---|---|---|---|---|---|---|---|
| | | | | | | | | | |
| | | | | | | | | | |
| | | | | | | | | | |
| | | | | | | | | | |
| | | | | | | | | | |
| | | | | | | | | | |
| | | | | | | | | | |
| | | | | | | | | | |
| | | | | | | | | | |
| | | | | | | | | | |
| | | | | | | | | | |
| | | | | | | | | | |
| | | | | | | | | | |
| | | | | | | | | | |
| | | | | | | | | | |
| | | | | | | | | | |
| | | | | | | | | | |
| | | | | | | | | | |
| | | | | | | | | | |
| | | | | | | | | | |

Medform Revised   /   /     Patient Name:

## MEDICATION HISTORY

| Patient name: | | | | | | | | | | | Year: | |
|---|---|---|---|---|---|---|---|---|---|---|---|---|
| **Medication** | / | / | / | / | / | / | / | / | / | / | / | / |
| | | | | | | | | | | | | |
| | | | | | | | | | | | | |
| | | | | | | | | | | | | |
| | | | | | | | | | | | | |
| | | | | | | | | | | | | |
| | | | | | | | | | | | | |
| | | | | | | | | | | | | |
| | | | | | | | | | | | | |
| | | | | | | | | | | | | |
| | | | | | | | | | | | | |
| | | | | | | | | | | | | |
| | | | | | | | | | | | | |
| | | | | | | | | | | | | |
| | | | | | | | | | | | | |
| | | | | | | | | | | | | |
| | | | | | | | | | | | | |
| | | | | | | | | | | | | |

## PROCEDURE CHRONOLOGY

**Patient:**

| Date | Procedure | Site* | Status | Reason | Ordering Doctor |
|------|-----------|-------|--------|--------|-----------------|
|      |           |       |        |        |                 |
|      |           |       |        |        |                 |
|      |           |       |        |        |                 |
|      |           |       |        |        |                 |
|      |           |       |        |        |                 |
|      |           |       |        |        |                 |
|      |           |       |        |        |                 |
|      |           |       |        |        |                 |
|      |           |       |        |        |                 |
|      |           |       |        |        |                 |
|      |           |       |        |        |                 |
|      |           |       |        |        |                 |
|      |           |       |        |        |                 |
|      |           |       |        |        |                 |
|      |           |       |        |        |                 |

* Site Legend:

# TRACKING FORM

**PATIENT:** **PROVIDER:** **YEAR:**

| SVC DATE | BILLED AMT | PPO AMT | INS EOB DATE | INS AMT PAID | DED AMT | OOP AMT | COPAY AMT | PERS DUE | PERS PAID | PERS DTE PD | TOTAL PAID | BALANCE DUE | COMMENTS |
|---|---|---|---|---|---|---|---|---|---|---|---|---|---|
| | | | | | | | | | | | | | |
| | | | | | | | | | | | | | |
| | | | | | | | | | | | | | |
| | | | | | | | | | | | | | |
| | | | | | | | | | | | | | |
| | | | | | | | | | | | | | |
| | | | | | | | | | | | | | |
| | | | | | | | | | | | | | |
| | | | | | | | | | | | | | |

# Index

AARP. *See* American Association of Retired Persons
accept assignment, 91–92, 114–115
actuarial risk, 21, 25
additional Medicare reading material, 92
advocacy, 77, 127, 130, 188, 205, 211. *See* Advocacy Program. *See* Advocate
Advocacy Program, 102, 155, 182, 186, 225. *See also* advocacy, advocate
advocate, 77, 127, 130, 182, 187–188, 194–204, 211. *See also* advocacy, Advocacy Program
agreements
    Medicare agreements, 120, 148–150, 186, 214, 216
American Association of Retired Persons, 102, 110, 154, 225, 228
annual deductible, 22, 25, 59, 88, 90–91, 96, 97, 107–108, 111, 193–194, 202, 218
arbitration, 77, 130
attained-age rates, 109, 119. 148, 211

Better Business Bureau, 109, 123, 147
billing and reimbursement system, 188
billing service, 32, 196, 204
block grants, 100–101, 148, 211
Board Certified, 38, 74, 128–129
Board eligible, 38
Boards, 22, 25, 38, 74, 128

cap, 22, 25, 211
capitation, 22–23, 25, 43, 80, 135, 211
carve-out, 23, 25, 44, 212
Case Management, 39, 47, 212
chronic illness, 170, 182, 212
claims office, 28–35, 49, 58, 62, 64–66, 79, 83, 132, 193, 195–196, 208, 212–213, 218
claims processing, 35, 212

clinics, 14, 42
COBRA, 10, 24, 212
coinsurance, 76, 98, 121, 130, 186, 193–197
communications, 28, 79, 132, 165, 167, 174, 179–181, 190, 207
community rates, 109
Consumer Information Center, 94, 105, 228
*Consumer Reports,* 97, 109, 155, 224, 229
Consumers Union, 97, 109, 155, 224
contracts, 37–38, 42–45, 47, 119, 214
copay. *See* copayment
copayment, 22, 24–25, 28, 46, 60, 63, 64–65, 76, 89, 91–92, 97, 106, 114, 130, 190, 193, 196–197, 202, 212. *See* copay
Coverage Summary, 187, 195
CPT code, 182, 189, 212
credentialing, 37–38, 47, 212
Custodial Care, 91, 103, 148, 155, 212

dangerous attitudes, 2
date of service, 31
decision process, 20, 52, 54, 67, 69, 70, 72, 81–83, 94–95, 125, 137–138, 146
    Medicare decision process, 137
deductible, 11, 22, 25, 59–66, 88, 90–91, 93, 96–97, 107–108, 111, 113, 190, 193–194, 196–197, 202, 212, 218
dental coverage, 118
Department of Consumer Affairs, 188, 204
Direct Contract Model HMO, 47
disability insurance, 152–153, 155–156, 212
disability premium waiver, 152, 156, 212
disabled, 9, 15, 87–88, 101, 121, 149, 152, 156, 179, 212, 216
disallowed charges, 182, 193, 213
Discussion Topics, 168. *See also* Office Visit
dunning notices, 197, 203–205

durable medical equipment, 88
Durable Power of Attorney for Health Care Decisions, 164–165

effective patient, 2, 51, 160, 180
Eldercare locator, 101
emergency care, 40–42
employer, 10, 13–14, 19–21, 24, 27–28, 30, 32–36, 46, 48, 51–52, 54, 67, 70–71, 87, 118, 147, 154, 195
employer insurance, 98
encounter, 67, 82–83, 213
enzyme, 182, 213
EOB. *See* Explanation of Benefits
evaluating options, 20, 95
Exclusive Provider, 32–34, 37, 50, 213
experimental, 19, 73, 120, 127
Explanation of Benefits, 4, 28–29, 35, 79, 182, 190–191, 193, 197–198, 203, 205, 213
eye examinations, 114

facilities, 42, 214
facility sources, 42, 44, 213
Family Deductible, 59
Family Out-of-Pocket, 60
Federal Identification Number, 182, 189–190
Fee-For-Service, 12–14, 20–21, 25–30, 32, 34–37, 42–46, 48–51, 59, 60–61, 63, 66, 72, 95, 117–118, 160–161, 185–186, 188–190, 192, 194, 196–197, 205, 213
  Fee-For-Service Summary, 36
forms, 4, 67, 72–73, 82, 125–126, 177
Formulary, 39, 47, 70–71, 123–124, 214

Gatekeeper, 34–35, 40, 214
glasses, 92, 114, 118
grievance procedure, 187
group contracted, 42, 44
Group Model HMO, 37, 41, 47
Group Practice, 37, 42–43, 45, 47, 50, 214
gynecologist, 21, 40–41, 45–46, 74, 128

Health care and insurance terminology, 25, 35, 46–47
Health Care Plan Enrollee Questions, 78, 132
Health Care Plan Evaluation, 67–69, 81–82
Health Care Prepayment Plan, 120–121, 148
Health Care Reform Act of 1996, 24
health care system, 9, 11, 15
Health Insurance Counseling and Advocacy Program, 102, 155, 225
Health insurance decision process, 54, 95, 146

Health Insurance Information and Counseling offices, 102
Health Insurance Portability and Accountability Act, 10
Health Maintenance Organization, 2, 4, 9, 12, 14, 20–23, 25, 28, 32, 34, 37, 39, 35–52, 54, 56, 58–63, 66–67, 69–82, 94–95, 97, 99, 103, 106, 117–135, 137–138, 146–150, 159–161, 170, 174, 182, 185–188
  Health Maintenance Organization Summary, 45
Health Plan Employer Data and Information Set 46, 48, 214
HEDIS. *See* Health Plan Employer Data and Information Set
HICAP, 102, 155, 225
HMO. *See* Health Maintenance Organization.
HMO and Insurance Company Questions, 73–77
HMO Contracted, 213
HMO Provider, 63
home health care, 90–91, 93, 112, 149, 214
hospice, 90–91, 149, 215
hospital, 23, 37, 42, 56, 64, 88–93, 96, 99, 106–107, 111, 115, 152–153, 156, 161–162, 164, 175, 188
Hospitalization Supplemental Insurance, 153, 155, 156

ICD-9, 183, 189–190, 215
Impact of health care changes on our doctors, 159
indemnity insurance company, 21–22, 25, 215.
Independent Physician Association, 37–38, 41–42, 45, 47–48, 50, 118–119, 215.
individual doctor HMO contracts, 50
Individual Out-of-Pocket, 60
Information Directory, 221
information sources, 103
inpatient, 88–89, 96, 106, 111, 113, 153, 161, 169
insurance company, 28, 31, 33, 74, 76–77
insurance options, 14, 51, 56–62, 195
  Insurance Options Summary, 56–62
insurance plans, 14, 20, 25–26, 34, 47, 51
insurance plans and terminology, 20, 51
IPA. *See* Independent Physician Association
IPA Model HMO, 37, 47, 215
Issue Age Rates, 109, 119, 149, 215

Key Points, 5, 15, 26, 29, 32, 34, 41, 45, 51, 71, 82, 103, 116, 122, 136, 148, 155, 165, 181, 205
Kipling, 53–54, 123

laboratories, 42, 162
laboratory reports, 174–175
limits, 73, 89, 108, 127–128, 188
List of Providers, 175–176, 181
local physician network, 32–34
long term care, 89, 97, 103, 153–156, 215
long term insurance, 154–156, 215, 222
long-term nursing home, 89, 92, 100

managed care, 12, 14, 20, 26–27, 32, 35–36, 49–50, 59, 61–63, 72, 94, 117, 119–120, 122, 150, 159, 161, 215
Managed Care Plan, 20, 32, 35
Managed Care Provider, 63
maximum lifetime benefit, 73, 127
Medform, 171–173, 175, 181, 183, 215
Medicaid, 2, 9, 97, 99, 103, 149, 154, 207, 215, 222
Medical Database Access and Report Services, 5, 103, 174, 222. *See also* Information Directory
Medical Director, 188
medical expenses, 56, 67, 69, 71, 81, 93, 95, 124, 146
medical savings account, 11
Medicare, 2, 4, 9–10, 13, 87–99, 101–103, 105–149, 153–154, 159–160, 188–191, 199, 205, 207, 216, 224
Medicare beneficiary, 87–88, 109
Medicare carrier, 92, 110, 115, 147
Medicare Cost Plan, 149, 216
Medicare gaps, 96–98, 146
*Medicare Handbook*, 94, 102, 115
Medicare HMO, 9, 95–97, 118–120, 122, 124, 132, 134–149, 216 *See also* Senior Plans
Medicare HMO agreements, 120, 149, 216
Medicare HMO contracts, 119–120
Medicare HMO Member Questions, 96, 133–134
Medicare HMO No Premium Plan, 96, 118, 122
Medicare Part A, 87–90, 95–96, 103, 138–141, 149, 153, 216
Medicare Part B, 87–89, 91–93, 95–96, 103, 138, 142–145, 149, 153, 216
Medicare Risk Plan, 149, 216
Medicare Select Plan, 120–121, 150, 216
Medication History, 175, 177, 180–181, 271
Medigap, 2, 4, 9, 95, 97–99, 102–103, 105–116, 118–120, 122–148, 185, 199, 224, 228–229
  Medigap plans. *See* Medigap.
Medigap Carrier and Medicare HMO Questions, 126–131
*Medpard Directory*, 91

member, 10, 12, 20, 22–23, 25, 35, 37–40, 43–45, 78, 117–118, 132, 134, 174, 185–187
Member Services, 186–187
Membership Agreement, 39–41, 44–45, 216

National Association of Insurance Commissioners, 98
National Committee for Quality Assurance, 48, 77, 131, 217
National Health Care System, 11
NCQA. *See* National Committee for Quality Assurance
Network Model HMO, 47, 218
nursing home, 89, 92, 96–97, 99–101, 106, 146, 154–156, 215

office visit, 25, 59–60, 64–66, 167, 181, 183, 189, 217. *See also* Discussion Topics
OOP. *See* out-of-pocket
open enrollment period, 4, 54, 98, 121, 154
other facilities, 42
other Model HMOs, 41–42, 44–45, 217
out-of-pocket, 14, 22, 25, 57, 59–66, 83, 190, 193–194, 196–202, 217
outpatient, 59, 64, 76, 89, 92, 111, 113–114, 138, 153, 161–162, 169, 175, 178

Part B. *See* Medicare Part B.
patient ID, 189
PCP. *See* Primary Care Physician
pediatrician, 40–41, 46, 74
pending charges, 183, 192–194, 200, 202
per diem, 23, 26, 217
physician sources, 43–44
Point of Service, 46–47, 49–50, 118, 186, 217
post-authorization, 187
PPO. *See* Preferred Provider option
PPO Plan, 30, 63, 217
PPO Provider, 57, 60
pre-authorization, 23–24, 40–41, 48, 76, 186–188, 217
preexisting conditions, 71, 124
Preferred Provider, 30–32, 35, 42–45, 65, 160, 197, 202, 217
Preferred Provider Option, 20, 27, 30–32, 35, 37, 50, 59–63, 66, 72, 79, 185, 191–192, 197, 199–200, 202, 205
Preferred Provider Plan, 35, 217
premium, 21–24, 56, 87–88, 91, 96, 109, 116, 118–119, 122, 151–153, 156, 179, 195, 213
prescription drugs, 124
prescription drug benefit, 39, 76, 130

preventive, 14, 20–22, 43, 49, 59, 66, 92, 97, 99, 108, 117, 159, 161, 170
Primary Care Physician, 12, 21–22, 33–35, 38–41, 45–46, 49, 62, 74, 78–79, 128–129, 186, 218
procedural limits, 73, 127
procedure, 22, 37–38, 48, 73, 76, 91, 97, 127, 162, 178, 186–189
Procedure History, 175, 177–178, 181
Procedure List, 177–178
prolonged hospitalization, 96
protocols, 11, 37, 39, 48, 218
Provider List, 174, 176

qualified physicians, 38
qualified specialists, 38
Quality Compass, 46, 48, 218
quality measurements, 46
Questions to Ask Your Doctor, 79–80, 96, 134–135, 147
Questions to Grade and Compare, 72, 124

Range of Available Options, 20–21, 26
reserve days, 89–90, 107
respite care, 156, 218. *See also* Custodial care, Nursing home.
rising cost of health care, 13–14
risk sharing, 21–23, 37, 44, 51
rules, 23–24, 37, 39, 43, 54, 70, 75, 81, 92, 95, 100, 105, 108, 121, 161, 170, 186, 188, 194–195, 205

S/P. *See* Status Post
Sample Example, 58–66, 67, 70, 81, 96, 124, 147, 191, 207
score, 72–80, 82, 125–136
second opinion, 75, 130
Select Plan 120–121, 150
self-insurance, 98
self-refer, 20–21, 23, 26–27, 49, 218
Senior Plan, 2, 117–118
Skilled nursing, 89–90, 97, 106–107
Skilled nursing facility, 90, 110, 112, 138
Social Security Administration, 87–88, 91, 94, 98, 102, 115–118, 122, 146, 152, 222, 224–225
Social Security Disability Insurance, 152–153
special needs, 71, 124
specialist, 12, 21, 23, 27, 30, 36–38, 43–44, 74–75, 78, 128–129, 134–135, 174
SSA. *See* Social Security Administration.
staff, 37–39, 42, 45, 50, 118–119, 218

Staff Model HMO, 37–43, 46–47, 49–50, 118–119, 218
Status Post, 183, 189–191, 218
status report, 175, 179–181, 183
stop-loss, 22, 26, 218
Supplemental Insurance, 2, 146, 151–155
System for Evaluating Insurance and HMO Plans through Questioning, 71
  Medigap and Medicare HMO, Use Questions to Grade and Compare, 124

third-party administrator, 183, 195, 218
TPA. *See* third-party administrator
Tracking Form, 191, 196, 199, 201–203
Traditional Medicare Supplement Policy (Medigap), 120, 150, 218

U.S. Health Care System. *See* Health Care System
usual and customary, 28–29, 35, 218, 219
utilization management, 38, 48
utilization review, 4, 48

vital sign, 170–172, 183, 219
weighted score, 72–80, 125–136, 219
wellness, 14, 22, 25, 49, 66
worldwide health care coverage, 73, 128

Your Doctor's Questions, 79–80, 134–135
*Your Medicare Handbook 1995*, 117
*Your Medicare Handbook 1996*, 115

# Index to Forms and Diagrams

## Diagrams

Fee-For-Service, 28
Fee-For-Service with a Preferred Provider Option, 31
Exclusive Provider, 33
Staff Model HMO, 40
Other Model HMO, 44
The Range of Available Plans, 50

## Examples

Discussion Topics (Office Visit), 169
Explanation of Benefits (EOB), 192, 200
Insurance Options Sumary, 57
Status Report, 180

## Illustrations

Mrs. Sample Chiropractic Costs, 61
Mr. Sample Preferred Provider Costs, 64
Mr. Sample and Sons Preferred Provider
 Costs, 65
Mrs. Sample's Explanation of Benefits
 (EOB), 192

## Insurance Questions

Health Care Plan Enrollee Questions (15),
 78–79
HMO and Insurance Company Questions (40),
 73–77
Questions to Ask Your Doctor About Commercial HMOs (10), 80

## Medigap and Medicare HMO Questions

Medicare HMO Member Questions (14),
 133–134
Medigap Carrier and Medicare HMO Questions (48), 126–131
Medigap Policyholder Questions (10), 132–133
Questions to Ask Your Doctor (10), 135

## Sample Forms

*See also* Appendix D for reproducible forms
Health Care Plan Evaluation, 68
List of Providers, 176
Medform, 171
Medical Expenses, 55
Medication History, 177
Procedure List, 178
Tracking Form, 201

## Tables

Detailed Medicare-Medigap, 111–115
Medicare Part A Coverage, 90
Medicare Part B Coverage, 93
Medicare—Medigap—HMO Coverage and
 Cost, 139–145
Medigap Overview, 107

# The McNally Method Educational Services

It's important that we stay informed of health care industry developments because they ultimately affect us. With this is mind we have developed a full spectrum of informational and educational services. We offer a newsletter, brief presentation, and two classes, all of which are presented from a consumer's point of view and can be tailored to the needs of the audience.

- *The McNally Method Newsletter*
  There are a number of bills in congress to control all HMOs because of those HMOs who would deny us the benefits of health maintenance by putting profit ahead of patient care. The Health Care Reform Act of 1996 also known as the Health Insurance Portability and Accountability Act, is about to be implemented. There are some questions that won't be answered until the law is implemented. Medicare and Medicaid are going be changed as the administration and the congress write the details of the budget agreement they reached on Friday, May 2, 1997. We need to stay current on these and other health care market developments and legislation. I continue doing day-to-day research to stay personally informed and help keep you up-to-date by publishing an inexpensive bimonthly newsletter for subscribers. To help you decide if you want to subscribe, we will send you additional information and the current newsletter. To receive your free newsletter, check *The McNally Method Newsletter* on the form at the bottom of the page, fill in your name and address, and send to the address shown.

- *The Health Care World We Live In and What We Can Do About It*
  This presentation is designed to acquaint groups with the new and changing world of medical care. It relates today's care to "the good old days," stressing that we must be active participants in managing our health care today. The speaker will share some techniques you can use to be an effective patient. This program is designed to last 45–60 minutes, depending on audience participation.

- *The McNally Method Seminar*
  This is a half-day or evening session. Our trainer presents the topics in *The McNally Method for Managing Your Health Care*, covering the examples and tables in detail as time pemits. It serves as a good introduction to the topic or as classroom reinforcement for those who have read the book.

- *The McNally Method Workshop*
  The purpose of this program is to take someone, who has not read the book before enrolling, through a 12–16 hour classroom workshop, going through the entire text. During the class all workshop exercises will be completed using the enrollee's medical and insurance data. The goal of the workshop is to have every student using the system in class and continuing to use *The McNally Method* after the class.

Please complete the following form, cut it out, and send it to: **MYHC Distributing, Inc.; 4960 Almaden Expressway, #194; San Jose, California 95118**.

---

Please send me a free *McNally Method Newsletter* and information on the items I checked below:

____ *The McNally Method Newsletter* and subscription information

____ *The Health Care World We Live In And What We Can Do About It*

____ *The McNally Method Seminar*

____ *The McNally Method Workshop*

Last Name _____ First Name _____ M.I. _____

Address _____

City _____ State _____ Zip _____

# Managing Your Health Care:
## A Consumer's Guide to Navigating Today's Health Care Systems

*Write:*  Warde Publishers, Inc.
3000 Alpine Road
Portola Valley, CA 94028

*Toll-free order line:*  (800) 699-2733

---

**ORDER FORM**

Please send me _____ copy(ies) of *Managing Your Health Care* by William F. McNally at $19.95. (Add $4.50 for first copy and $.50 for each additional copy for packing and shipping). California residents, please add $1.65 sales tax per book ordered). Make check payable to: Warde Publishers, Inc.

Total Enclosed: $_____

Name: _____

Address: _____

Address: _____

City: _____ State: _____ Zip: _____


May we send information on *Managing Your Health Care* to a friend, family member, or associate?

Name: _____

Address: _____

Address: _____

City: _____ State: _____ Zip: _____